SUBJECTS OF RESPONSIBILITY

Subjects of Responsibility

Framing Personhood in Modern Bureaucracies

Edited by

Andrew Parker, Austin Sarat,
and Martha Merrill Umphrey

FORDHAM UNIVERSITY PRESS

New York 2011

Fordham University Press has no responsibility for the
persistence or accuracy of URLs for external or third-party
Internet websites referred to in this publication and does not
guarantee that any content on such websites is, or will
remain, accurate or appropriate.

Fordham University Press also publishes its books in a
variety of electronic formats. Some content that appears in
print may not be available in electronic books.

Library of Congress Cataloging-in-Publication Data

Subjects of responsibility : framing personhood in modern
bureaucracies / edited by Andrew Parker, Austin Sarat, and
Martha Merrill Umphrey.—1st ed.
p.   cm.
Includes bibliographical references and index.
ISBN 978-0-8232-3322-9 (cloth : alk. paper)
ISBN 978-0-8232-3323-6 (pbk. : alk. paper)
ISBN 978-0-8232-3324-3 (ebook)
1. Bureaucracy. 2. Responsibility. I. Parker, Andrew,
1953– II. Sarat, Austin. III. Umphrey, Martha Merrill.
JF1501.S83 2011
302.3'5—dc22
2010033995

Printed in the United States of America
13 12 11   5 4 3 2 1
First edition

To Esther and Herb Cohen, responsible subjects (A.P.)
To my son Benjamin, with gratitude for the joy he brings to my life (A.S.)
For Thomas A. Green, with deep affection (M.U.)

ACKNOWLEDGMENTS

The essays collected in this book were first presented at a conference held at Amherst College on September 28–29, 2007. We are grateful for generous financial support provided by the College's President's Initiative Fund. We are also grateful for the enthusiastic participation in that conference of our colleagues Catherine Ciepiela, Thomas Dumm, Marisa Parham, and Adam Sitze. Finally, we wish to acknowledge the valuable research assistance provided by Tovah Ackerman and Michael Donovan.

CONTENTS

INTRODUCTION

Andrew Parker, Austin Sarat, and Martha Merrill Umphrey

Responsibility. What's your policy?™

LIBERTY MUTUAL INSURANCE COMPANY[1]

Bringing together the writings of scholars in anthropology, law, literary studies, philosophy, and political theory, *Subjects of Responsibility* asks how and why the concept of responsibility—confused and contested throughout its peculiar history—has come today to pervade the fabric of Western, in particular American, public and private life. Ideas of responsibility are instantiated in, and constituted by, the workings of social and political institutions; appeals to responsibility are used to define the parameters of inclusion in American culture, and those appeals become standards against which new social arrangements are judged. Since state bureaucracies play crucial roles in fashioning the forms of responsibility enjoined on the populations they serve, this collection suggests that efforts to cultivate an ethos of individual responsibility constrain or mask the exercise of power. We inquire in particular into the obscure origins and paradoxical functioning of types of private insurance, which, some claim, undermine the responsibility they appear to promote. How do government and market constitute subjects of responsibility in a culture so enamored of individuality? What kinds of subjectivities are created in this process? Are such subjects truly responsible?

These concerns are, of course, not new. They can be traced at least as far back as Hannah Arendt's famous invocation of the "banality of evil" as a framework for understanding the Holocaust.[2] But in an increasingly bureaucratized world, taking up Arendt's interest in the subject of responsibility remains important, because appeals to ideas of individual responsibility continue to saturate discourses of state, commerce, and family in liberal democracies. Thus, in his first inaugural address Bill Clinton told Americans: "It is time to break the bad habit of expecting something for nothing, from our government or from each other. Let us all take more responsibility, not only for ourselves and our families but for our communities and our country."[3] Or, as Barack Obama put it in a speech before the NAACP in July 2008: "I know some say I've been too tough on folks talking about responsibility. NAACP, I'm here to report, I'm not going to stop talking about it. Because as much I'm out there to fight to make sure that government's doing its job and the marketplace is doing its job . . . none of it will make a difference—at least not enough of a difference—if we also don't at the same time seize more responsibility in our own lives."[4]

Despite such emphasis in public discourse, the concept of responsibility itself has received little sustained attention outside the fields of moral philosophy and legal theory and almost none from the interdisciplinary perspective adopted in this volume.[5] In seeking to broaden and reframe critical inquiry into responsibility (its past, present, and future) by examining its meanings and functions within various discursive contexts, we asked our contributors to reflect on a series of interrelated questions. What does it mean to claim, assume, or bear responsibility? Is it, in fact, ever bearable? Who would be the subject of this act? If to be responsible is to engage in a performance, what would be the modalities of that performance? What notions of agency and intention does responsibility imply (or, indeed, presuppose)? When, and under what circumstances, did subjects become responsible?

One measure of the confusion usually attendant to considerations of responsibility is the absence of scholarly consensus concerning the very history of the term. Depending on whom one consults, responsibility is either one of the most venerable of philosophical concepts or one of the most recent. "Philosophic reflection on moral responsibility has a long history," writes Andrew Eshelman in the *Stanford Encyclopedia of Philosophy*—a history that reflects, in his view, a persistent and "widely shared conception of ourselves as members of an importantly distinct class of individuals—call them 'persons.'"[6] For proof of the concept's longevity, Eshelman points to Aristotle's discussion in *Nicomachean Ethics* (1110a) of the conditions under which actions can be considered voluntary as the first in a line of theories of moral responsibility running from the ancient to the contemporary world.[7] In this sense, responsibility has no history, properly speaking, since the term is held to reflect invariant aspects of human agency and ethical capacity.

Bernard Williams takes this assumption further in enlisting *The Odyssey* as evidence to reject the notion that the ancient Greeks thought differently than we do about the nature of responsibility. What distinguishes us from Homer, he argues, is less a different conception of responsibility than a different conception of *law*—"a different view, not of responsibility in general, but of the role of the state in ascribing responsibility, in demanding a response for certain acts and certain harms."[8] Unchanging in its structure, responsibility, for Williams, will always be composed of "four basic elements": "cause, intention, state, and response." These latter "really are universal materials" though they can and will combine in different ways depending on their particular context.[9]

Against this universalist account, *Subjects of Responsibility* plumbs the contingencies that have shaped and continue to shape the history of responsibility. Linguistic evidence suggests that the term's history has hardly been continuous over time. The noun "responsibility" is of relatively recent origin in English, French, and German—its first appearances can be traced to Alexander Hamilton, James Madison, and John Jay, who argued in *The Federalist* nos. 63–65 for the accountability of elected officials to their constituencies—and its use remained restricted largely to political discourse throughout the eighteenth century.[10] Although it may be surprising to learn that responsibility "should be of such recent origin and not really well established within the philosophical tradition," most historians agree that the concept began to receive philosophical attention only in the mid-1850s.[11] Kant, significantly, never analyzed what Germans today call *Verantwortlichkeit* (which was coined in 1832 by Heinrich Heine), though in retrospect we often mistake his interest in the nature of duty (*Pflicht*) and imputation (*Zurechnung*) for an inchoate theory of responsibility.[12] While "accountability" and "imputation" dominated eighteenth-century philosophical debates concerning the determination of guilt and the administration of punishment, these controversies did not yet concern *responsibility*, which, in the decades to come, encompassed and exceeded the restricted meanings of its predecessors.[13]

What made "responsibility" significantly different from the terms that it replaced was, first and foremost, the nineteenth century's pervasive project of distinguishing the public from the private.[14] By 1884, Lucien Lévi-Bruhl could simply assume that difference as the underlying basis for his distinction between two different types of responsibility, the legal/objective and the moral/subjective.[15] A century later, Hannah Arendt reversed this bifurcation—for her, the legal aligns with the individual, the moral with the public—but retained the structure of opposition in her notion of collective responsibility: "Where all are guilty, nobody is. Guilt, unlike responsibility, always singles out; it is strictly personal."[16]

Most recently, in a synoptic essay tracing the vicissitudes of the term, Paul Ricoeur noted that moral and legal versions of responsibility continue to orbit each other, though one of the two seems of late to have reached escape velocity:

> This essay is motivated by the sort of perplexity I was left with following an examination of the contemporary contextual uses of the term "responsibility." On the one side, this concept seems well delimited in its classical juridical usage: in civil law, responsibility is defined by the obligation to make up or to compensate for the tort one has caused through one's own fault and in certain cases determined by law; in penal law, by the obligation to accept punishment. We can see the place given to the idea of obligation: an obligation to compensate or to suffer punishment. A person subject to these obligations is someone who is responsible. All this seems clear enough. But, on the other side—or rather, from several other sides—a kind of vagueness invades the conceptual scene. . . . The current proliferation and dispersion of uses of this term is puzzling, especially because they go well beyond the limits established for its juridical use. The adjective "responsible" can complement a wide variety of things: you are responsible for the consequences of your acts, but also responsible for others' actions to the extent that they were done under your charge or care, and eventually far beyond even this measure. At the limit, you are responsible for everything and everyone. In these diffuse uses the reference to obligation has not disappeared; it has become the obligation to fulfill certain duties, to assume certain burdens, to carry out certain commitments. In short, it is an obligation that overflows the framework of compensation and punishment. This overflowing is so forceful that it is under this meaning that the term imposes itself today on moral philosophy, to the point of occupying the whole terrain and of becoming for Hans Jonas, and to a large measure for Emmanuel Lévinas, a "principle." This overflowing runs in many directions, thanks to the chance assimilations encouraged by the polysemy of the verb "to respond": not just in the sense of "to answer for . . ." but also as "to respond to . . ." (a question, an appeal, an injunction, etc.).[17]

While Ricoeur's view of the supposed clarity of the legal record is surely open to question,[18] his exasperation with the contemporary "excessiveness" of moral responsibility has been widely shared, especially among moral philosophers. For if our sense of moral obligation no longer is fully commensurate with and limited by our older legal frameworks of compensation and punishment,[19] if we have become responsible for everyone and everything, then how can we know—Ricoeur seems to ask in protest—what responsibility *can* mean? What remains of responsibility if its semantic reach has grown beyond the agency or intentions of any particular human subject?[20]

Answers to that question will depend, of course, on how one conceives of the latter category, "the members of an importantly distinct class of individuals—call them 'persons.'" Moral philosophy has tended to assume that, under ordinary circumstances, such persons are responsible when they are alive, human, conscious, sane, mature, and free to be the cause of their own acts—and, to that extent, accountable for them. Requiring the fulfillment of *all* of these conditions, responsibility makes for a highly tenuous norm. Indeed, as in this remarkably subjunctive-heavy passage from Isaiah Berlin, responsible subjects seem to depend more for their existence on the force of their *theorist's* desire than on their own intentions:

> I wish my life and decisions to depend on myself, not on external forces of whatever kind. I wish to be the instrument of my own, not other men's, acts of will. I wish to be a subject, not an object; to be moved by reasons, by conscious purposes, which are my own, not by causes which affect me, as it were, from outside. I wish to be somebody, not nobody; a doer—deciding, not being decided for, self-directed and not acted upon by other men as if I were a thing, or an animal, or a slave incapable of playing a human role. That is, of conceiving goals and policies of my own and realizing them. This is at least part of what I mean when I say that I am rational, and that it is my reason that distinguishes me as a human being from the rest of the world. I wish, above all, to be conscious of myself as a thinking, willing, active being, bearing responsibility for my choices and able to explain them by reference to my own ideas and purposes. I feel free to the degree that I believe this to be true, and enslaved to the degree that I am made to realize that it is not.[21]

If, from this perspective, our actions turn out to be predetermined or otherwise not "our own," then our notion of ordinary circumstances would need revising. But even so, say many moral philosophers, determinism need not be incompatible with our ability to assess responsibility.[22]

On the other hand, what *is* incompatible with the responsible person as typically conceived by moral philosophy is her or his psychoanalytic counterpart—and incompatible precisely because, for Freud, neurotics *are* ordinary persons:

> An obsessional neurotic may be weighed down by a sense of guilt that would be appropriate in a mass-murderer, while in fact, from his childhood onwards, he has behaved to his fellow-men as the most considerate and scrupulous member of society. Nevertheless, his sense of guilt has a justification: it is founded on the intense and frequent death-wishes against his fellows which are unconsciously at work in him. It has a justification if what we take into account are unconscious thoughts and not intentional deeds.[23]

Freud asks us here to ponder, in these "ordinary circumstances," the difficulty of assessing responsibility when the neurotic confesses his guilt for a deed he has *and* hasn't performed. If this neurotic is not free in Berlin's sense, do we then say that she or he can't be responsible? Who, after Freud, *could* possibly claim responsibility if the latter is conceived solely on the basis of conscious intention?

But even if the fact of my unconsciousness keeps me structurally from ever attaining the status of "a thinking, willing, active being, bearing responsibility for my choices," I may not be thereby rendered *ir*responsible. I may instead become, as a diverse group of continental thinkers would have it, responsible *otherwise*. Though Heidegger, Levinas, and Derrida were often profoundly at odds with one another, they all sought to redefine responsibility in ways that are "irreducible to and rebellious toward the traditional category of 'subject'" with all of its traditional predicates.[24] What if, they asked, the subject were conceived as the effect and not as the agent of responsibility? What if "I" can come into being only in responding to an Other who precedes any subject/object distinction? "Only in responsibility does the self first reveal itself," Heidegger averred, a self that does not exist before or apart from its answerability.[25]

Derrida continued that thought with the recognition that "*I cannot assume responsibility*," since it is responsibility that precedes and enables "me."[26] In this sense responsibility no longer depends, as in moral philosophy generally, on consciousness, freedom, or any other imputed attributes of an autonomous subject. That subject, according to Maurice Blanchot, is instead created and undone by responsibility, created in the very undoing of the subject's autonomy:

> Responsible: this word generally qualifies—in a prosaic, bourgeois manner—a mature, lucid, conscientious man, who acts with circumspection, who takes into account all elements of a given situation, calculates and decides. The word "responsible" qualifies the successful man of action. But now responsibility—my responsibility for the other, for everyone, without reciprocity—is displaced. No longer does it belong to consciousness; it is not an activating thought process put into practice, nor is it even a duty that would impose itself from without and from within. *My* responsibility for the Other presupposes an overturning such that it can only be marked by a change in the status of "me," a change in time and perhaps in language. Responsibility, which withdraws me from my order—perhaps from all orders and from order itself—responsibility, which separates me from myself (from the "me" that is mastery and power, from the free, speaking subject) and reveals the other in place of me, requires that I answer for

absence, for passivity. It requires, that is to say, that I answer for the impossibility of being responsible—to which it has always already consigned me by holding me accountable and also discounting me altogether. And this paradox leaves nothing intact—not subjectivity any more than the subject, not the individual any more than the person.[27]

Blanchot clearly disdains here "the successful man of action" who, bourgeois through and through, "calculates and decides" without recognizing that his cherished responsibility is catastrophic to his selfhood. Though this derisive attitude may remind us more of Nietzsche than Heidegger or Lévinas, Blanchot could find inspiration for his argument in *The Genealogy of Morals*, which similarly proclaims that the subject is more the effect than an agent of responsibility:

> To ordain the future in advance in this way, man must have first learned to distinguish necessary events from chance ones, to think causally, to see and anticipate distant eventualities as if they belonged to the present, to decide with certainty what is the goals and what the means to it, and in general be able to calculate and compute. Man himself must first of all have become *calculable, regular, necessary*, even in his own image of himself, if he is to be able to stand security for his own future, which is what one who promises does!
>
> This precisely is the long story of how *responsibility* [Verantwortlichkeit] originated. The task of breeding an animal with the right to make promises evidently embraces as a preparatory task that one first makes to a certain degree necessary, uniform, like among like, regular, and consequently calculable.[28]

From a Nietzschean perspective, then, we are called on to describe the work of constituting subjects who are "regular, and consequently calculable." Nietzsche reminds us that this is an ongoing project, one that must be renewed in every epoch and in its grand narratives of heroism as well as its stories of evil. *Subjects of Responsibility* examines that project in the contemporary United States, providing examples from the Bush administration's use of torture after 9/11, the continuing debate about civil rights and welfare reform, and the discourse surrounding medical error and medical malpractice. Here we will describe how bureaucratic imperatives shape the creation of responsible subjects as well as the ways that notions of responsibility shape bureaucratic practice. While some of our contributors are optimistic about the capacity of an ethic of responsibility to shape that practice, others worry that the discourse of responsibility, in effect, enables bureaucracies to function without effective accountability.

If, for Nietzsche, responsibility makes calculating subjects of us all, this notion was later taken up by Michel Foucault and his associates, who found in the history of insurance a paradigmatic, nonmoral form of subject formation:

> Whereas an accident, as damage, misfortune and suffering, is always individual, striking at one and not another, a risk of accident affects a population. Strictly speaking there is no such thing as an individual risk; otherwise insurance would be no more than a wager. Risk only becomes something calculable when it is spread over a population. . . . Moral thought uses accident as a principle of distinction; an accident is a unique affair between individual protagonists. Insurance, on the other hand, functions through a quite different mode of individualization. A risk is first of all a characteristic of the population it concerns. . . . Insurance individualizes, it defines each person as a risk, but the individuality it confers no longer correlates with an abstract, invariant norm such as that of the responsible juridical subject: it is an individuality relative to that of other members of the insured population, an average sociological individuality.[29]

Taking off from this idea of the displacement of the "responsible juridical subject," Jonathan Simon argues that insurance approaches risk in ways that objectify and aggregate individuals.[30] Insurance, including the kind of social insurance exemplified in the welfare state, is based on "actuarial" tools that have their roots in calculations of probability. In this sense, insurance is less interested in what any particular individual does than in what people *like* him or her *might* do. As such, insurance constitutes thin rather than thick subjects, subjects with tendencies, likelihoods, and risks rather than with will, calculation, and responsibility.

The tension between actuarialism and traditional ideas of responsibility manifests in various ways during the late modern era. One of the most important of those manifestations concerns the domain of criminal justice. With his collaborator Malcolm Feeley, Simon notes that "clinical diagnosis" and "retributive judgment" increasingly give way to risk calculations and risk assessments. They see a paradigm shift from a focus on individuals, guilt, and responsibility to what they call a "new penology" based in actuarial justice. Holding individuals responsible becomes less important than calculating risks and devising efficient strategies to identify and manage dangerous people.[31]

In this context, whether Simon's analysis of the rise of risk is or is not accurate is less important than it is in setting an agenda of inquiry, in calling for an analysis of the meaning of the risk mentality and its effects on the constitution of responsible subjects. *Subjects of Responsibility* takes up that agenda, examines the ways that ideas of responsibility are deployed in our collective life, and analyzes the way that insurance fits in a society in which identifying responsible subjects and fixing responsibility has played such an important role.

Section I, "Responsibility, Bureaucracy, and Accountability in Social and Political Life," begins with an essay by Leonard Feldman, who argues that, rightly understood, responsibility can have a disciplining effect on the uses of political power. To make this case, he takes up the question of what it means to be responsible "in a circumstance of necessity." Necessity, he argues, seems to simultaneously supersede responsibility (either as a justification or an excuse to avoid criminal liability) and "burden people with a greater responsibility" (to ignore the law when necessary). Thus, Feldman contends, "necessity both intensifies and subverts responsibility."

In an attempt to parse the implications of necessity, Feldman explores the different domains of responsibility for "the political leader, the bureaucrat, and the citizen." For an analysis of the responsibility of political leaders, Feldman turns to Max Weber and Michael Walzer. Weber argues that "necessity and the violent means used to cope with it intensify the ethical responsibility of leaders, understood as responsibility for the likely consequences." Walzer adds that "this ethic of responsibility makes the politician a suffering hero." Instead of adopting a "free-floating ethic of responsibility warranting dirty hands," Feldman focuses on what separates political leaders from other public officials and the difference between "an ethic of responsibility and an ethic of conviction." These two concepts illuminate some of Feldman's chief concerns: that actions taken under circumstances of necessity may turn into "immunizing legal norms," and that the language of necessity may mask convictions of absolute moralism that lead to unjustified violence. He sees both at work in the post-9/11 Bush administration.

On the topic of how pleas of necessity interact with and may replace standing legal norms, Feldman focuses on the arguments of the political theorist Jean Elshtain, who suggests that necessity should be treated not as a justification but rather as an excuse. Actions taken out of necessity, she argues, should not be legalized, normalized, or justified; they represent a "temporary suspension of law," not a new legal norm. Feldman is somewhat wary, however, of leaving customary legal prohibitions in place while an unwritten understanding allows them to be violated out of necessity. He cautions that this stance will create "an extralegal zone in which the judiciary has no place [and] will be filled in with bureaucratic content: nonjudicial but nevertheless regularized bureaucratic protocols."

Feldman suggests that an ethic of responsibility may offer a solution to this problem, calling, as it does, on "the responsibility of the public to either validate or condemn the extralegal actions committed by their officials." The responsibility of citizens to hold officials accountable can help prevent unjustified actions from becoming ongoing norms. This may help ensure that the actions are in fact only taken out of necessity. The responsibility of bureaucratic officials, Feldman notes, is based in carrying out the instructions of leaders. If leaders engage in extralegal action under the rubric of necessity, then their "ethic of responsibility . . . migrates down the civil service ladder." In this context, "extralegal invocations of necessity function in a bureaucratic context as a recursive . . . process" in which the legal system validates its actions by turning back on itself, and those actions move from being unjustifiable decisions made outside law to norms existing inside law.

To illustrate the way that necessity may erode responsibility, Feldman takes up the Bush administration's uses of torture following 9/11. Beginning with the Bybee memo, which claimed necessity as a justification, the administration immunized state officials from legal sanction for actions violating the ban on torture. A December 30, 2004, memo from Acting Assistant Attorney General Daniel Levin replaced Bybee's. It provided "a strong condemnation of torture," but instead of repudiating necessity justifications, it merely claims that torture was "unnecessary."

These post-9/11 understandings of necessity help us see what happens to an ethic of responsibility aimed at leaders when it "migrates into a bureaucracy." Only, Feldman concludes, when there is a strong culture of responsibility in the public and in the state bureaucracy can arguments about necessity be disciplined and can necessity intensify rather than erode responsibility.

From Feldman's interest in necessity and his optimism about the value of responsibility in disciplining public power, we move next to S. Lochlann Jain's analysis of the discourse of responsibility in regard to medical error and her worry that responsibility does not effectively limit the incidence of such errors. Like Feldman, Jain is interested in bureaucracy, but here she looks at the hospital rather than at governmental bureaucracy.

As Jain explains, errors occur quite frequently, although "given the low rates of litigation . . . the recent legislation limiting compensation to $250,000 . . . and the lack of other systems of accountability, very little incentive exists for medical systems to improve—and so these errors continue, leaving issues of responsibility to individuals and individual incidents."

Jain describes one case where chemotherapy medication was accidentally and fatally administered to a young man through his epidural shunt. In its public statements, the hospital "took full responsibility" for the incident, but the press releases, Jain notes, "did not discuss what responsibility might mean in this context: compensation to the victim's family, redesigning the drug delivery systems at all Kaiser hospitals, or punishing or firing the individual involved in the killing." However, Jain continues, "the incident raises a new aspect of an emergent public relations adoption of the term responsibility, one that is found in the increasing demand on doctors to offer apologies to patients."

Some argue that those apologies give a human face to the bureaucratic system. Others argue that apologies force doctors to accept responsibility for mistakes that are not necessarily their own but rather are those of the hospital bureaucracy. As Jain sees it, in the presence of claims of responsibility we must ask: "on what basis, to whom or what, and with what goals, can wrongs be assigned? At the level of structural change: if no one is responsible for the moral—rather than economic—wrongs, then how can improvement in what is clearly a broken system of healthcare delivery be fulfilled? Is responsibility merely a public relations moment, something that is realized through the speaking of it?"

In fact, studies show that the attitude of physicians matters immensely in an injured person's decisions to litigate. Patients often want an acknowledgment of responsibility and an apology for a mistake rather than any monetary reward. Yet as Jain sees it, "apology implies a level of responsibility that may not exist or implies that some action might be taken when it will not." As a result, it remains utterly unclear what the apology has to do with responsibility and so, at the social level, what, precisely, medical responsibility entails. Jain believes that medical apology adds another level of complexity to the question of whether or not medical injuries are avoidable, since the question of compensation and structural change in healthcare delivery rests on attributions of responsibility. Attributing responsibility to an individual doctor, she notes, may satisfy the injured party but, at the same time, obscure structural problems and hinder broad reform. Jain concludes that Americans' readiness to accept individualized attributions of responsibility for medical error "leaves them (us) with virtually no rights or means of recovery" in the face of bureaucratically routine medical error.

Unlike Feldman and Jain, who examine the efficacy of discourses of responsibility in disciplining public and private power, Carol Greenhouse's essay describes the way that arguments about responsibility are used in the public sphere as tools to discipline citizens—or at least particular classes of citizens. Greenhouse notes that discussions of responsibility have pervaded some of our most important political controversies, namely those surrounding civil rights and welfare reform. In these domains, unsurprisingly, the discourse of responsibility has been racialized.

As Greenhouse sees it, race has become one of the most important lenses through which subjects of responsibility are identified in contemporary American politics. Race, she writes, has been "drawn into contention by the policy debates of the time—functioning simultaneously and paradoxically as an object of federal power *and* as the mark of extreme social marginality." During the 1990s, race palpably marked a contradiction between a booming economy and the persistence of poverty: "*palpable* in its direct reference to stereotypical excesses of consumption (i.e., entitlements, dependency) and equally stereotypical deficiencies with respect to the status of the so-called urban underclass in relation to forms of productivity and exchange central to capitalism." In this way, subjects of responsibility became inextricably tied to both consumption and federal power.

To illustrate her point, Greenhouse takes up debates surrounding the Civil Rights Acts (CRA) of 1990 and 1991 and the Welfare Reform Act of 1996. She treats them as key sites where issues of race were "honed around consumption and glossed with official sanction." The CRA of 1990 sought to rectify a Supreme Court ruling that assigned the burden of proof in employment discrimination cases to the plaintiff to prove that they had been discriminated against. In the legislative debate that followed, both advocates and critics invoked the civil rights landmarks of the 1960s: "The rhetorical common ground in the Johnson-era legislation cast important segments of the debate as judgments of history itself . . . a discursive turn that simultaneously offered a language of collective responsibility." Greenhouse continues, "advocates of the CRA of 1990 read *Griggs* [the Supreme Court case] as putting that burden on the employer—just as (from the standpoint of agency) *Brown* and the CRA of 1964 had put the burden on school boards and others responsible for public facilities. . . . Critics, on the other hand, saw the bill as a fishing license for plaintiffs and their lawyers—acknowledging the pervasiveness of the disparate impact of hiring practices but also denying the relevance of those statistics in relation to *individual* hires." Critics argued that the appeal to federal assistance in itself undermined the legislation, claiming that existing law was sufficient to allow "motivated," responsible individuals to "find their own pathways to opportunity." Thus the CRA provided an occasion on which politicians could stage a debate about responsibility and its limits.

Eventually, President George H. W. Bush vetoed the 1990 bill, and its proponents set out to redraft a compromise bill in 1991. This bill dropped the attempt to resettle the burden of proof on the employer. In doing so, it ultimately reconfigured "*race* as the attribute of an individual to be *erased* by civil rights—as opposed to the underclass that by dint of social shift and psychological pathologies were outside the law's reach. This discursive shift—crystallized in the [1990] CRA bill's critics' position on the burden-of-proof issue—was ultimately important to the mobilization of bipartisan support for the new welfare law, as the disparate impact of that legislation could by then be presented as race neutral, targeting *cultural* problems rather than minority individuals or racial communities." The cultural problems that the legislation targeted were figured as problems of personal irresponsibility, of lives lived aimlessly, of wills misdirected, and of subjectivities in need of the responsibilizing discipline of work.

The 1991 CRA and the 1996 Welfare Reform Act carried forward rather traditional views of responsible subjects and reinforced a familiar linkage of race and responsibility. As Greenhouse notes: "In the end, liberals were able to renew the affirmation of equality only to the extent that its implementation did not impose financial burdens on the private sector or 'the taxpayers'—in this context, a proxy term that evokes the state through a condensation of the national public to a contributive fiscal identity. . . . The debate over the new civil rights legislation showed that there was no liberal consensus over equality when it was set up as a trade-off against profitability. The debate over welfare officialized a highly pejorative view of the urban poor—stereotypically African American—as illegitimate consumers in a universe of limited goods." These acts closely allied property value with moral value and the national economy with individual morality.

Public responsibility, it seemed, could only begin where personal responsibility ended. The political work necessary to limit the former thus involved reaffirming and expanding the latter. Responsible subjects neither need nor value federal power and government intervention. To value either was to mark oneself as outside the American mainstream. The logic of antidiscrimination or public welfare was seen as incompatible with the project of fashioning and maintaining responsible subjects.

Part II of this book, "Responsibility, Risk, and Insurance," begins with Eric Wertheimer's discussion of the rise of insurance and the constitution of responsible subjects. Like Greenhouse, Wertheimer reads a set of social actions for what they signify about responsibility. "The history of insurance," he says, "demonstrates that responsibility's sources are tough to exhume and hard to disentangle; whatever its genesis and current incarnation, responsibility is difficult to fulfill. I argue that this elusiveness is a product of the tensions built into the figure of the 'socialized individual,' whose every decision involved calculations and calibrations related to the various and obsessive measurements of inward gain and outward protection."

Wertheimer writes that in the seventeenth and eighteenth centuries, the insurance policy invented a form of responsibility that we still recognize today. He notes that "the marketplace for such insuring texts made available new access to . . . individual and collective responsibilities by economically valuing the virtues of personal precaution. Insurance's concepts renamed and restructured the silent field of conditions that precede every insurance contract's 'whereas,' and that demand our consent, tacit or verbal." The "whereas" in an insurance policy, he argues, marks a meeting point between private and public interests and responsibility. "While the social individual achieves virtue by balancing her prudent measure of individual interests, obligations, and risks against collective forces," Wertheimer argues, "the *socialized* individual merges individual and collective, redistributing one's interests and risk into the capitalized pool of the collective." The socialized individual thus mitigates his singularity by the "outward marketability of trust."

Insurance also served as a status display that would reflect the virtues of a broader responsibility to the general public: "The florid and specialized way in which the policies named and announced their contracted subjects and objects were indications of the precise negotiations such texts made with individual obligation and public consent."

Like Greenhouse, Wertheimer sees race playing a key mediating role in the American discourse about responsibility. Thus he claims that insurance's odd relation to responsibility arises from its emergence in the same era as arguments for the abolition of slavery. The two rhetorics—personal care and commercial probity of insurance, and personal liberation and communal salvation of abolition—clashed, but Wertheimer believes their co-emergence was more than coincidental, since both invoke similar relationships between the individual and the group, though sometimes in opposing ways: "Abolitionism and merchant capitalism cultivated an anxious proximity because of their shared sense of responsibility—one a responsibility entailed by a transcendent notion of human freedom and the other by the obligations of contracts."

These linkages of insurance, property, and personhood are still being played out today. For example, in August 2000, the California legislature passed a statue enabling state entities to use slave-insurance policies from the slaveholding era in the archives of insurance companies as evidence of ill-gotten profits from slavery. In the insurance policies that were found, Wertheimer argues, slaves were reduced to a statistic or record and were lost as full human beings. In this way, "the matter of responsibility, when seen as a textual process that redounded on the parties tied to property definitions, becomes uniquely difficult to fulfill."

As in Feldman's essay, Wertheimer himself relies on the language of responsibility, calling on us to take responsibility for our past, a past that links the rise of insurance and our troubled racial history to the constitution of particular kinds of subjects. This work, he says, "is worth something, even if the words and categories that would resurrect and reference . . . (our past) offer no easy redemption. Scholars and archivists, in reminding us of this enduring attention to word and historical record, demonstrate the never-finished work of memory and obligation in contemporary political life. Such work is the only real insurance."

The next essay, by Susanna Blumenthal, takes up the constitution of the subject of responsibility in the context of nineteenth-century judicial decisions concerning insurer liability for suicide claims. These cases arose because life insurance companies typically included an exclusionary clause in their policies stating that the insured forfeited payment if he "died by his own hand." The meaning of that phrase was continually challenged by plaintiffs seeking to collect on policies that the insurance companies claimed fell within the exclusionary clause. The debates that followed inevitably raised questions about the insured's capacity to differentiate right from wrong, insanity, and the relationship of actions committed by affected individuals and the responsibility of those individuals. Blumenthal uses a variety of cases to demonstrate the inconsistency of judicial opinions in this area and to support her argument that context is crucial "in determining the constitution of the responsible (human) subject."

She begins with *Breasted v. Farmers' Loan and Trust Company*, which she argues exposed "basic tensions and ambiguities in conceptions of the responsible subject." In that case, the court determined that if the insured was not capable of distinguishing right from wrong at the time of his suicide, he could not be said to be responsible for his death, and thus the insurer was liable. Yet "the judges diverged considerably in their interpretations," and thus the case ultimately raised "the question of what constituted the *self* in self-destruction." Some judges maintained that the act of taking one's own life was sufficient to prove insanity and thus warranted payment on the policy, while others feared that "to require payment on the disputed policy was . . . essentially rewarding and thereby encouraging a rather monstrous form of financial planning" among insured individuals who sought to provide for their dependents by ending their own lives. Blumenthal argues that "the American judiciary . . . never [arrived] at a settled consensus on the applicable rules of responsibility in cases of self-destruction. In case after case . . . the alleged suicide had a destabilizing effect on the doctrinal landscape."

In 1862, *Dean v. American Mutual Life Insurance Company* held that a state of insane delusion was immaterial so long as the suicide was "an act of volition." In contrast, four years later, *Eastabrook v. Union Mutual Life Insurance Company* held that any suicide committed in a state of insanity cannot be considered an act of the insured. In 1869, *St. Louis Mutual Life Insurance Company v. Graves* held that the insurer was not liable if the insured intentionally destroyed his life, unless if at the instant of the act he was subordinated to moral insanity.

In those cases, courts concluded that it was irrelevant whether the insured was sane or insane; as long as the insured intentionally and voluntarily died by his or her own hand, the insurer was relieved from making payment. The dissenters, however, lamented that these rulings "treated the insured as a responsible agent despite his want of moral capacity, unaccountably deviating from the rules of responsibility in cases of crime." Blumenthal argues that these "divergent interpretations should occasion no surprise, especially in view of the ambivalence about suicide that persisted in the broader culture after criminal penalties for the act were lifted."

Ultimately, Blumenthal contends that judicial attempts to define the responsible individual in the cases of suicide and life insurance reveal contradictions and instabilities in the idea of responsibility itself. They indicate how the logic of risk prevention became tethered to the various categories through which responsibility had traditionally been assigned to individuals. Judges used whatever legal mechanisms they had at their disposal to identify elements of responsibility or its absence in instances of self-destruction. Their futile efforts imply that, at least in the context of suicide-exclusion clauses, far from displacing responsibility as a central cultural construct, the growth of insurance intensified efforts to identify and pin it down.

The last essay in this book revisits the discussion of responsibility, bureaucracy, and accountability but this time locates that discussion in the context of the codification of compensatory relationships in and through insurance. Ravit Reichman uses E. M. Forster's novel *Howards End* to discuss how insurance "at its loftiest . . . creates (or at the very least, fortifies) community when catastrophe threatens to turn a nation into a collection of individuals, each concerned only for his or her own well-being." She provides an example of this idealism by citing Winston Churchill's response to the attacks on London during World War II, in which he focused on who would take responsibility by sharing the burden for what had been lost, thereby adopting a "principle of due care rather than financial compensation." Forster, Reichman argues, goes a step further by asserting that compensation does not necessarily fulfill the main condition for "a just society."

Reichman questions whether the codification of compensatory relationships reinforces responsibility or undermines it. She argues that insurance may propel us into "a world where compensation rather than responsibility forms the basis of justice," a world in which personal relationships are abandoned for business relationships, as individuals become more concerned with themselves than with others. She agrees with Maurice Blanchot that "one of the most glaring losses in a bureaucratized world is individual responsibility."

Howards End, she claims, "depicts the ebbing of an old world of personal accountability against the rising tide of bureaucratized responsibility," forcing each character to make choices on the security–risk spectrum. Some characters are careful; others choose to be reckless. In the end, however, "the caution woven into the best-laid plans—insurance policies, wills—are undone through the unpredictability of friendship, fear, passion, and anger." Like Forster, Reichman favors the cultivation of personal responsibility over corporate compensation. For her, in the face of accidents or catastrophes a shared sense of responsibility to others must prevail.

Yet Reichman argues that Forster's novel "ultimately seeks out the meeting points of such tendencies [legal arrangements and human relationships], the conditions under which the documented and the emotional life fuse into something more robust and genuine." The novel binds caution and risk through the interaction of different characters who make different choices. Reichman sees in the larger social context of the novel a "trend that replaced personal accountability with corporate compensation." She argues that with the adoption of insurance policies, events that would have mattered in a community become nonevents. Individuals ceased to be responsible and, as a result, personal interactions now "bear no consequence" as long as both parties have insurance.

Like Jonathan Simon, Reichman points out the absurdity of the new "logic of insurance, in which things . . . are fungible and compensation rights a wrong." Like Jain, Reichman criticizes the new "economic community where accountability has no place" and where the unfortunate fates of individuals are attributed to chance and unavoidable circumstances. In the end, she fears that the logic of risk reduction erodes responsibility and under that logic an enlivening spirit of care is replaced by mere prudence.

Taken together, the work collected in *Subjects of Responsibility* provides a wide variety of views concerning the condition and fate of responsibility in the modern era. This work locates the subject of responsibility in various institutional embodiments: in executive and legislative actions, in the work of hospitals and insurance companies, and in the discourses of law and literature. It shows how responsible subjects are imagined and constituted in those actions, work, and discourses. It asks us to consider whether a world moved from responsibility to necessity, calculations of risk, and action governed by prudence would indeed be a better world. Throughout, our contributors highlight the contingent and constructed character of subjects of responsibility, and together they call us to think "responsibly" about the subject of responsibility itself.

PART I

Responsibility, Bureaucracy, and Accountability in Social and Political Life

CHAPTER I

Assuming Responsibility in a State of Necessity

Leonard C. Feldman

Introduction: Necessity and Responsibility

What does it mean to be responsible in a circumstance of necessity? On the one hand, necessity seems to release people from responsibility: whether necessity justifies or excuses, it renders people immune from criminal liability. On the other hand, necessity seems to burden people with a greater responsibility: the responsibility to violate the law when extreme circumstances warrant it. Thus my central question: what does it mean to be responsible in a circumstance of necessity? This question cannot be answered without attention to the situatedness of different political actors. In this essay, I examine how that responsibility is figured differently for the political leader, the bureaucrat, and the citizen.

Necessity is a condition in which the central tensions of the legal versus the ethical and freedom versus determinism are played out. On the one hand, necessity implies a kind of causal determinism that subverts the assumption of free will upon which responsibility rests. On the other hand, a situation of necessity calls upon the actor to act courageously, to risk one's life or, short of that, legal sanction, to do what is either normally not expected or normally not allowed. In the common law, whereas the defense of duress situates the actor as deprived of free will, the necessity defense is presented in terms of a "choice of evils."[1] Necessity places us on the boundary between freedom and compulsion. One may think of this boundary as a site where ethics and law collide, or one may think of this boundary as a site where normativity confronts exigency. One gets a sense of this duality when a person does something truly extraordinary and heroic in a situation of great peril. Such an actor earns praise for their (not causally determined) response to necessity but often deflects such praise with a question: "what choice did I have?" Another way to put this is that necessity has the experiential quality both of a "being compelled" and of an excruciating choice. Necessity both intensifies and subverts responsibility.

It is in Max Weber's lecture "Politics as a Vocation" that the link between necessity, understood in traditional terms as reason of state, and responsibility comes to the fore. For Weber, necessity and the violent means used to cope with it intensify the ethical responsibility of leaders, "ethical responsibility" understood here as responsibility for the likely consequences. Such an ethic emphasizes responsibility for the foreseeable consequences of one's actions, as opposed to an "ethic of conviction" that emphasizes purity of motive and an absolutist ethic.[2] An ethic of responsibility grapples with the dangerousness of specifically political means—violence—and "the possibility or even probability of evil side-effects."[3] As Michael Walzer elaborates, this ethic of responsibility makes the politician a suffering hero: "the reader never doubts that this mature, superbly trained, relentless, objective, responsible, and disciplined political leader is also a suffering servant."[4]

The work of Weber remains an important touchstone for the debate over political responsibility in a state of necessity, and it is so for my essay as well. But rather than endorse a free-floating ethic of responsibility warranting dirty hands, I turn to two other aspects of Weber's discussion of political responsibility: his distinction between the responsibility of political leaders and the responsibility of officials, and his distinction between an ethic of responsibility and an ethic of conviction. These two contributions, I argue, help make sense of the real-world politics of necessity and, in particular, how pleas of necessity can become immunizing legal norms and can betray not a "dirty-hands realism" but moralistic conviction.

"Necessary" Torture and the Ethic of Responsibility

Weber's ethic of responsibility has emerged in the contemporary debate over torture. Jean Elshtain elaborates: regarding the politician who authorizes the torture of the prisoner who has knowledge of a ticking bomb, "he is good enough to do what is wrong but necessary in order to provide for the common defense—to protect the citizens he has a particular responsibility to protect—and he is guilty, as he should be, and as any decent person would be, at what he felt compelled to do, given his vocation of statecraft."[5] For Elshtain, necessity functions as something more like an excuse than a justification: the decision to torture is never justified—it is a choice of evils that is nevertheless never made legal (or moral), and the torturer remains guilty.

Indeed, Elshtain burdens her torturer with a heavy responsibility, which she describes with the rather jarring term "asceticism": "A certain asceticism is required of those who may be required, in a dangerous and extreme situation, to temporarily override a general prohibition. They should not seek to legalize it. They should not aim to normalize it. And they should not write elaborate justifications of it."[6] Necessity here is what requires the temporary suspension of law, the willingness of the torturer to act lawlessly when the circumstances require it. Necessity also burdens the official with responsibility for extralegal action, a responsibility that Elshtain argues cannot be shifted or shared via legal justification, procedures, torture warrants, or a "tick-list."[7]

Richard Posner also criticizes codifying torture from the extralegalist (pro-torture) perspective: "If legal rules are promulgated permitting torture in defined circumstances, officials are bound to want to explore the outer bounds of the rules; and the practice, once it were thus regularized, would be likely to become regular. Better, I think, to leave in place the customary legal prohibitions, but *with the understanding that of course they will not be enforced in extreme circumstances.*"[8] But Posner, like Gross and Elshtain, does not explore the extent to which such an extralegal zone in which the judiciary has no place will be filled in with bureaucratic content: nonjudicial but nevertheless regularized bureaucratic protocols for torture once a declaration (or acknowledgement) of "extreme circumstances" has been made.

Elshtain's support for extralegal torture is a call for executive discretion, in a double sense: first, the discretion of the sovereign (or petty sovereign, or perhaps vigilant citizen—as I discuss below, Elshtain does not distinguish different ethics for differently situated actors) to act outside the law when extreme circumstances (necessity) require it, and second, the discretion (being discreet) not to talk about it, not to provide "elaborate justifications" that risk instantiating a new norm.[9] Elshtain does not demand total silence, however:[10] it is the *before-the-fact* process of rationalization that she opposes. But after the extralegal act is committed, the torturer should be called to account. Elshtain writes, "the norm remains; it may have to be broken; the one who broke it for a strong reason must nevertheless make amends in some way. In other words, the interrogator must, if called on, be prepared to defend what he or she has done and, depending on context, to pay a penalty."[11] Necessity for Elshtain exists outside of law and, to the greatest extent possible, outside of language as well. In Elshtain's rendering, necessity is something closer to an excuse than a justification. The problem with justifications for Elshtain is that they become new norms—they change the law. Excuses, by contrast, only release one from a legal obligation.

Like Elshtain, Oren Gross burdens executives with an ethic of responsibility to act extralegally when crises demand it. Gross supplements Elshtain's account by developing in greater detail what might be involved in the after-the-fact judgment.[12] Elshtain does not elaborate on the situations that might require punishment versus those that do not or on the political processes by which such punishment is meted out. Gross's work is an improvement on Elshtain's position precisely because it attempts to work out the details of such accountability. Gross does so via a second "ethic of responsibility": the responsibility of the public to either validate or condemn the extralegal actions committed by their officials.

In contrast to Elshtain's Weberian politics of necessity that emphasizes almost exclusively[13] the ethics of responsibility of political officials, Gross develops an "Extra-Legal Measures Model," which emphasizes the dynamic relationship between the *pragmatic* responsibility of political elites and the *moral* responsibility of a judging, democratic public. Gross agrees with Elshtain that necessity should not be inscribed into law (as in the case of Alan Dershowitz's "torture-warrant proposal"): "Going completely outside the law in appropriate cases preserves, rather than undermines, the rule of law in a way that bending the law to accommodate for catastrophes does not."[14] Inspired by Locke's theory of prerogative power, Gross supplements the prerogative-power model with the requirement of after-the-fact public deliberation and review. Thus it is not only leaders who are made responsible by a circumstance of necessity—the public is as well. For instance, Gross writes: "The proposed solution emphasizes an ethic of responsibility on the part of not only public officials but also the general public."[15]

Gross's model requires a pragmatic-Weberian responsibility by political leaders (who must decide what he calls "the obvious question") *and* a different sort of responsibility from citizens after the fact (the responsibility to judge what he calls "the tragic question"). The obvious question concerns whether or not necessity requires extralegal action, including, according to Gross, torture in the case of the "ticking bomb." But unlike others who accept the legitimacy of the ticking-bomb hypothetical, Gross seeks to build in a process of uncertainty and evaluation: citizens are responsible for ratifying or condemning such extralegal action, and state officials must act with the uncertainty of such subsequent evaluation. Gross writes, "even when counter-emergency actions are deemed necessary under the obvious question, such actions may still be considered unjustified or nonexcusable from a moral or legal perspective, as they run afoul of a community's fundamental principles and values."[16] Gross argues that while extralegal action might be widely accepted as necessary from the pragmatic perspective, the public may, nevertheless, "decline to approve such action from legal, political, social or moral standpoints."[17]

The model hinges upon executive honesty. Extralegal action "must be openly, candidly, and fully disclosed to the public."[18] This assumption of honesty has been criticized as unrealistic by several commentators who argue that any approach to the politics of necessity must recognize that political leaders are likely to either keep their activity secret or claim that it is, in fact, fully legal.[19] (The secrecy and legal contortions of the Bush administration are, of course, exhibit A.) I would argue that the assumption of executive honesty makes sense only to the degree that the judging public *itself* embraces an expansive logic of necessity, prudence, and emergency as rendering normal law obsolete. To the extent that the judging public in his model holds fast, instead, to rule-of-law values (or even to the narrower model of necessity as excuse), the model fails, because elected leaders are more likely to pretend that their actions were fully consistent with normal law or cloak them in secrecy.[20] In other words, to the extent that Gross's model assumes a sovereign public fiercely committed to constitutional and legal values, it must then assume an executive whose superhuman morality makes her willing to confess, *against her own interests*, the extralegality of her actions. To the extent that the judging public does not hold fast to rule-of-law values, the extralegal-measures model falls short because no agent of constraint exists to check extralegal action. Executives are most likely to confess the extralegality of their actions when the public culture of their society has already fully accepted an expansive logic of necessity as a norm.[21]

While Gross and Elshtain take their inspiration in part from Weber's hard-nosed "ethic of responsibility" required of politicians, they ignore two other important contributions that Weber makes to the discussion of

political responsibility. The first is the distinction that Weber makes between the responsibility of the politician and the responsibility of the civil
service bureaucrat. The second is Weber's complication of the distinction
between an ethic of responsibility and an ethic of conviction when discussing the dangers of an ethic of conviction that, rather than refusing to dirty
its hands, engages in violence with a moralistic confidence. In the next
section, I discuss these contributions in turn, each paired with an aspect of
the Bush administration's torture scandal.

Weberian Responsibility, Bureaucratic Hierarchy, and the Torture-Memo Scandal

Elshtain's ethic of responsibility migrates indifferently between political
executives and their bureaucratic underlings. It is attached to "the political
leader," "political and military leaders," and, in the end, simply "officials."[22] While Gross complicates the picture by adding an ethic of responsibility on the part of a judging public, he too fails to rigorously distinguish
between executives and lower-level bureaucrats when discussing the
commission of extralegal acts. Gross declares, for instance: "When catastrophic cases occur, governments and their agents are likely to do whatever is necessary—whether legal or not—to neutralize the threat."[23] Thus,
despite linking his extralegal-measures model to a tradition of thinking
about executive prerogative power, Gross applies his model to the much
more expansive category of "public officials" and "government agents."[24]
Gross's examples of the extralegal-measures model include, for instance,
police officers. As David Dyzenhaus notes in his critique, Gross "appears
to give the power to determine that there is an emergency *to any public
official* who is prepared to take the risk that he will not receive after-the-
fact legal validation for his illegal acts."[25]

Weber's account of the distinctive ethic of responsibility of officials as
distinct from the ethic of responsibility of leaders raises questions about
this elastic approach to the "sovereign decision" and its extension to
"petty sovereigns." Concentrating on the specific ethic of responsibility
of the civil service bureaucrat, Weber asks, what kind of responsibility
does the professional officer of the state have in comparison to the politician? Even when the civil servant views the demands of a higher-up to
be wrong, "his honor lies in his ability to carry it out, on his superior's
responsibility, conscientiously and exactly as if it corresponded to his own
convictions." This norm is in sharp contrast to that of "the political

leader" who "acts exclusively on his *own* responsibility, a responsibility that he may not and cannot refuse or shuffle off onto someone else."[26] Weber's discussion is provocative in this regard, positing starkly different conceptions of responsibility.

Elshtain's and Gross's relative indifference to the question of institutional hierarchy appears problematic in light of Weber's distinction. When an ethic of responsibility to act outside of law in circumstances of necessity migrates down the civil service ladder, it risks mutating into a form of immunization. Let me be clear: I am not arguing that Weber's description of bureaucratic responsibility be accepted as the sum total of official obligations. Such a view obviously invokes the specter of Eichmann and all the bureaucratic defenses of mass atrocities. I am rather suggesting that *sociologically* Weber reminds us of the difficulties inherent in transposing an ethic for politicians into a bureaucratic structure where institutional actors seek norms and their consistent application. As David Dyzenhaus writes, "a significant problem for the Extra-Legal Measures model is that if it is adopted as a model, as a prescriptive set of considerations for officials who face or think they face an emergency, it is likely that they will come to anticipate and anticipate correctly that the legal response to their extra-legal activity will be an Act of Indemnity or its equivalent."[27]

The processes of indemnification and immunity surrounding torture, beginning with the Bybee "torture memo" in 2002, its leaking in 2004, its withdrawal and replacement by the "Levin memo" in 2004, the McCain amendment of 2005 (subsequently passed as the Detainee Treatment Act), and Military Commissions Act passage in 2006 demonstrate that extralegal invocations of necessity function in a bureaucratic context as a *recursive legal process*. In contemporary use by a few sociolegal scholars, the notion of law as recursive tends to designate a cyclical pattern to law creation in which complex interactions and iterations produce changes in law.[28] But recursivity also indicates a certain paradoxical relationship: Drucilla Cornell describes legal recursivity as when "the legal system . . . grounds the validity of its own propositions by turning back on itself."[29]

Before examining how the infamous "torture memo," sent from Jay Bybee to Alberto Gonzales and dated August 1, 2002 (and written by John Yoo), functions recursively to indemnify state agents, I turn briefly to summarize its substance. The memo contains three main arguments. First, the Bybee memo restricts what counts as torture through a reinterpretation of the Convention Against Torture and the federal criminal prohibition against torture. As is well known, the memo claims that "physical pain amounting to torture must be equivalent in intensity to the pain accompanying serious physical injury, such as organ failure, impairment of bodily function, or even death."[30] The memo gets there by, as David Luban puts it, "scour[ing] the federal laws for anything that used the term 'severe pain.'"[31] The point of this was to distinguish between torture, on the one hand, and "cruel, inhuman or degrading treatment," on the other hand, to claim that the legal status of the latter is far murkier than the former and that "there is a wide range of techniques that will not rise to the level of torture."[32] The memo, though subsequently withdrawn (through a process that I will discuss later in the essay) set the pattern for the Bush administration's approach to torture: drastically narrow what counts as torture, then allow various "enhanced interrogation techniques" that fall outside of this definition.

Second, in an argument that generated as much scathing criticism as his extraordinarily narrow definition of torture, Bybee asserts a constitutional foundation for executive power to authorize any kind of interrogation in pursuing war. Bybee asserts that the Convention Against Torture cannot constrain executive war powers: "Any effort to apply [the federal torture statute] in a manner that interferes with the President's direction of such core war matters as the detention and interrogation of enemy combatants . . . would be unconstitutional."[33] This became known as a commander-in-chief "override"—the asserted ability of the executive to immunize state officials from criminal charges.

Third, the memo discusses possible defenses for state agents accused of violating laws governing interrogation practices. Even if a method of interrogation constituted torture, and even if the application of the torture ban was not held to be an unconstitutional limitation on the president's war-making powers, agents of the state could raise two kinds of defenses: necessity and self-defense. In other words, after restricting what counts as torture to "the most extreme forms of physical and mental harm" in an effort to provide legal cover for other forms of coercive interrogation usually considered to be torture, Bybee invokes necessity to justify such torture and "eliminate criminal liability."[34] Here, at the end of the memo, a version of the ticking-bomb hypothetical makes an appearance. "Standard criminal law defenses of necessity and self-defense," Bybee writes, "could justify interrogation methods needed to elicit information to prevent a direct and imminent threat to the United States and its citizens."[35] Necessity appears as the final outlet for extralegal action—if all other legal arguments and maneuvering fail, the doctrine of necessity may be invoked to justify the violence of torture.

The key here is the term "justification." The Bybee memo does not claim necessity as an excuse but rather as a justification. A justification means that the action is claimed as morally right, not as a moral wrong that, given the circumstances, should go unpunished.[36] As a justification, the necessity defense is premised on a version of the ticking-bomb scenario, which Bybee suggests is the post-9/11 reality:

> On September 11, 2001, al Qaeda launched a surprise covert attack on civilian targets in the United States. . . . According to public and governmental reports, al Qaeda has other sleeper cells within the United States that may be planning similar attacks. Indeed, al Qaeda plans apparently include efforts to develop and deploy chemical, biological and nuclear weapons of mass destruction. Under these circumstances, a detainee may possess information that could enable the United States to prevent attacks that potentially could equal or surpass the September 11 attacks in their magnitude.[37]

Interrogations that do violate the ban on torture might then be justified in these circumstances. The justification is stronger, Bybee claims, the greater the certainty of state actors that "a particular individual has information needed to prevent an attack" and the "the more likely it appears that a terrorist attack is likely to occur."

A working group's authorization of "enhanced interrogation techniques" in April 2003, signed by Donald Rumsfeld, followed directly from the Bybee memo and repeated many of its arguments.[38] This report repeats and expands the Bybee memo's defense of presidential prerogative, as rooted in the U.S. Constitution, defending the "President's complete discretion in exercising the Commander-in-Chief power," including the "interrogation of unlawful combatants." The Working Group Report adds, in the conclusion of its discussion of presidential prerogative, what is arguably the real purpose of the discussion: the generation of a legal paper trail to immunize state officials in advance: "As this authority is inherent in the President, exercise of it by subordinates would be best if it can be shown to have derived from the President's authority through Presidential directive or other writing."[39]

The report also reproduces verbatim Bybee's discussion of the necessity defense. It adds a discussion of "superior orders" as a defense for a subordinate accused of engaging in torture. The report declares that "the defense of superior orders will generally be available for U.S. Armed Forces personnel engaged in exceptional interrogations except when the conduct goes so far as to be patently unlawful." But this report adds a discussion of the necessity defense in relation to military courts martial and cautions that "military courts have treated the necessity defense with disfavor."[40] According to Jane Mayer, "in March, 2005, the Pentagon declared the working-group report a non-operational 'historical' document."[41]

The Bybee memo also became nonoperational when it was withdrawn in 2004[42] and replaced by a superseding memo. However, the memo still functioned recursively despite its withdrawal; the discussion of possible, future necessity defenses that could be raised in a criminal prosecution looped back onto law: both the memo's grounding of presidential prerogative in a theory of constitutional necessity and its elaboration of a necessity defense for accused torturers form the backdrop of the Detainee Treatment Act's immunity provision.

The official withdrawal of the Bybee memo, one week before Alberto Gonzales' confirmation hearings, occurred in what has been called a "confirmation conversion." The withdrawal was prompted by the political controversy surrounding the memo after it was leaked in June 2004. This leak occurred in the wake of the Abu Ghraib torture scandal following the *60 Minutes* exposé and Seymour Hersh's *New Yorker* article on (and photographs of) prisoner abuse. The withdrawal of the Bybee memo did not occur until December 2004, but it was presaged by critical comments made by Gonzales. On June 22, 2004, then–White House Counsel Gonzales criticized the memo at a press conference. Gonzales suggested that the memo might have overreached: "There was an analysis on a question that was not presented, which was the President's constitutional authority as Commander-in-Chief. He hasn't exercised that authority. It's unnecessary. And so that would be one example of something that is being looked at."[43] Then, in December 2004, the week before Gonzales' confirmation hearings to become Attorney General, the Justice Department officially withdrew the Bybee memo and replaced it with a new one. Daniel Levin's superseding memo[44] is overwhelmingly devoted to the issue of defining what counts as torture, rejecting Bybee's restrictive definition and providing a strong condemnation of torture. For instance, Levin writes: "Although Congress defined 'torture' under sections 2340–2340A to require conduct specifically intended to cause 'severe' pain or suffering, we do not believe Congress intended to reach only conduct involving 'excruciating and agonizing' pain or suffering."[45]

By contrast, the Levin memo's comments concerning presidential power to immunize torture as commander-in-chief and the ability of accused torturers to raise the defenses of necessity and self-defense are briefer and echo Gonzales's statement. Levin writes: "Because the discussion in that memorandum concerning the President's Commander-in-Chief power and the potential defenses to liability was—and remains—unnecessary, it has been eliminated from the analysis that follows."[46] In other words, the memo does not repudiate the necessity and self-defense justifications but simply declares them "unnecessary." As Luban argues, the retraction of the Bybee memo was perhaps the most minimal retraction possible. "Levin includes no indication that torture lite, or even torture medium, is prohibited by the statute. Nor does Levin retract the Bybee memo's analyses of self-defense or necessity; it simply declines to discuss defenses."[47]

Elshtain's caution that we should not write "elaborate justifications" for torture appears to be the lesson learned by the Bush administration by the time of the Levin memo. The deleted sections regarding presidential power and criminal defenses were not deleted as bad law but as "irrelevant," "inappropriate," and "unnecessary." In other words, the retraction of the torture memo did not repudiate the necessity defense. Rather, it declared that discussion of the necessity defense is itself "unnecessary." Why is it unnecessary? The first possibility is that these sections were unnecessary because, as Levin himself declared, "we do not torture." Levin asserts that Bybee's discussions of commander-in-chief powers and the necessity defense are unnecessary because the president has made "an unequivocal directive that United States personnel not engage in torture."[48] But if this is the reason, why not explicitly rule out the defenses of necessity and self-defense?

But there is another unstated reason why these discussions of necessity might be considered "unnecessary": when faced with intense political criticism and contestation, necessity may migrate back from the legal domain to the extralegal domain. Those sections of legal analysis are unnecessary because necessity places us in the domain of the extralegal. Necessity knows no law and sovereign power will do what it needs to do.[49]

And if the retraction seeks to reinstate the illusion of a liberal legal order without violence, it also retains, through its silences, through its *discretion*, the figure of the responsible torturer. Necessity compels him to embrace, ascetically and with a heavy heart, those mechanisms of violence that have no place within the law. The claim that the necessity, self-defense, and commander-in-chief portions of the Bybee memo were "unnecessary" returns us to a silent necessity. As Sanford Levinson writes, "the administration's position is that discussion of the president's legal authority to torture is irrelevant because the United States simply does not torture. This is almost certainly a lie. . . . I have no doubt that the administration's position is precisely that set out by Professor Yoo and Judge Bybee in the withdrawn memo, though it is now what might be termed a 'secret' position."[50]

Indeed, the compromise reached by McCain and Bush incorporates the logic of the Bybee memo, despite that it had been withdrawn and replaced, with those necessity sections deemed "unnecessary." The Detainee Treatment Act's immunity provision reads:

> In any civil action or criminal prosecution against an officer, employee, member of the Armed Forces, or other agent of the United States Government . . . arising out of the officer, employee, member of the Armed Forces, or other agent's engaging in specific operational practices, that involve detention and interrogation of aliens who the President or his designees have determined are believed to be engaged in or associated with international terrorist activity . . . and that were officially authorized and determined to be lawful at the time that they were conducted, it shall be a defense that such officer, employee, member of the Armed Forces, or other agent did not know that the practices were unlawful and a person of ordinary sense and understanding would not know the practices were unlawful.[51]

The justification for a state official committing torture has now shifted. It is no longer based on a set of certainties or perceived certainties about necessity but rather on a set of uncertainties or perceived uncertainties about the law. The Bybee memo originally tried to rewrite the law of torture; its apparent repudiation in the Levin memo and Detainee Treatment Act incorporate the simple fact of the memo's existence as a defense against laws banning torture.[52] The success of this paper trail in leading to legal immunity is further demonstrated by the passage of the Military Commissions Act in 2006, which gives legal immunity to state officials engaged in torture before the passage of the McCain amendment in 2005.

What this process revealed is that necessity claims might not function in the real world as singular excuses. Rather they might become new justificatory norms to govern agents in a bureaucracy who, far from confronting the hypothetical ticking-bomb exception (and all the certainty of knowledge that this fantasy entails),[53] seek bureaucratically validated procedures to govern the interrogation of various detainees about whom little is known. But movement in the other direction is at least possible as well, when necessity claims are rejected and when "reason of state" meets public contestation in democratic politics. It is political work on norms and expectations and background understandings that can expand and legitimate necessity claims, and it is the pressure of political opposition and contestation that can narrow necessity claims.

If the lynchpin of Gross's extralegal-measures model is executive honesty, the necessary condition for such public contestation of necessity in the real world may be bureaucratic disobedience and the practice of leaking sensitive information anonymously. Indeed, a different concept of responsibility can be seen in the very act that gave the public access to key information in the torture scandal. Against both Elshtain's ethic of responsibility for leaders and Weber's notion of bureaucratic responsibility, a third necessitarian ethic of responsibility can be perceived in the "extralegal" whistle-blowing actions of executive-branch bureaucrats. Indeed, where Gross and Elshtain posit the need for extralegal action such as torture in conditions of necessity, in a political regime devoted not to candid disclosures of extralegality[54] but secrecy, the relevant, courageous, and risky extralegal action by "responsible" civil service agents may be the action of unauthorized disclosure.

The "Torture Memo" and the Ethics of Conviction

Elshtain is arguing against three positions: the Kantian deontological moralist who says "no torture ever"; the utilitarian who makes torture the clean result of a simple calculation; and Alan Dershowitz's torture-warrant idea, which accepts as its basis the ticking-bomb hypothetical but in contrast to Elshtain's approach supports juridical, legal processes for managing the exceptional case. About the deontologist, Elshtain thinks this position is not based on a view of responsible politics but rather on a version of what Weber describes as "an ethics of conviction": his moral absolutism makes him unwilling to dirty his hands. He would let thousands die to avoid "violating his own conscience," while the leader with an ethic of responsibility "acts in the light of harsh necessity [and] does not rank his or her 'purity' above human lives."[55]

Elshtain, then, contrasts the responsible politician and the politician who privileges his or her moral purity in a way that parallels Max Weber's distinction between an ethics of responsibility and an ethics of conviction. But Elshtain neglects to mention another possibility—a disturbing one— which Weber explores in "Politics as a Vocation." While a concern with moral purity (the ethics of conviction) is *logically* connected to a moralist's nonviolence, to the refusal to dirty one's hands (as in the example of the deontologist), in *practice*, according to Weber, it is often connected with the most severe and unconscionable forms of political violence. This is puzzling. After all, for someone with an ethics of conviction, purity of motive, purity of intention is everything, so how can he or she justify the use of violence? For someone operating from such an ethics of conviction, the only logical approach would be to reject all politics and its violent means. As Weber writes, "it logically has only one possibility. That is to *repudiate every* action that makes use of morally suspect means, logically."[56] However, according to Weber what is most disturbing about politicians operating with only an ethics of conviction is the extent to which they are, in practice, willing to employ violence: "In the world of realities, of course, we see again and again how the representatives of an ethics of conviction suddenly become transformed into chiliastic prophets. For example, people who have just preached 'love against force' are found calling for the use of force the very next moment. It is always the very *last* use of force that will then bring about a situation in which *all* violence will have been destroyed."[57]

This type of "conviction" politician is all too willing to employ violent means. However, he should not be confused with the stylized Benthamite utilitarian politician often raised by philosophers (including Elshtain herself) as the classic case of the type of leader who violates persons' rights in the name of a greater good, justifying torture with a summing up of individual utilities. Rather, it is the purity of his moral conviction and not the calculation of consequences that lies behind the violence: "Such a man believes that if an action performed out of pure conviction has evil consequences, then the responsibility must lie not with the agent but with the world."[58] A politics of pure conviction, of passionate commitment to a moral cause, can become a politics of extreme violence.

Simon Critchley captures this dangerous combination when he characterizes the Bush administration as "crypto-Schmittian," a combination of a politics attuned to (or actively producing) the dynamics of violence, security, and the friend/enemy distinction and an antipolitical, moralistic ideology of freedom. Critchley suggests that this ideology works by constructing enemies and mobilizing fears of terrorism with great skill while at the same time deploying these tactics within a depoliticizing (and, for Schmitt, all the more dangerous) set of universalistic ideals of humanity, freedom, and God's will:

> On the one hand, the concept of the political is based on the fantasy construction of the enemy and maintains the economy of terror that allows order to be secured in the so-called homeland. On the other hand, the decisive feature of the current US administration is a thoroughgoing hypocrisy about the political. . . . Contemporary US power espouses an utterly moralizing, universalist, indeed millennial ideology whose key

signifier is freedom. . . . A political decision of the classic friend-enemy variety was made on the basis of the depoliticizing instance of God's will. The power of this kind of political thinking is that the enemy is not just, as in classical war, unlike us, or advancing a territorial claim. . . . On the contrary, on the crypto-Schmittian view, the enemy is evil and becomes, in Schmitt's words, an outlaw of humanity who can therefore legitimately be annihilated.[59]

Elshtain hints at a similar danger when she argues that Dershowitz's torture-warrant proposal "partakes of the same moralistic-legalism as the statesperson who values his pure conscience above all else and who will not violate a moral norm under any circumstances."[60] A defense of torture that appears to be driven by a reluctant, realist sensibility betrays a lurking moralism that transforms a necessary evil into a moral right.

Similarly, Bybee's torture memo *appears* like it belongs in the "ethics of responsibility" vein and its tragic recognition of necessary wrongdoing by politicians. But lurking underneath the posture of tough-nosed realism lies something much closer to Weber's ethics of conviction, with its emphasis on the goodness of intentions and absolutist ethical principles. And the underlying ethic of conviction appears in a surprising place: in Bybee's discussion of the necessity defense and its bizarre juxtaposition of torture and abortion. At the conclusion of the discussion of the necessity defense, Bybee raises one context in which a necessity defense would be *impossible*: when the exception had been already ruled out explicitly in the relevant legislation. Bybee's example—abortion law—comes out of the blue:

> If Congress explicitly has made clear that violation of a statute cannot be outweighed by the harm avoided, courts cannot recognize the necessity defense. LaFave and Israel [*sic*] provide as an example an abortion statute that made clear that abortions even to save the life of the mother would still be a crime; in such cases the necessity defense would be unavailable. . . . Here, however, Congress has not explicitly made a determination of values vis-à-vis torture.[61]

This odd example is a telling slip—a brief glimpse into the intensely moralistic "ethic of conviction" that lies beneath the apparently tough-nosed rhetoric of realism about the "unprecedented" situation after 9/11. While it is true that a "no-exceptions" abortion statute is the only example that LaFave and Scott raise in the text itself under this point about legislative provisions ruling out necessity claims (the footnotes raise a case involving a nuclear power plant as well), their full discussion is slightly more complex:

Thus the legislature might, in its abortion statute, expressly provide that the crime is not committed if the abortion is performed to save the mother's life; under such a statute there would be no need for courts to speculate about the relative value of preserving the fetus and safeguarding the mother's life. Conversely, the abortion statute might expressly (or by its legislative history) provide that the crime is committed even when the abortion is performed to save the mother's life; here too the legislature has made a determination of values and by its decision thereon foreclosed the possibility of the defense that the abortion was necessary to save life.[62]

LaFave and Scott's own cited cases either come pre-*Roe* (a 1939 case in which a doctor was exonerated after performing an abortion by "necessity" because of the health of the mother) or concern the necessity defense as raised by *pro-life demonstrators* who claim that civil disobedience was necessary to save the life of a fetus. While the Bybee memo does not distort LaFave and Scott's main point, the selective citing of the text is illuminating in how it purges from the discussion any hint of ideological complexity. Furthermore, the discussion is especially curious in the way it juxtaposes the almost unlimited exceptionality defended vis-à-vis laws against torture with an absolutist, no-exceptions, hypothetical abortion statute that even rules out necessity defenses to save the life of the mother. The moralism of necessity here is revealed in the way that underlying notions of innocence (the fetus) and guilt (the terrorist) frame the choice between a rigid legalism (a no-exceptions abortion ban) and a porous "legal grey hole"[63] surrounding violent interrogation. Exceptions and absolutism orbit around overdetermined categories of guilt and innocence. The fetus, as a form of life constituted as pure innocence, triggers a purist's legality without exceptions. The enemy combatant, by contrast, triggers the suspension of normal law, including what had appeared to be absolute prohibitions against torture.

Conclusion

There is a broader institutional point to be made here about the question of political responsibility in circumstances of claimed necessity. It is that we need to take seriously the notion of complexity within the executive branch of government. The normative debate about emergency powers has tended to rest with an outdated notion of executive power—ironically, left-wing critics and right-wing defenders seem to agree on an image of a "unitary executive." Then the debate proceeds to evaluate the relative merits of legislatures and courts in constraining (or authorizing) a "dirty-hands" executive. Lockean princes and Roman dictators loom large as precedents. But perhaps we are looking in the wrong places.[64] As William Scheuerman writes: "Despite the traditional metaphor of the single executive, the machinery of the modern executive is a complex and multiheaded creature, made up of oftentimes competing bureaucratic fiefdoms. Conflict and disagreement are no less common there than within the legislature or judiciary."[65] Taking as a starting point the distinct roles and norms within the executive bureaucracy, it is imperative that we examine what happens to an ethic of responsibility aimed at leaders when it migrates into a bureaucracy and remain attuned to bureaucratic dissidence as a source of constraint on executive extralegalism. Finally, for bureaucratic acts of dissidence to work as a source of constraint requires the cultivation of a public culture of citizen responsibility. On this (though not on the problematic assumption of an executive's confession of extralegal activity) I am in full agreement with Oren Gross. But such a public culture is undermined, not assisted, by those recursive legal processes that turn "extralegal" necessity into legal indemnity.

CHAPTER 2

How to Do Responsibility: Apology and Medical Error

S. Lochlann Jain

In a ghoulish misreplication of the clichéd diagnosis in which a patient is told he has only a short time to live before cancer kills him, a young man at Kaiser Permanente in San Jose was recently told that he had only three days to live after hospital staff mistakenly administered cancer treatment into his epidural shunt in the place of another drug. Accidents involving toxic chemotherapy drugs have happened before, for example, a highly publicized lethal overdose was given to a young *Boston Globe* journalist a few years ago.[1] Chemotherapy drugs have evolved from nitrogen mustard gas, originally used as a chemical weapon. They have been used since the early 1940s in hospitals, and one might wonder, given the combination of their relatively long history of use and their extreme toxicity, why such seemingly avoidable errors happen with some frequency.

One could imagine that in many hospital settings, doctors will be rushed, nurses undertrained, and pharmacists sloppy. Indeed, mistakes in pharmaceutical delivery have been recorded for hundreds of years, and they offer some of the earliest cases in the burgeoning area of law involving medical error. One might well ask why drugs aren't color coded such that certain classes of drugs can go only into certain colors or designs of containers. One might wonder about designing epidural-shunt systems that would differ from chemotherapy-delivery ports, such that potentially poisonous drugs could only match one particular type of hookup, making it physically impossible for a nurse to put the wrong type of chemical into the wrong patient. One might consider this issue as an issue of design—of labeling, bottle shape, storage cupboard organization—as well as one of human error. Further, one can project this kind of systematic error—no one's fault and no one is noticing—all the way back into the delivery systems, the drugs' manufacture, and the initial research. How can we trust that the active ingredients are in the pills we take or that the cell line with the right cancer is being used in the basic research?

Some reports estimate that well over one hundred thousand people a year die in the United States due to medical errors—and these account for only immediate deaths, not those who develop short- or long-term disabilities or delayed yet still premature deaths.[2] In addition, there is no good way to collect this data, since it relies on the self-reporting of physicians and hospitals, who may have an interest in underreporting. However, given the low rates of litigation (only about 2 percent of injured patients ever attempt a lawsuit), state-by-state legislation limiting plaintiff compensation to only $250,000 in California (not even enough to cover the cost of the medical malpractice trial itself), and the lack of other systems of accountability, very little incentive exists for medical systems to improve.[3] What, then, does responsibility in medical practice mean, particularly in relation to the recent fashion of medical apology?

The case outlined above is a more egregious and obvious one than many: it's hard to justify or evade fault for the unexpected deaths of young people in a clear case of drug misadministration. The aspect that I dwell on in this essay concerns the hospital's publicity statement that it took "full responsibility" for the incident.[4] The press releases did not discuss what responsibility might mean in this context. One imagines that it might cover offering compensation to the victim's family, redesigning the drug-delivery systems at all Kaiser hospitals, or punishing or firing the individuals involved in the deadly error. However, the incident raises a new aspect of an emergent public relations adoption of the term responsibility, one that is found in the increasing demand on doctors to offer apologies to patients. From a legal-studies perspective, the medical apology offers one place to better understand what responsibility means in conditions of bureaucratic for-profit medicine. Specifically, we will see how it relies on contradictory modes of care and corporate relations that balance and rely on a logic of individuated notions of neoliberal responsibility, an intense desire for a human and personal interaction, and principles of cost spreading central in different ways to risk management and tort.

Insurance companies present the option of the apology to doctors as a way of limiting medical malpractice claims. The doctor is asked to lend a human face to what might be considered a medical bureaucracy—a bureaucracy that controls how much time the doctor will spend with patients, which tests and treatments the insurance companies will pay for, and how carefully and competently the delivery of those treatments will be done. One might suggest that the generally high compensation enjoyed by physicians includes taking on this role: providing a human touch to the system while simultaneously negotiating conflicting patient and industry interests. Others might suggest that such apologies force physicians to become fall guys for the medical bureaucracy. Such role slippages in the physician's job description let us reflect on medical responsibility in the contexts of humanist aspects of apology and the material expense of medical error for patients, physicians, and bureaucracies.

A paradox lies at the core of current discussions about medical error in accounts of both apology and medical malpractice law. It has to do with the human imperfections of even the best and most motivated physicians. On the one hand, doctors indisputably make mistakes in diagnosis and procedure that could have been avoided. Quite simply, doctors can maim and kill people with the slightest slip-up, the tiniest moment of inattention. Doctors make mistakes: some doctors many more than others, some with more or less grace, and some with more or less associated attention and care. It is also virtually impossible for a nonspecialist to know or find out how good a physician is, since good manners do not mean good medicine—nor, necessarily, do loving patients make a competent physician. Data on physician skill and efficacy are not collected. On this side of the paradox lie claims that vary as widely as the observation that mistakes will inevitably be made (to err is human, after all) and the claim that apology is simply a conceptual and linguistic impossibility in a power dynamic within which one person's oversight can kill another person. Still, on this side of the equation, claims that doctors should have no responsibility for intentional or unintentional mistakes and that the responsibility should lie solely with the system seem too indemnifying.

On the other hand, fault for error can often be distributed in many ways, as one sees with the Kaiser Permanente example. Does fault lie with the system designer who neglected to use a system of color coding, the nurse who didn't check the drug name, the technician who misfilled the prescription, or the person who misstocked the shelves? Was it the doctor whose handwriting was illegible, or were the names of the drugs too similar? Was it the insurance company that would only pay for only a few minutes to administer the drug, rather than for the thirty minutes that adequate attention might have required? In this sense, claims to individual fault miss the structural nature of injury production.

The use of the medical apology exemplifies the contradiction at the heart of contemporary corporate medical provision, and this contradiction is rarely foregrounded and examined in the context of differing notions and presumptions of responsibility. At the level of analysis, one question becomes: on what basis, to whom or what, and with what goals can wrongs be assigned? What political models do such assignments rely on and presume? At the level of structural change: if no one is responsible for the moral—rather than the economic—wrongs, then how can improvement in what is clearly a broken system of healthcare delivery be fulfilled? Is responsibility merely a public relations moment, something that is realized through the speaking of it? The conditions of modern medical bureaucracy call for the development of new ideas and analyses of responsibility, ideas different from those offered by either medical malpractice law (which has utterly failed in regulating the provision of medical care) or the medical apology (which does not indicate any responsibility toward systematic improvements to reduce medical error).

Tracing Fault

Even the best doctors carry malpractice insurance in order to protect them from personally having to pay the costs of rectifying errors made when peoples' lives are at stake.[5] It also protects them from having to pay for defending themselves in court in the case of a frivolous or misguided claim. Study after study has shown that juries tend to be predisposed in favor of physician-defendants, but even the winner of the case will incur significant costs if the case goes to trial, largely because of the high charges levied by medical experts and the high hourly wages of defense lawyers hired by the insurance firms (plaintiffs' lawyers work on a contingency-fee basis).[6] Ideally, medical malpractice insurance also protects a physician's patients, potentially allowing a way for medical errors to be paid for without bankrupting the physician. Medical malpractice insurance accounts for about 2 percent of healthcare costs and is folded into the costs of healthcare, and in this ideal world, these costs are merely part of the cost of doing a dangerous business. Most business owners carry insurance in case their customers are injured. Bugaboo Sports, in Santa Cruz, for example, carries insurance for one million dollars, the same amount carried by most

California primary-care physicians, lest a shopper slip on the floor and break a leg. In this sense, the medical malpractice system offers an insurance system, albeit an expensive and wasteful one.

These theoretical underpinnings of medical malpractice law recognize that some medical errors are inevitable and that neither should physicians be held criminally responsible nor should patients go untreated or personally pay for physician mistakes. This theory suggests that mistakes might be kept to a minimum through careful medical practice and that the threat of litigation would ensure deterrence and systematic changes where necessary. Insurance premiums would be priced a little above the costs of payouts, and no one would make undue financial profit or find themselves overcome by greed.

However, medical malpractice law is more typically understood as a system of blame, and doctors tend to take claims personally. This point is absolutely critical in understanding the culture and politics of medical malpractice law and the confluence of what one might expect to be very different investments in patient health. Of the many places to turn to understand this personalization, I look here at Atul Gawande's comments in his universally acclaimed book *Complications: A Surgeon's Notes on an Imperfect Science*, which reached a wide audience in the United States after having been serialized in the *New Yorker*. Among the first of a genre of popular books by physicians, Gawande writes a compelling account of his training to become a surgeon.

In some sense, the book offers a revolutionary account of surgery. While various internal debates in the profession have drawn an audience outside itself, particularly where patients have come to request higher standards of evidence that surgical interventions are not overly aggressive (as in the women's health movement), by and large the professional debates have remained inside the field of practitioners. Surgery's particular mode of physical labor, requiring cutting into other humans, the enormous risks of such endeavors, as well as leaps of faith in its efficacy against the huge costs and side effects of surgery, nearly seems to require the "great man" philosophy after which the profession has modeled itself.[7] Gawande manages both stylistically and through the details of his medical training to remain inside of the surgical profession while commenting on it as an interested and informed observer. In this sense, he occupies a space that is both insider and not quite insider as he narrates his coming-of-age story as a surgical resident.

To be sure, his narrative brings all the elements of a good adventure—life, death, blood, close calls, quick decisions, emergencies, and attempts to save lives in a system that seems often to work against him. In one instance, Gawande recounts his inability to successfully give an emergency tracheotomy to a patient.[8] He readily admits his own shortcomings in the event: he does not call for help soon enough out of hubris, he doesn't have enough light or suction, and he is so inexperienced that he makes a cut horizontally rather than vertically. The patient only survives through a pure, last-minute stroke of luck, when another physician inserts a pediatric breathing tube.

Who knows if Gawande would have written about this case had the patient died. But this example, coming early in the book, does critical work on several levels. First, it factually records a simply horrifying instance of an improperly trained doctor with ego and insecurity pressures and insufficient institutional or professional support involved in a potentially fatal procedure. Second, the reader understands this instance as a commonplace event in hospitals, and Gawande spills a fair amount of ink convincing his readers that the training of surgeons requires such risk and cost to real flesh. Third, the incident provides an opportunity for Gawande to explain the procedure for the hospital's safety and disciplinary review of such events. And fourth, the story and others interpellates the reader into Gawande's account, through its use of some key literary strategies by which the power differentials between doctor and patient are disavowed. (For example, he comments that once his patient is able to breathe, Gawande is as well, as if actual and metaphorical breathing were the same, or as if the held breath of a stressed professional were equivalent to a patient actually suffocating on the table.) Through this inauspicious conversational tone, *Complications* makes a hard-hitting political argument. The reader cannot *but* sympathize with this autobiographical narrative, in which the honest surgeon as upstanding citizen does his heroic best in a system that could be better.

The disciplining that Gawande receives after this failed tracheotomy consisted of a reprimand by a senior colleague, and what becomes important in the retelling is Gawande's feelings and the private interactions among the surgeons. There was no informing (or even the discussion of informing) the patient or the family of the long period of oxygen deprivation and extraneous cuts and stitches, no apology to the patient, no discussion of compensation, and no consideration of systematic changes that could have avoided the situation in the first place. In thinking through surgical discipline and responsibility Gawande does not discuss those things but rather turns to a posture about medical malpractice law:

There are all sorts of reasons that it would be wrong to take my licenses away or to take me to court. These reasons do not absolve me. Whatever the limits of the M&M [the meeting of physicians that reviews the errors of the week, including that one], its fierce *ethic of personal responsibility for errors is a formidable virtue.* No matter what measures are taken, doctors will sometimes falter, and it isn't reasonable to ask that we achieve perfection. What is reasonable is to ask that we never cease to aim for it.[9]

The reader learns little about what this "personal responsibility" actually means, though certainly in a sense it seems to be something that surgeons have to each other rather than to the patient, though the patient ostensibly benefits when the surgery goes well. Responsibility in this case did not mean disclosing the events to the patient; nor did it mean completing a structural analysis of the factors that led to what would have been a death or serious disability.

Gawande sidesteps the two most controversial questions raised by his book. First, what *should* happen to those patients who provide the meat on which surgeons practice their highly remunerated craft? While readers may agree that practice on real patients is a necessary evil, they may want some recognition of the human costs of that practice. In discussing how people unwittingly donate their bodies to the cause of training surgeons, he readily admits that he would never allow a surgical student to work on him or his family. He thus raises a question he does not pursue, questions that raise but also exceed class and education differentials in the receipt of medical care.

In the world beyond the training of Atul Gawande, those least able to afford the extra financial costs, lobby their carriers for coverage for the extra health problems caused by surgeons in training, and bear the physical costs of ill health are the ones who unknowingly are donating their health to this cause. But if we as analysts want to put our sympathies with the patients who will bear the costs, it is worth remembering that once inside the medical system, no one is immune to the basic fact that bodies are simply work objects that sometimes must bear mistakes, errors, and sloppiness. Second, had the botched tracheotomy ended in a death, how would it have been explained? As an unpreventable accident? As an acceptable outcome of an emergency situation? As a compensable medical error?

Physicians have been unable to "murder" patients in the normal course of medical treatment since the mid-nineteenth century, when the law determined that anyone who called himself a physician would be legally protected from criminal charges.[10] This led to the subsequent development of more clear professional training and certificate programs and to the ongoing externalization of alternative and "quack" medicine. Since that time, patients have had a legal right not to the best care but simply to average care. As a jury in 1857 was charged, since every physician cannot by definition give superior care, to require such care would mean that many people would simply get no medical attention at all: "That the law did not require of the defendants eminent or extraordinary skill; that this kind of skill is possessed by few. An absolute necessity requires that the wants of a community must be supplied with the best medical knowledge its means and location will command. To require the highest degree of skill would deprive all places, except large cities, of medical men."[11] It is never clear in Gawande's tale whether the successful emergency tracheotomy is considered average or exceptional medical care.

Contemporary medical malpractice plaintiffs still must prove that the care they received did not meet the professional "standard of care," for which they depend on other physician experts to testify. Only very occasionally will a court attempt to push the profession to adopt higher standards, as in one case in which a judge ruled that even if it were not the standard of care to count sponges after a surgery, it should have been. By and large, physicians are the gatekeepers to the standards of their profession.

How, then, do nodes of responsibility (in terms of how deaths are attributed to certain kinds of behaviors or intent) determine how deaths are categorized? A murder is different from an error, different again from an accident. Gawande's text provides an important clue as to how deaths are scripted as acceptable or not. Gawande presents ideas about what a patient—or rather a population of patients—can reasonably expect, except that what he leads us to expect in the best-case scenarios is that these decisions are made behind closed doors, during the surgical M&M meetings. Surgeons will make mistakes, and in his view, when they do, they should not be taken to court.

Medical malpractice law operates on a parallel but opposite basis. The legal theory supposes that since, statistically, some people will suffer inevitable mistakes, the costs of the mistakes should be spread across the population, such that each person pays a little bit for the inevitable mistake that one person will suffer. Medical malpractice law offers a means of distribution such that the cost of the error does not fall to just one person. In this view, it is indeed precisely when a doctor injures a patient that the court should be called on to ensure that amends are made.

In this sense, Gawande confuses several critically important issues. First, he mistakes the individual surgeon who has to learn and who will make mistakes throughout his career for someone who should be responsible only to the profession (and not to the patient) for those mistakes. He overrides the enormous costs of those mistakes, acknowledging them only through his own efforts to try to avoid them. He further confuses the compensatory function of law for a moral system of blame. While he admits to feeling shame (feelings in a man are good, although how would such sentimentality have gone over had the author been one of the 3 per- cent of surgeons who are women?), he completely ignores the questions of patient knowledge of error, whether patients being practiced on should pay reduced rates for care, how the systematic analysis of error might help correct current problems with healthcare delivery, such as a lack of light, jammed suction equipment, or, as in another case he mentions, a lack of resources for quick research into which emergency medical procedure might yield the best results and what backup plans would be appropriate. Aiming for perfection is certainly an admirable goal, but ultimately, in Gawande's book, perfection remains a noble individuated fantasy.

The medical system has notoriously little oversight. One physician re- ported to me that she receives tremendous resistance from physicians in trying to set up a system for analyzing medical error at her clinic. Dr. Yvez (name changed for privacy) attempts to employ "root-cause analysis": in any given situation, she asks the doctors at her clinic which parts of the error were preventable, potentially preventable, or not preventable.[12]

In her view, medical errors are often built into the system. For example, the two vastly different drugs, magnesium sulphate and morphine sul- phate, are written the same in prescription shorthand. Or often very dif- ferent drugs are stored in similar packaging and placed near each other in storage areas. The way that American health insurance works also means that patients change doctors often, making it virtually impossible to build relationships between physicians and patients or even to maintain com- plete patient records. Physicians, then, may not have the history and rela- tionship necessary (an understanding of how an individual might present symptoms, a desire to spend some extra time with a patient when neces- sary, or a sense of the patient's personal and work life) to make good diag- noses. The National Academy concluded that the high number of deaths due to medical error is simply the "price we pay for not having organized systems of care with clear lines of accountability."[13]

The potential success of the root-cause method of understanding medi- cal error was demonstrated in the 1970s, when the death rates of patients undergoing anesthesia in the United States was one in ten thousand.[14] Simple mistakes were leading to the deaths of 3,500 Americans a year, even with a doctor dedicated solely to administering the drug and watching the patient during surgery. In early 1978, the engineer Jeff Cooper published a paper documenting his study on anesthesia, "Preventable Mishaps: A Study of Human Factors." He reported:

> Most of the preventable incidents involved human error (82 per cent), with breathing circuit disconnections, inadvertent changes in gas flow, and drug-syringe errors being frequent problems. . . . Equipment design was indictable in many categories of human error, as were inadequate experience and insufficient familiarity with equipment or with the specific surgical procedure. Other factors frequently associated with incidents were inadequate communication among personnel, haste or lack of precaution, and distraction.[15]

The paper was notable in the sense that it was written from the perspective of an engineer and took system design into account. While widely discussed in the late 1970s, there was no move to change the systems, and the statistics became a stand-in for one of the acceptable risks of surgery. Oxygen monitors, for example, had been available for years, but no one used them. The machines were not standardized: on some, one turned the knob to the left for more oxygen, and on others one turned the knob to the right. Shortly afterward, ABC's *20/20* showcased the issue, reporting that thousands of people had been permanently disabled from anesthesia. Finally, Ellison Pierce, the president of the Society of Anesthesiologists, mobilized the society to focus on the problem after a friend's daughter died during a routine procedure.

Science and Technology Studies (STS) has developed some ideas of how responsibility can be shifted between objects and actors in technical systems. Peter Galison, in tracing accident reconstruction in airline accident investigation, writes that "there is an instability between accounts terminating in *persons* and those ending with *things . . . it is* always possible to trade a human action for a technological one: failure to notice can be swapped against a system of failure to make noticeable."[16] Where blame rests—with the person or the thing—is an intensely political question. It becomes more complicated when the thing being blamed is a service—and one given not in the context of a contract where a patient has fully informed consent but in the context of a tort, in which a patient has a right not to be injured. How might we think further through these notions of individual responsibility, bureaucratic systems, and patient injury? The medical apology provides one venue for such analysis.

Apology

Nearly everyone agrees that the medical malpractice system rarely works
in its stated goals, either to fairly compensate those injured or to encourage systematic changes in healthcare provision to reduce injury rates. One
recent approach adopted by insurance companies to reduce the incidence
of medical malpractice litigation trains physicians to apologize immediately after a medical error. These apologies generally take the form of a
carefully worded statement that takes "responsibility" for an incident and
offers a small settlement. While leaving open the precise meaning of responsibility, this approach to medical error is based on studies demonstrating that the attitude of physicians matters a great deal in injured peoples'
decisions to initiate litigation. Many times patients want an acknowledgment of the harm done and an apology rather than an actual monetary
award, and the law does not allow for apology.

Despite the legal theory of tort that sees the law's role as something
of a cost-spreading mechanism, the determination of the injured's status
requires the physician and patient to take an oppositional stance, one in
which each side argues their case as strongly as possible in an effort to
"win." Thus, doctors and patients, parties that were initially assumed to
be working together toward the higher goal of patient health, take a stance
that may be highly uncomfortable for both. In this legal positioning, the
patient rarely receives an apology and the doctor rarely has a chance to
acknowledge an error.

Commentators on the right and the left have welcomed apology as a
means of healing and avoiding these oppositional and expensive compensatory regimes. However, these commentators have missed the critical and
high stakes and thus have diminished the role of the apology in constituting new models of medical responsibility. On the one hand, the apology
offers a sort of human touch, and patients who welcome it might well find
that the system is at its most "human" precisely when it is attempting to
limit its liability. On the other hand, apology implies a level of responsibility that may not exist, or it implies that some action might be taken when
it will not. And so it remains utterly unclear what the apology has to do
with responsibility, and at the social level, it remains unclear what, precisely, medical responsibility entails.[17]

Tort rather than contract law officially guides the terms of responsibility that inhere in medical practice (this came about in the mid-nineteenth
century). Tort and contract offer differing notions of chance and of the
parties' agency. Thus, the legal relationship between patient and doctor is

not one of mutual agreement about the possible costs and benefits of a treatment but rather one in which the patient has a right not to be injured and a right to sue if the care received does not reach standards set by the profession. The apology seems to be at odds with the legal framing of the relationship.

The apology offers a highly formalized mode of speech intended to promote social healing. Lucian Leape, a main advocate of the medical apology in the United States, writes that an apology serves six functions for the person to whom an apology is directed. The apology heals, he says, by (a) restoring dignity and self-respect to the injured party, where a lack of apology intensifies the humiliation of injury; (b) providing assurance of shared values and reaffirming the injurer's commitment to the rules and values of the relationship; (c) assuring the patient that he is not at fault; (d) assuring the patient that he is now safe and that steps are being taken to ensure no further injury; (e) showing that the doctor is also suffering, thereby leveling the playing field; and (f) demonstrating an understanding of the impact of the injury.[18]

Leape's explication makes several assumptions about the doctor-patient relationship that remain implicit. For example, he seems to assume that suffering levels the power differential between doctor and patient or that modes of suffering are in some way equal. Nevertheless, Leape proffers that a true apology can have an exonerating quality, theoretically similar to the effect of money in a legal damage award, through which everyone can feel heard and attended to. In this sense, as the philosopher of language J. L. Austin writes, apology is a performative act in which the verbal act of apologizing brings a new relationship into being.[19] Often in reporting on the apology, patient narratives are held up in support of its value. One patient, who settled with the hospital after he received an apology for a sponge left inside his body cavity, explained: "They honored me as a human being."[20]

Although the theory behind tort law differs from that of the apology, both doctor and patient can also feel that the costs of the mistake have been made up by a compensatory award negotiated through litigation. In this sense, by negotiating an apology, the insurance companies merely attempt to make the apology happen sooner, in a slightly different form and less expensive way. An apology that enables an early settlement saves money for both plaintiff and defendant at a time when a potential plaintiff may be more inclined to settle for less. Citing reasons that vary from the healing effects of apology to the costs of litigation, many states have encouraged this mode of conflict resolution by disallowing apologies to be used as evidence of wrongdoing in courts, thus protecting doctors and hospitals from having "admitted" to any mistake.[21] In that sense, the honoring of the human is a temporary initiative.

The kinds of errors that occur vary vastly in scope, seriousness, likelihood of being detected by patients or colleagues, and regulation. Certain injuries must be reported to regulatory boards and investigated, such as removing the wrong limb. These cannot be "apologized" for.[22] But for the vast majority of injuries, which have no regulatory infrastructures, insurance companies have significantly reduced their costs by using apologies. Such apologies typically claim responsibility in a vague way (rather than offering specific directives for how they will change practices or procedures) and are used as an alternative method of negotiating settlements for injuries that a hospital's public relations department might describe as "unanticipated medical outcomes" or "possible risks of the procedure."[23]

Citing multiple sources, Liz Kowalczyk wrote in 2005 that:

> Colorado's largest malpractice insurer, COPIC, has enrolled 1,800 physicians in a disclosure program under which they immediately express remorse to patients when medical care goes wrong and describe in detail what happened. . . . Since 2000, COPIC has reimbursed more than 400 patients an average $5,300 each for bad medical outcomes, or a total of about $2 million. . . . Malpractice claims against these 1,800 doctors have dropped 50 percent since 2000, while the cost of settling these doctors' claims has fallen 23 percent. The University of Michigan Health System has cut claims in half and reduced settlements to $1.25 million from $3 million a year since developing a disclosure policy in 2002."[24]

A complicated explication of medical malpractice law and insurance policies discussing the decisions and variability of medical malpractice defense strategy is beyond the scope of this essay but is worth noting, as these insurance strategies make it nearly impossible to interpret the numbers cited by Kowalczyk. But my goal is not to enter the fracas about whether and why medical insurance rates are skyrocketing or discuss how the apology saves and costs money. Rather, I am interested in the politics of adding this particular mode of human interaction into the explication of error and the compensation for injury.

One of the factors that make *Complications* such a compelling read is the way that Gawande negotiates what he understands to be a central mystery of medical practice: the fact that a doctor simply will not perform perfectly every time. Statistically, a doctor will make mistakes every so often while performing relatively simple procedures. As he repeats throughout the book: a doctor may strive for perfection, but she will never reach it. Thus, since error is inevitable, he struggles with how fault should be understood.

The medical apology adds another level of complexity to this question, for the questions of compensation and structural change in healthcare delivery rests on the attribution of responsibility. In the case of medical error, the rescripting of injury is particularly interesting, because the profession already requires a fine balance between the skills of each individual physician and her ability to rely on and work within circumscribed medical protocols (an oncologist would be remiss not to recommend chemotherapy in many instances, even though its actual efficacy for several cancers remains controversial) while bringing her unique judgment and expertise. Even the highest-ranked physician in an operating theater will be dependent on the infrastructure of services and materials available. Thus Gawande analytically and ethically struggles with his apotheosis of the individual surgeon and how to understand him in relationship both to the social organization of the hospital and the social aggregate of patients.

To be sure, Gawande gives examples of the ways that these statistics can be altered. He writes of a hernia hospital in Toronto that perfected a particular surgical procedure, bringing the error rate close to zero, with the implication that error rates for all kinds of surgeries could be brought to zero with attention to questions of structural design and technique. Elsewhere he has written about hospitals' refusals to adopt simple measures such as standardized handwashing and draping procedures that have been shown to diminish infection rates to practically zero. Nevertheless, in *Complications*, statistics perform something of a mystic discourse that helps ground his assertion that surgeons will never reach perfection.

Constructing this language of chance requires a rendering of medical errors as detached from any particular actors or systems. Rendered at the level of the aggregate, a language of chance absorbs the particular circumstances of a wrong cut or a lost sponge, and then these incidents are ritualized into the language of accident. Any injury may be at once predictable at the level of the aggregate and explicable through certain sets of particularized instances. This critical slippage stands in for a sort of humanist bind for Gawande: we want to do right, but we can't. Since we can't, we are doing our best and so should not be sued. The bind is one of action and being acted upon: the doctor is both the person in charge yet still only human in situations that do not "cover" for that humanity through the careful design of technologies and systems.

Only through the concept of the population can an injury be understood as accidental—on the individual level there is always a reason for it.

A driver who runs over a pedestrian is nearly never criminally charged, since the structure of automobiles and intersections seems nearly to require the predictable six thousand annual pedestrian deaths. As I have argued elsewhere, changes to automobile design, changes to modes of responsibility, or changes to intersection policies could reduce these rates at the structural level. In lieu of those social changes, pedestrian fatalities remain predicable. We don't know who it will be, but it *will* be someone, and each time we walk outside we imply our consent that it might be us.[25]

Medical apology cannot be understood outside of the broader attack that insurance companies have led in encouraging tort reform. The insurance industry lobbied extensively to cap damage awards on medical malpractice claims, leaving many people unable to retain a lawyer for their injuries. In California, the maximum award for any medically induced injury is $250,000. Insurance companies have launched a media blitz ridiculing "frivolous claims" and set up in-house legal departments enabling them to battle claims and settle only on the courtroom steps, deliberately driving up costs and scaring contingency-fee plaintiffs lawyers from taking cases. As one plaintiffs' lawyer claimed, a "doctor's apology [will] get the case settled for a lower amount of money, but if there is no immediate settlement, they will aggressively defend their cases."[26]

In these circumstances, what is the potential for the kind of "real" apology described by Leape? Lee Taft, an apology theorist, writes that "the remorse and regret conveyed by the words 'I'm sorry' imply a willingness to change, a promise of forbearance, and an implicit agreement to accept all the consequences, *social, legal, and otherwise*, that flow from having committed the wrongful act."[27] The medical apology seems to be a linguistic and logical impossibility. Medical apologies are carefully scripted. One article reports that doctors are told: "Don't say, 'I'm sorry I cut the wrong blood vessel,' say, 'I'm sorry you had bleeding.' "[28] According to apology theorists, this set of phrases cannot be considered an apology. First, it does not acknowledge the reason for the bleeding. Second, it completely elides the question of responsibility that an apology by definition must address. As I mentioned above, the doctor/patient relationship is one guided by the law of tort. Yet the apology explicitly offers an attempt to avoid the tort system.

In a debate framed around a moot surgery in which an error leads to the patient's death, one commentary enlisted two doctors to argue the cases for and against medical apology. The case against it is particularly illuminating. Keith Naunheim, a medical doctor, argues that when a patient is killed during a procedure, the dead patient will not gain anything from the reasons for apology enumerated by Leape. Further, Naunheim dismisses the benefits of compensation: "Thus, the only 'patient benefit' or goal that might be fulfilled is the potential for 'fair' compensation via litigation. Somehow the words 'fair' and 'litigation' just don't seem to belong in the same sentence in the 21st century medico-legal world."[29] While it is true that Naunheim too easily dismisses medical malpractice law, that is not what I want to dwell on here. What seems like a glib dismissal of the value of apology and an attempt to wriggle out of responsibility actually holds the kernel of an idea worth spelling out further, for Naunheim essentially argues that you can't apologize if you are in no position to.

In this case, Naunheim explains, the doctor is in no position to apologize for three reasons. First, the patient is dead and so cannot play the critical performative role of receiving the apology. Second, medicine is a group project, and so the head surgeon simply cannot be responsible for everything that happens (and so why should he have to apologize?). Third, surgeons will make mistakes, as a basic fact of medicine. In other words, the goals of insurance and tort law aside, a surgeon's words can never meet the linguistic and ethical requirements of apology.

The critical point that Naunheim makes, unintentionally I think, since he does not discuss apology theory and dismisses law out of hand, is that an apology requires a prior relationship between two people, one that simply does not exist in the relationship between doctor and patient (even when the patient is alive). Without that relationship, a nonsensical apology cannot be harnessed to do the work described by Leape, Taft, or Austin.

In claiming that apologies are nonsensical in the case of surgery because doctors will make mistakes, Naunheim reiterates Gawande's quandary. How do we think about well-intentioned physicians making mistakes: what does responsibility mean, and how should it manifest in the statistically necessary mistake? In claiming that physicians should not be blamed for these statistical errors—and, critically, should not be sued—the doctors mistake legal compensation for a moral system of blame rather than seeing it simply as a cost-spreading mechanism similar to any insurance scheme. But the quandary can be taken a step further in thinking about the apology.

This confusion between personal blame and paying the costs of an error can only happen because, as we see with Naunheim, the nature of the relationship between doctor and patient is so easily mischaracterized. A logical sleight of hand between the ethical and legal frameworks of the nature of the doctor-patient relationships plays out such that responsibility, chance, and compensation muddle among one another. In fact, the *legal* relationship, as established in medical malpractice law, is very clear.

This mistaking of the relationship between doctor and patient matters here because the argument is so easily replayed by tort reformers and insurance companies to cut back on the compensation gained by injured patients—it makes sense, because we want to sympathize with the doctor and we don't want them to be blamed. We also live in a culture that privileges wellness and that hides sickness away—and so it is hard to fully grasp how powerless sick people are. But the costs of error don't disappear; they just become easier to hide, because patients have to absorb them.

Recall that legally, a tort relationship is one in which the patient has a right to a certain standard of care—it isn't very high; it's just an average standard of care. The patient has the right to a surgery in which mistakes are not made. When mistakes are made, as they inevitably will be, the patient has a right to compensation. Torts provide a cost-sharing mechanism whereby everyone pays into a pot that pays out to the one or two people who suffer statistically necessary errors. In that sense, tort offers a deeply biopolitical version of the distribution of accidents that takes into account the industrialization and inevitability of accident and injury distribution. Tort law allows both threads: statistical probability over the population *and* the right of each individual patient not to be injured.

This relationship differs from the sort of contractual relationship that Gawande and Naunheim wrongly imply as guiding the doctor-patient relationship. While the chance of an error may have been accepted by a patient in an informed-consent document, the relationship is still guided legally under tort rather than contract law. No matter how predictable the mistake, no matter how careful the surgeon, the patient has a right to compensation by law. The attempt to circumvent the law as the motivating force for issuing the apology nullifies it by definition. Naunheim's dismissal of law leads him to misunderstand his own legal obligations here, not of apology but of responsibility. According to him, each surgeon performs under a sort of professional contract to the best of his ability. If you are the patient on whom a mistake is made, too bad for you, but that possibility lay in the contract from the beginning. Naunheim is simply wrong there, no matter how difficult it may be, in the real world, for the plaintiff to defend that right.

Thinking that an apology can be inserted into the tort relationship is like putting icing on a rubber tire and trying to eat it for dessert. It mistakes the relationship and tries to make both into things they are not.

According to Taft, an apology implies a willingness to accept consequences, including those in law. However, the purpose of the medical apology is precisely to *interrupt* the distribution of legal consequences.

Thus the apology, while posing as a humanist interchange of sentiment, produces a version of responsibility and professionalism based in a highly individuated subjectivity. The value of the "human" gesture of the apology lies in its use as a technique of neoliberal free-market governmentality. The apology builds on an older model of responsibility, one that is a verbal expression of regret and an acceptance of fault. In this case, the insurers—the very bureaucracy that asks the doctor to defend his actions in a medical malpractice case (rather than accepting the insurance function of medical malpractice)—require the doctor to play out the apology as a means of indemnity of legal responsibility.

In this sense, the very context of responsibility shifts in relation to a preservation of the profitability of medicine and the maintenance of the bureaucratic status quo of insurance-driven medical care. The physician is caught in a set of contradictory loyalties between the health of the patient and the need to protect herself in a system that may not be in her personal or professional interest to criticize or change. The medical apology, then, keeps the doctor-patient relationship on a personal level, which has two effects. On the one hand, this move makes it easier to misunderstand the medical malpractice claim as a personal attack rather than as an insurance system designed to cover injured patients. On the other hand, it does add a human exchange into a system that can be extraordinarily dehumanizing precisely at the moment that people feel the most vulnerable. An apology in that context can be incredibly disarming. The new version of apology, as something of a public relations move, monopolizes the notion of responsibility while also giving it away, either by not fully valuing the personal costs to those who suffer from errors or by explaining them away in terms of population and the inevitability of error. Either way, no more knowledge about how and why errors occur is gained, and neither is any pressure put on the system to produce structural and design understandings of medical error.

J. L. Austin claimed that apologies, as perlocutionary acts, are never false. They either create effects or they do not. In the case of the medical apology, the effects extend beyond the actual apology, creating potentially large-scale political effects that ironically may undercut patients' rights by sentimentalizing the doctor-patient relationship in a way that neglects to understand the institutional framing of medical practice. Both doctors and

patients have an investment in believing in this relationship, and it provides a handy way for lucrative systems that frame this relationship (insurance, hospitals) to keep it personal even in a situation of vastly unequal
power dynamics.

The rights and role of the medicalized body offers a morass of conflicting ethical, economic, and educational/expertise frameworks that constitute the doctor-patient relationship. After all, if a dead person cannot
"receive" an apology, can a sick person? Can someone in a coma? Can a
person under general anesthesia? If the apology cannot work in the way
that Austin and Leape outline—that is, it cannot have effects in the relationship in which it is given—then how can responsibility be understood
in these situations where someone's life, body, and consciousness is at
stake? The patient brings money into the system, and a lot of it: what
rights should this market relation carry? The patient also carries her
body—as a work object, a practice object, and a site in need of particular
kinds of care—into a system with many conflicting goals. These issues are
nearly universally ignored in discussions about medical apology.

From the perspective of critical anthropology, apology serves a unique
humanitarian role and is a human gesture that may at times be authentic
(as an expression of the physician's trauma) and at others rhetorical (such
as when the doctor pats the patient on the shoulder or calls her "dear").
But if the term "responsibility" is to carry meaning as the backbone of
apology, surely the acknowledgment that an action caused an injury lies at
the core of figuring out ways for the responsible party to make amends. In
the real-life context of insurance and medical provision in the United
States, the apology cannot be extricated from its value as a technique of
neoliberal free-market governmentality, where "I'm sorry I cut the wrong
vein" becomes—indeed, *must* become—"I'm sorry you are bleeding."

But the *form* of the medical apology (divorced from its content) as an
expression of moral sentiment can be read precisely as a technique of governmentality as Foucault outlined it: as a confession of fault and regret
pressed into the service of an administration of life that is outside of law.
In this case of medical apology, medicine (with its highly paid experts and
its delivery of high-tech procedures within low-tech/high-error systems)
presents the perfect lens through which to view how the apology has been
harnessed by corporate public relations.

The nearly nostalgic version of human interaction embedded in contemporary apologies, one that cites and emulates concern without actually
expressing fault or responsibility, tends not, except in the most obvious
cases, to acknowledge the cause of physical wounding; in other words, it

elides the definitional requirement of an apology. Here, the confession of moral fault and regret produces an indemnifying or exculpatory effect in the wider domains of law, such that, paradoxically, the rhetorical admission of moral and personal responsibility becomes a mode of absolving oneself of legal responsibility. The absolving effect of these apologies, then, is precisely the opposite of the social function of apology as described by Taft and other apology theorists, for whom the law provides the moral and necessary backing of the apology.

The universal embrace of Gawande's narrative, with its complete deletion of the patients' concerns about and entitlement to their physical bodies, indicates how deeply Americans have bought into this version of medical practice and medical apology, a version that—together with the steady erosion of medical malpractice law—leaves them (us) with virtually no rights or means of recovery as receivers of the medical procedures that so misleadingly, innocently, and routinely present as healthcare.

CHAPTER 3

Responsibility and the Burdens of Proof

Carol J. Greenhouse

This chapter looks back at the early 1990s, when the U.S. home front of the "new world order" was absorbed in major political confrontations over civil rights and welfare.[1] By 1990, major civil rights legislation was before Congress, with welfare reform soon to follow. Debate was starkly partisan, and novel forms of insecurity associated with globalization added new tensions to the proceedings. Although civil rights and welfare involved debates of long standing, I look to the legislation of the 1990s as benchmarks in the history of social security in the United States. My focus is on the politicization of responsibility over the course of the congressional hearings that produced the Civil Rights Act of 1990 (hereafter CRA 1990) and the Personal Responsibility and Work Opportunity Reconciliation Act ("Welfare Reform Act") of 1996.[2] The Civil Rights Act of 1990 was vetoed by President George H. W. Bush in a major defeat for congressional Democrats. The Welfare Reform Act became the centerpiece of a broad bipartisan congressional consensus under the Clinton administration.[3] The outcomes of the legislation had massive social effects in terms of constricting the defensive resources available to civil rights advocates[4] and delivering a major blow to the welfare rights movement, essentially bringing it to an end at the federal level.[5] The legislative processes that yielded those outcomes featured extensive discussion of *responsibility*—offering rich evidence of the political stakes in the discursive maneuvering around that key term at the time.

My thesis is that understanding the significance of *responsibility* in the committee rooms of the House and Senate in relation to civil rights and welfare is crucial to understanding a central chapter in the political mainstreaming of U.S. neoliberalism. The two pieces of legislation punctuate important moments in that chronicle. Under the Reagan administration (1980–1988), critics of New Deal and Great Society liberalism asserted their positions in ideological discourse strongly colored with libertarian appeals (i.e., against "big government" in the name of freedom). The antiregulatory idiom of the George H. W. Bush administration (1988–1992) was softer in tone (though no less ideological) in its common-sense invocations of productivity and efficiency. By the mid-1990s, the rhetorical focus had turned to government spending and waste. Questions of *costs* increasingly prevailed against claims of *rights*. But even where costs were discussed in hearing rooms or on the floor of either congressional chamber, it is important to recognize that they were for the most part treated symbolically—that is, as a symbol of the relationship between the direct beneficiaries of the rights in question and taxpayers entitled to a return on their dollars. The symbolic content of those debates was part and parcel of the discursive trend that made consumption the new index—a sort of quality measure—of citizenship.[6] If citizens had become consumers, taxpayers had become shareholders, and shareholder value became the new template for federal social policy. *Responsibility* was discursively rendered by rights advocates as a counterdiscourse to marketization, emphasizing civil rights as the collective expression of a national commitment. For rights critics, responsibility was rendered in a way that symbolically consolidated two images of the citizen: the mythic figure of the rugged individualist and the modernist figure of the global consumer. The symbolic focus of the civil rights and welfare debates was on the discursive control of the meaning of responsibility.

The hearings over civil rights were mainly about standards of proof in cases of race and gender discrimination in employment.[7] The main hearings on welfare were mainly meant to address the claims that the welfare system was producing strong disincentives for job seeking and work (in the hearings, this was often discussed in terms of incentivizing out-of-wedlock childbearing). In different ways for the two laws in question, the legislation centrally involved the relationship of law to labor markets. As the testimony in the congressional hearings on the bills makes clear, those who supported the Civil Rights Act of 1990 or opposed termination of federal welfare entitlements saw labor markets by themselves as inadequate means of delivering American families out of poverty or of bringing equal opportunities for self-sufficiency and advancement regardless of race and gender. Critics of the civil rights bill and proponents of the welfare reform act adopted as their unstated premise a view of labor markets as infinitely open to individuals' strivings.

That view is based on a fiction, not only in the fundamental sense envisioned by Polanyi with respect to the very notion of a self-regulating market for labor[8] but also specifically in relation to the economy of the time—as several witnesses explained in detail over the course of the welfare reform hearings. By 1990, the U.S. economy had become a bimodal (high- and low-end) service economy, and occupational sectors classically associated with upward mobility (certain manufacturing sectors, for example) had been "globalized" offshore or technologized out of existence.[9] Even among corporate executives, downward mobility was a prominent feature of the mergers-and-acquisition era. In general, income gaps widened and the dollar lost significant purchasing power.[10] The political climate was strongly antiregulatory—the Bush-Quayle administration having won the 1988 election with slogans that made economic productivity and competitiveness into national security issues.

As an ethnographic premise in what follows, it is important to consider that the symbolism of responsibility was not simply some natural confluence of cultural ideas along the channels of ordinary language but was instead a keyword chosen from alternatives and honed with a strategic view toward intended effects.[11] An analysis of the political work that sustained the symbolic content of the debate in the public hearings is beyond the scope of this chapter. Much of that work would have taken place off stage, inaccessible through these documentary sources—and not feasible to address here. Still, some of that political work is evident in the transcripts, as speakers make conspicuous efforts to manage the symbolic load of their chosen imagery in jockeying for their side in the debate. Accordingly, in my selections from hearing transcripts, I focus on passages where political discipline is particularly evident in the exchanges between witnesses and members of Congress and integral to their political contests. The critics answered the proponents' discourse of *responsibility* with *the same discourse*, drawing on the conventions of nationalist narrative to distinguish individuals from communities and the modern present from the darkness of the past—and thence to make their opposition from within.

A second premise in my analysis is that while symbolic meanings may be the focus of pitched battles for control, meaning is never wholly subject to political control—or any centralized control, for that matter.[12] The nature of language—alive and densely enmeshed in open-ended associations—precludes this. Law works in discourse and selectively determines its significance, for example, but law does not produce discourse—nor the reverse.[13] Thus, even when a rhetorical gambit succeeds strategically, rhetoric cannot explain outcomes; it can only point to their situation in context. For the same reason, questions of meaning surpass outcomes. Such surplus is not necessarily unintended, unexpected, or unwanted in terms of political calculus—indeed, it may well be part of the calculus. But for theoretical purposes, it is important to acknowledge that meaning emerges interpretively from outside the text, as echoes from that wider terrain where the text's key terms and associations circulate in other institutional channels and with other effects. In their testimonial roles in these hearings, political actors are gambling their legitimacy and efficacy on the "echo-effectiveness" of their rhetorical appeals among the public.[14]

In the context of the legislation in question here, an important register of surplus meaning for the keyword *responsibility* is the way that it was stretched and flexed so as to echo incommensurate constructions of the idea of *race*. This is evident in myriad ways throughout both sets of hearings, but with particular vividness in relation to the civil rights bill.[15] In that context, proponents of the bill referred openly to the ongoing history of racism and continuing need for civil rights legislation to achieve racial equality, while critics decried the bill as reverse discrimination. For the bill's proponents, everyone is raced and some are disadvantaged by race; for critics, race was implicitly coded "black" and had no implication of class status unalterable by responsible personal choices. This was a fundamental difference, since for the bill's proponents, race discrimination requires legal remedies; for its critics, the proposed remedies created a special advantage for African Americans. For the bill's proponents, new legal remedies for race and gender discrimination were a prerequisite for national economic vitality; for its critics, they imposed undue burdens on productivity. The critics represented their position on the bill as the continuation of civil rights law—as further progress toward equality; for proponents, it was a reversal. *Reversal* is not a metaphor here (although the discourse of responsibility lent itself to judgments of history several times in the hearings). Rather, it was the legal question at the core of the debate. But we are getting ahead of ourselves.

The divisions revealed and concealed by the symbol of responsibility during the civil rights and welfare hearings form the theme of what follows. The new discourse of responsibility was by no means written on a blank sheet, but through what it became in these hearings, these legislative outcomes gave the state's warrant to neoliberalism as a moral discourse and contributed to moralizing the rationale for disembedding government from society—the central tenet of neoliberal philosophy.[16] In making *responsibility* the theme of President Obama's 2009 inaugural address, the new administration signaled the meaning of the moment in a reappropriation of that keyword.

Discrimination and Disparate Impact: Problems of Persuasion

In the middle of the George H. W. Bush presidency, the Democrats— then in control of Congress—struck back against what they saw as the retrenchments of the U. S. Supreme Court with two major legislative proposals, bills that were eventually passed under the titles "Americans with Disabilities Act" (hereafter ADA) and the "Civil Rights Act of 1990" (hereafter CRA 1990). The congressional hearings over the ADA and the CRA 1990 turned out to be tests of the practical limits of liberalism in what became a highly public political theater, and their passage entailed some striking political surprises. The ADA, despite adding a federal layer to what was already law in most states, ran into extensive opposition on the grounds of potential costs to businesses. Instead of confirming the national appetite for a renewal of equal protection rights, the debate over the ADA proved to be a portentous rehearsal of the arguments against rights-based equality subsequently lodged against the civil rights act. The CRA 1990, drafted as a clarification of the Civil Rights Act of 1964 in connection with antidiscrimination rights in employment, also passed Congress but was vetoed by President Bush. The following year, another version of CRA 1990 was signed into law as the "Civil Rights Act of 1991" (hereafter CRA 1991).[17]

In proposing CRA 1990, the Democrats' stated purpose was to make a midcourse correction relative to recent U.S. Supreme Court opinions in discrimination cases. In particular, CRA 1990's proponents singled out *Wards Cove Packing v. Atonio*. In *Wards Cove*, the court had ruled in favor of an employer accused of discrimination, on the grounds that the current law's standard of proof was defective and tantamount to a quota system.[18] The effect of *Wards Cove* was to reassign the "burden of persuasion" in cases of disparate impact (i.e., the filtering effects of a firm's hiring practices) from employers to disappointed candidates. Under the previous standard, firms were responsible for proving that discrimination *had not* occurred by referring to patterns of hire in relation to the characteristics of the candidate pool. Now, plaintiffs would be required to show that discrimination *had* occurred as a matter of intentional individual exclusion. In the year since the ruling in *Wards Cove*, the case had been cited as the rationale for overruling over three hundred employment discrimination cases,[19] prompting Democrats to move to restore the burden of persuasion to employers in this new legislation.

Edward Kennedy (Democrat, Massachusetts), as chair, opened the Senate Committee on Labor and Human Resources hearings on the CRA of 1990 by announcing a project of reclaiming for Congress a civil rights agenda that had been led off course (he asserted) by the Supreme Court: "When the Court misinterprets the legislative intent of Congress, Congress can correct the mistake by enacting a new law. And that is what we intend to do."[20] He continued, referring to the effects of *Wards Cove*: "In *Wards Cove*, the U.S. Supreme Court unwisely and unfairly shifted the burden of proof . . . from employers to employees. By shifting the burden, the U.S. Supreme Court has made it far more difficult and expensive for victims of discrimination to challenge the barriers that they face. . . . It is a mockery of civil rights and the fundamental principle of equal justice under law for opponents of this legislation to raise the false hue and cry of quotas."[21]

Senator Orrin Hatch of Utah, the ranking Republican member of the committee, responded. Where Kennedy had referred to the restoration of civil rights, Hatch cast the new bill as an "overhaul [of] the American legal system."[22] Where Kennedy spoke of access to justice, Hatch saw "a litigation bonanza for lawyers."[23] He subtly shifted the referents of symbolic "fundamental principles" and "rights" from job seekers to employers. Among his specific objections, he listed the following: "Hiring the most qualified applicant may no longer be an acceptable defense to a charge of discrimination. . . . There ought to be a right to hire the most qualified applicant. . . . [The same sections] conflict with the fundamental principle that one is innocent until proven guilty. . . . We must not legislate by label."[24]

In the ensuing statements by members of the committee and witnesses, advocates and critics alike invoked the civil rights landmarks of the 1960s as their baseline reference. For example, Senator Howard Metzenbaum (Democrat, Ohio) introduced *Brown* this way: "Since 1954, when the U.S. Supreme Court issued its landmark *Brown v. Board* decision, women and minorities have been able to look to the U.S. Supreme Court as a safe haven for the protection of civil rights. I am saddened that, some 35 years later, that safe haven for women and minorities has been closed. . . . We must tell the U.S. Supreme Court in no uncertain terms that turning back the clock on civil rights protection is unacceptable."[25] Senator Strom Thurmond (Republican, South Carolina), co-sponsor of the administration's bill countering S. 2104, was more general in claiming that "much progress has been made in our Nation to ensure that any individual will not be discriminated against in employment opportunities or adversely affected on the basis of race, color, religion, sex, or national origin, in keeping with the precepts of Federal statutes."[26] For Shirley Hufstedler, a federal appeals court judge and former secretary of education under President Carter, the 1960s were also the baseline but its goals were still on the horizon: "We still have a long way to go. . . . Take a look at the plantation economy in *Wards Cove*. It looks very much like the Old South did before the Civil Rights Act became effective."[27]

The rhetorical common ground in Lyndon Johnson–era legislation cast important segments of the debate as judgments of history itself—defining a discursive turn that pitted historical accounts of collective responsibility against presentist accounts of individual responsibility. The leading witness for the bill was William Coleman, a lawyer in private practice, formerly secretary of transportation under President Ford and chairman of the NAACP Legal Defense Fund for Education. His opening statement looked back to the history of slavery:

> Black Americans today seek in our own country precisely what brings thousands of new immigrants to our shores every year, to achieve the dream of being fully integrated into the society.
>
> From the beginning . . . even when slaves were forbidden to learn to read or to seek jobs of their own choosing, blacks understood that a good education and a decent job were the keys to full participation in our democratic society. Blacks recognized from the beginning that education and employment remain the essential tools by which black Americans can avoid, for themselves and for this great Nation, crime, inadequate housing, insufficient medical care, poor government in the community, high rates of illegitimacy and illiteracy, and all the other evils which shamefully are still visited upon blacks in our country in greater proportion than upon whites.
>
> And I think that is why it is very appropriate that this legislation is before this committee, because part of this is trying to help blacks achieve those conditions that everybody else in this room thinks is part of the American way.[28]

Glenn Loury, then a member of the faculty at Harvard's Kennedy School of Government, turned the question of responsibility and proportionality the other way, to "blacks" who, "despite the long-term upward trend," remain in poverty for reasons that put them (in his view) beyond the reach of civil rights legislation:

> In the case of blacks, the relative labor market gains of individuals have not been matched by comparable gains in the resources available to families. This is because the proportion of families headed by a single parent has risen dramatically among blacks during the same period in which individuals' earnings have improved. As well, the percentage of black children residing in households in which only one parent is present has risen sharply. . . . More generally, the emergence of what some have called an "urban underclass" has been noted in many of our cities. Blacks are disproportionately overrepresented in this population, where the problems of drugs, criminal violence, educational failure, homelessness and family instability are manifest. It is my conviction that these problems constitute the most important and intractable aspect of racial inequality in our time. Unfortunately, these problems are unlikely to be mitigated by civil rights legislation, because they do not derive in any direct way from the practice of employment discrimination.[29]

In the civil rights hearings, competing explanations of persistent poverty and its demographics were keyed to opposed positions on the limits of federal antidiscrimination law. They were again major axes of symbolic competition in the hearings on the welfare reform act five years later, when Loury was once again a witness.[30] Meanwhile, discrimination and disparate impact emerged in the debate over CRA 1990 in dappled light— sometimes claimed as mutually relevant, sometimes floating apart— depending, respectively, on how speakers construed *responsibility*.

Responsibility by the Numbers

At stake in the contest over the burden of persuasion (or, as Kennedy and others refer to it, *burden of proof*) was the question of how a potential plaintiff could make a case on discrimination grounds. The critics of the bill did not object to the CRA's requirement that employers provide data to account for minority hires at rates disproportionate to rates in the pool of candidates. And advocates of the bill never claimed that disparate impact should be treated in the same way as intentional discrimination. These were not always easy positions for the two sides to sustain, given the tendency of production requirements (i.e., the obligation to provide statistical information) to spill over into persuasion requirements (the rationales for the practices that yielded those statistical profiles). This was the context in which the question of continuity or reversal hinged on the differences between *Wards Cove* and an earlier case, *Griggs v. Duke Power Company*.[31]

The bill's proponents resisted separating the burdens of production and persuasion and disparaged attempts to do so as a misreading or misunderstanding of existing law. On the first day of the hearings, William Coleman's colloquy with Orrin Hatch, notwithstanding its occasional punctuation with what appear to be calculated performances of collegial jocularity, concentrated on the question of the impact of *Wards Cove* on antidiscrimination lawsuits in the employment context and specifically in relation to *Griggs.* For Coleman, there was no question that *Wards Cove* overturned *Griggs*: "I am making the statement to you and I wish you would ask them, that nobody can read *Wards Cove* without coming to the conclusion that it overruled *Griggs.*"[32] Later, Coleman and Hufstedler sparred at length with Hatch over this question, ultimately urging him to read the relevant documents again. Hatch was cordial but deflected the suggestion: "Well, I will be interested in reading that," the senator replied, adding, "well, we will sit down and chat."[33]

When the witness table was turned over to the bill's critics, the exchanges turned once again to the impact of *Wards Cove.* And once again, the colloquy was led by Senator Hatch, in an exchange with Charles Fried, a member of the faculty at Harvard Law School and former solicitor general under President Reagan. Fried disagreed with Secretary Coleman as to his assessment of the impact of *Wards Cove* on subsequent discrimination cases. What Coleman saw as cases overruled on the basis of *Wards Cove*, Fried saw as the natural result of a finite backlog of cases that the court's clarification of *Griggs* had made ripe for resolution: "*Wards Cove* did not change the law, did not overrule *Griggs*, it focused it and clarified it where there was confusion before."[34]

The burden-of-proof debate involved two main issues. One was the standard to which employers would be held in accounting for their hiring practices. Should they be required to show that their hiring practices were *essential* from a business standpoint or (a looser standard) *consistent* with business necessity? Fried took the position that CRA 1990 introduced a new, more stringent standard than *Griggs* and that this standard placed unreasonably heavy burdens on employers:

> *Senator Hatch:* There are other parts [of the bill] that I think are objectionable, but nothing as serious as this particular new standard. And you agree it is a new standard.

Mr. Fried: The way I would put it is it doesn't too much matter what you say about how heavy the employer's burden is, just make it a burden which is clear and specific and not just this amorphous endless list, and that it is reasonableness, not "essential," which really that [*sic*] is an enormous innovation and very serious.

Senator Hatch: In the law that is a very important word, and that did not exist prior to Wards Cove.

Mr. Fried: I don't believe so.[35]

The question of novelty as a negative was echoed by the witness from the Justice Department speaking for the administration[36] and by other critics of the bill.

The critics' other main issue also stemmed from the "essential" standard, on the grounds that (in their view, echoing the court in *Wards Cove*) it was an unattainable standard unless employers were to hire by quota. Employers were likely to do so, they argued, so as to preclude litigation by plaintiffs trolling for advantage, or even court-managed personnel management. Hatch and Fried developed these points in their public dialogue:

Senator Hatch: Now, you indicated that if this law passes in its present wording, including the definition of business necessity a [sic] meaning essential to effective job performance, that employers are just going to have to protect themselves and hire on a proportional or quota basis.

Mr. Fried: Well, I believe that common sense would do that, because how are they doing to defend themselves? Plaintiffs' lawyers are very aggressive. They come in, they show the numbers are wrong, and they can point to an endless list of practices, and there is no defense.

Senator Hatch: But what if they cannot hire by quotas? What if they cannot hire by proportionality?

Mr. Fried: Because the people aren't out there?

Senator Hatch: That's right . . .

Mr. Fried: Well, the thing that troubles me is that by talking about essentiality, you are telling every business, nonprofit organization, school, museum, hospital, that the Courts will decide what the essential way to run their business is.

Senator Hatch: That's right.

Mr. Fried: . . . That is a very serious intrusion.[37]

As the administration hardened in its opposition to the bill, its proponents were driven to compromise in a way that set business interests as a tradeoff in relation to civil rights remedies.[38] Senator Hatch was explicit in this regard: "I want to do what is right for minorities in this country and women in this country, and, frankly, for everybody. I really want to do what's right for small business in this country, too, and this bill could have a devastating impact with that one standard [of proof] on small as well as large business in this country."[39]

The president, too, referred to having business in mind as he assessed the prospect of litigation if CRA 1990 were allowed to stand. In his veto message, he held up the specter of "years—perhaps decades—of uncertainty and expensive litigation," adding: "It is neither fair nor sensible to give the employers of our country a difficult choice between using quotas and seeking a clarification of the law through costly and very risky litigation."[40] Representing CRA 1990 as reverse discrimination, the bill's critics glossed their defense of business interests as a defense of equal rights, but as the president's language suggests, the implication of an unavoidable tradeoff between antidiscrimination law and business profitability was never far from the surface. Thus, the critics defended—successfully— business as the source of true equality on the grounds that its benefits extended to "everyone." In contrast, they argued, antidiscrimination law benefits only a particular group. This is the context in which their singular racial coding (race = black) is crucial, since it is only from that standpoint that the discourse of responsibility lends itself to reframing disadvantage as advantage, recoding *civil rights* as identity politics.[41]

Echoing the language of rights advocates in their own argument against CRA 1990, the administration's supporters reserved their concern for equal rights protection to employers who they claimed might otherwise be victims of reverse discrimination; their resolve was to preempt a quota system that (they argued) would be the inevitable result of the bill. Important for our purposes is the fact that the critics' opposition to the bill rested on nonlegal factors, mainly the untested assumption that employers would seek to avoid liability by establishing racial quotas in hiring. This was the basis of their claim that the bill was itself discriminatory. As noted above, it was also the president's claim in his veto message.[42] The bill's supporters were having none of this. They derided each of these points in searing terms on the Senate floor, when the body convened to consider overriding the president's veto.[43] The override failed. The following year, the Civil Rights Act of 1991 was signed into law with the administration's burden-of-proof provision, modeled on *Wards Cove.*

This is the context in which *race* was essential in the discursive shift from rights to markets. The evidence for that discursive function is not in the language of the bill itself but in the opposed framings of the debate and their wider associations. The fact that minority individuals can find opportunities for upward mobility was invoked to portray the so-called underclass as a culture outside the law. In the process, race was left to individuals of color as their visible characteristic—but one that should have no legal significance, no history, no collective associations. The responsible subject, it seems, travels alone.

Race, Poverty, and Responsibility

A few years later, the Clinton administration made *responsibility* its keyword for welfare reform—in the very title of the proposed legislation. The Bush administration's victory on the burden-of-proof question was relevant in this new context, as the subject of responsibility came to welfare reform as, in some ways, already a settled question. The premise of the welfare debate was that in welfare lay larger issues of *personal responsibility*, such that Congress ultimately claimed a "state's interest" in marriage and family life as preamble to the new law. Welfare reform hearings began in earnest after the 1994 midterm elections sent a Republican majority into the Congress.

The new Republican majority in the House of Representatives announced its platform as a "Contract with America."[44] Its welfare provision targeted a social pathology rooted in a culture of dependency. The welfare pathology was not always explicitly made out to be the problem of the African American urban poor in particular (though this was an association of long political habit), but the anecdotes and vignettes that illustrated proponents' claims were almost always illustrated by examples involving African Americans, some of them stunningly derogatory, especially when they involved young men. As in the civil rights context a few years earlier, history was in question: the War on Poverty (Lyndon Johnson's legislative program thirty years earlier) was for some at fault and for others needed modernizing. In particular, critics of entitlements (i.e., proponents of the new reforms) focused on what they claimed was a statistical correlation between welfare dependency and pregnancy among unmarried women and girls. Largely treated as axiomatic by members of the committee, this correlation became the main focus of discussion in the "Contract with America" hearings on welfare held by the House Ways and Means Committee.[45]

The exchanges between committee members and witnesses concentrated on the defense of the claimed correlation between welfare and unwed teen pregnancy. And, as in the civil rights context, the contest politicized the problem of proof. For example, Robert Greenstein, then executive director of the Center on Budget and Policy Priorities, sought to uncouple the causal link others were drawing between federal welfare spending and poverty:

> I think this whole discussion is offbase, I will tell you whether they are liberal or conservative, there are very few economists who would subscribe to this analysis. During the period that poverty is going way down, we had a booming economy. We had rapid rate growth. We had high rates of productivity growth.
>
> The very point on the chart where poverty stops going down, around 1973, this has been written by economists of all persuasions, is the point at which wage stagnation sets in and productivity growth in this country stops growing forward at a substantial rate. . . .
>
> You go to Wall Street and ask people if they think the Food Stamp Program or the AFDC Program rather than trends in the international economy and others are the reasons for the 20-year slowdown in the rate of productivity growth in the U.S. economy. People will look at you like you are a little bit offbase. These are fundamental issues that relate to the larger economy.[46]

Moments later, in the midst of another attempt to recontextualize the association between welfare and illegitimacy, a member of the committee, John Ensign (Republican, Nevada) deflected this expert assessment, interrupting Greenstein to insist that he give his *personal opinion*:

> *Senator Ensign:* Do you think that the illegitimacy rate in this country has gone up in any small part due to the welfare state?
> *Greenstein:* This is a matter on which there is a great deal of research and the—
> *Senator Ensign:* What is your opinion on that?
> *Greenstein:* My opinion is that the bulk of the research is . . . that there may be an effect from welfare here, but if there is, it is relatively modest. We find illegitimacy rates rising as rapidly among women with more education, people in other countries with different social welfare systems. In particular, I would note that if AFDC were the driving factor, then we would have expected as AFDC benefits eroded, as they have in the last 10 or 20 years, then rates of out-of-wedlock births would have slowed or gone down and they didn't.[47]

Indeed, at several critical junctures, committee members and witnesses negotiated (and sometimes sparred) over the question of whether and how the "technical literature" or "studies" supported particular claims as to causal links between welfare and certain behavioral demographics. The hearings frequently revolved around talk of, and displays of, numbers: levels, rates, comparisons, correlations. Proponents of the bill often relied on simple correlations (as in the example cited above), anecdotal evidence, or so-called common knowledge. For example, asked by Dave Camp (ranking Republican from Michigan on the House subcommittee on Human Resources) if he could "tell me why the rate of illegitimate births rose sharply in the late eighties," Glenn Loury responded: "Mr. Camp, no, I can't. I am not aware of any analysis that has specifically, in the technical literature, that has specifically addressed that question, nor can I think offhand of anything that has changed in the environment of the late eighties to which one could attribute."[48]

Later, Camp rephrased the question: "Would you agree with the statement that welfare subsidies sustain illegitimacy?" This time, Loury replied: "Yeah. The statement is true almost by definition."[49] In the same panel, Camp asked William Bennett (the former drug czar): "How has the current welfare system contributed to the rising crime rate and drug abuse in America?" Bennett's response referred to presumptive common knowledge: "Well, Mr. Camp, I think any police sergeant in the country will tell you the day the welfare checks go out is a big day for drug buys. That is just the way it is. That is just the way the world works, and it has been in the drug literature."[50]

Critics of the bill challenged these assessments by offering findings from more rigorous studies, by reversing the direction of causality in the proponents' correlations, or by recontextualizing the statistics in relation to broader economic and social trends (e.g., assessing poverty rates in relation to wage levels, not just welfare expenditure).[51] For minority (i.e., Democratic) members of the committee, this sometimes put them at risk of reversing roles with the more powerful witnesses for the majority. In an exchange with William Bennett, for example, Harold Ford (Democrat, Tennessee) challenged Bennett's account of "the social science evidence" for Bennett's claim of a causal link between welfare and illegitimacy: "According to the most respected social scientists, just the opposite is true. . . . Poverty and decay are the surest roads to illegitimacy." Ford went on to cite low rates of *intentional* pregnancy on the part of teens.[52] Bennett interrupted him at that point: "What is your question, sir?" and then twice more interrupted Ford to challenge his line of questioning.

Other critics of the bill presented their arguments in qualitative terms, drawing on the language of values and national traditions for appeals in terms of collective responsibilities for the poor, the idea of the nation, or the long tradition of federal sponsorship of social security. For example, the witness Lawrence Mead, from Princeton's Woodrow Wilson School, invoked citizenship as he concluded his argument in favor of retaining welfare as a federal program: "Welfare . . . is one of the ways in which we operationalize what citizenship means. That is of the highest national importance. It is for Congress to make decisions about it rather than turning this over to the States."[53] Katherine McFate, a social scientist, made a detailed argument to show that devolving welfare to the states would likely sharpen "regional and racial inequalities."[54] Other witnesses took up more specialized appeals, for example, on behalf of children and their mothers.[55] But in the environment of the hearings, at least inside the committee chamber, such statements were never dispositive. Moreover, the fact that numerous committees were involved with the welfare reform issue gave members considerable scope in cutting off discussion of some of these more wide-ranging appeals on the grounds of the specificity of their mandate and deference to other committees' jurisdictions.

Those who attempted to argue over the quality of a study (as in the exchange between Ford and Bennett cited above)[56] or who took a position in favor of reform that did not *also* ascribe to the existing welfare system the full range of social ills targeted by the majority were quickly pulled back into line. For example, the political scientist James Q. Wilson supported welfare reform but not the correlation between AFDC and illegitimacy, on the grounds that rates of illegitimacy were rising worldwide and that they were higher in the United States than in countries where welfare payments were higher. But his attempt to uncouple a causal connection between money and behavior in favor of cultural approaches quickly drew a censorious response from Jim McCrery (Republican, Louisiana), on the grounds that culture went beyond the committee's jurisdiction: "Unfortunately, some of those things aren't within the power of this Subcommittee. The welfare program is, though." McCrery then spoke for Wilson, retrofitting his testimony to the dominant discourse: "And so I am going to take the liberty of saying that you . . . agree with me that at least this would be a positive step toward fighting the problem of illegitimacy in this country. And if you disagree, I will give you a chance to say that."[57] Wilson did not correct the congressman, referring (perhaps ironically) to their respective expertise: "I don't know how to write bills. I am an ivory tower professor."[58]

Committee members who overreached in seeking to buttress the majority's position seemed to suffer no embarrassment. For example, the following exchange between Senator Bob Packwood (Republican, Oregon, and the committee chair) and Senator Tom Harkin (Democrat, Iowa, and a congressional witness) took place after Harkin, speaking as a witness, described an Iowa workfare program, advocating it as a potential model for federal legislation. Packwood changed the subject, seeking to return the conversation to the teen pregnancy issue:

> *The Chairman:* Just a quick question. . . . Do you know, or can you tell, if it is having any effect on illegitimacy?
> *Senator Harkin:* I do not know the answer to that question.
> *The Chairman:* What I am curious about is whether there is a relationship between jobs and job availability and legitimacy or illegitimacy. I do not know either.
> *Senator Harkin:* I do not know the answer.
> *The Chairman:* All right.
> *Senator Harkin:* We do not have the research on that . . .

But for those who sought to decouple illegitimacy and welfare, their skepticism was delegitimated as *ignorance.* For example, Senator Moynihan (Democrat, New York), ventriloquizing, mocked the doubts of those who rejected a causal connection between welfare and family structure: "A parallel view has been that, what we call the welfare system is simply a fallout of the change in family structure in our country. It is not at all clear why this has come about, and even less clear what we might do to change it."[59]

The discursive discipline that kept social debate narrowly focused on numbers (often simple correlations) made it easy to shift frames into questions of cost. The scale of federal expenditure on welfare in absolute terms as well as relative to other federal budget categories were dominant themes. One supportive witness, for example, presented a chart comparing welfare expenditures to the United States defense budget, projecting a widening gap (in favor of welfare) over the next five years.[60] While such a direct tradeoff between social security and national security was not usual, the implication was pervasive—if only in the continual references to damaged masculinity and the consequent vulnerability of women and children in the inner city. There were numerous references to welfare as imposing an undue drag on the global competitiveness of the U.S. economy or as a poor return on U.S. investment.

Such accountings were never very far from the issues of moral order and personal responsibility—indeed, they were mutually coded. For example, William Bennett referred to a "rapid and massive collapse of family structure" as being "without precedent among civilized nations,"[61] later adding: "Look at the body count. . . . Whatever you do, don't stay the course."[62] Senator Rick Santorum (Republican, Pennsylvania) referred to the Supplemental Security Income (SSI) as "killing people. . . . We are giving them money to do what? To stay drug-addicted and alcoholic for the rest of their life."[63] For Senator Alan Simpson (Republican, Wyoming), the risks were cosmic: "There is an interesting prayer which is, I believe, embraced by most faiths which begins with, Our Father, Who art in heaven. Now these people that we hear the statistics on do not even know what a father is." He then drew a connection to the bombing of the federal building in Oklahoma City by a domestic terrorist in 1995: "Then you see something like Oklahoma City come along, and what is the emphasis? It is on prayer and religion, care and nurture. Somewhere in there that has failed."[64]

"Welfare" went forward as a project in social engineering, based on the premise (recast as congressional "findings" in the law's text) that the state's interest in the welfare system was primarily in its potential to mold positive behaviors in relation to work and family life. As Dave Camp said in committee: "We want to send a strong signal from the Federal Government that taxpayers are no longer willing to provide a comprehensive package of public benefits to young men and women *who violate social convention by having children they cannot afford*."[65] The opening lines of the enacted bill, announcing Congress's findings, are not about welfare but marriage:

The Congress makes the following findings:

(1) Marriage is the foundation of a successful society.

(2) Marriage is an essential institution of a successful society which promotes the interests of children.

(3) Promotion of responsible fatherhood and motherhood is integral to successful child rearing and the well-being of children.[66]

The text of the bill then devotes two full pages to the statistics of teen pregnancy, child health, and crime (especially youthful criminal offenders)—all claimed as correlations with out-of-wedlock parenting and single-parent families. The three pages of findings culminate in a resolution: "Therefore, in light of this demonstration of the crisis in our Nation, it is the sense of the Congress that prevention of out-of-wedlock pregnancy and reduction in out-of-wedlock birth are very important Government interests."[67]

Responsible Subjects Redux

The symbolic focus on responsibility was pivotal in the legislative debate over civil rights and welfare in terms of dividing race from class, the past from the present, and—perhaps most manifestly—the public sector from the private sector; overall, the responsible subject was defined by the absence of a necessary connection between equality and security. In particular ways at the time of these legislative debates, the persistence of poverty in the midst of rising affluence was a pressing contradiction. In the congressional testimony and debate, that contradiction was lent material form in the twinned figures of responsible and irresponsible subjects, as if these were denizens of two worlds: the American world of individual enterprise and the alien world, dwelling in the so-called inner city, where the cultural icon was dependency.

As these figures were drawn into the public discussion, the strategic symbolic value of responsibility for the administration's position (on both bills) was its deferral of this contradiction. Both bills were about responsibility in the broader, ordinary-language sense of the word; the partisan framing was more narrowly figured around individuals' economic self-sufficiency. The particular qualities of their responsible subject borrowed heavily from popular literature and social science—the latter, notably, from the so-called Moynihan Report and, a generation earlier, Gunnar Myrdal's *American Dilemma*, both broadly familiar from their wide circulation.[68] For those on the other side of either debate, it was the demographics of poverty (and the stereotypes of welfare recipients) that made responsibility self-evidently a discussion of racial disparities; this association was repeatedly dismissed by members of the House panel in the welfare reform hearings.

The advocates of the legislation that eventually became the Civil Rights Act of 1991 and the Welfare Reform Act of 1996 put forward their proposals as explicit correctives to what they deemed to be the anachronisms of liberalism—its excesses, in their view, relative to the challenges of the new global economy. For the most part, neoliberalism came packaged as a modernizing rhetoric of *endorsement* and *reform*, not an explicit reversal or rejection of earlier programs. Thus, both sides of the debate over civil rights could express liberal endorsements of the values of *Brown* and the

Civil Rights Act of 1964, and all sides of the welfare debate could endorse New Deal and Great Society programs in their acknowledgments of public responsibility for the most vulnerable citizens. But such universalistic expressions of values crumbled under pragmatic political pressures (mainly costs). The Civil Rights Act of 1964 had opened access to legal remedies to race discrimination that the Reagan and Bush administrations strove openly to curtail. The congressional hearings over civil rights and welfare in the 1990s further tested the limits of rights against the new realities of neoliberal economics, as civil rights were discussed as a drag on productivity and welfare as spending. The responsible subject (as constructed in debate) offers a return on value to the *taxpayers*—a proxy term that condenses a national public to a contributive fiscal identity in the state.

These issues dominated the public sphere and put key images, logics, and prescriptions of value into wide circulation—with heavy material effects. The debate over the new civil rights legislation showed that there was no liberal consensus over equality when it was set up as a tradeoff against profitability. The debate over welfare officialized a highly pejorative view of the urban poor—stereotypically African American—as illegitimate consumers in a universe of limited goods. This is not merely a point about the hermeneutics of political persuasion. Through the congressional testimony and debate over these measures, specific constructions of race became hegemonic and, written into law, worked their effects on actual communities. Their hegemonic effect is less a question of the direct power of law but rather of the consequences of the highly public spectacle by which discourse is selectively consolidated from a diverse communicative field and attached to conditions of access to public arenas.[69] Writing at the time, Michael Sandel captures the sense of unsettlement:

> The main topics of national debate—the proper scope of the welfare state, the extent of rights and entitlements, the proper degree of government regulation—take their shape from the arguments of an earlier day. These are not unimportant topics; but they do not reach the two concerns that lie at the heart of democracy's discontent. One is the fear that, individually and collectively, we are losing control of the forces that govern our lives. The other is the sense that, from family to neighborhood to nation, the moral fabric of community is unraveling around us.[70]

He seems to register the civil rights and welfare debates as separate from "democracy's discontent"; however, in retrospect, they were central to it.

American individualism has never been just one story line. In the legislative debates discussed in this chapter, conservatives valorized business interests as the public interest and constructed dependency (i.e., illegitimate consumption) as the responsible subject's Other. The legislative processes described in this chapter advanced a notion of rights-based racial equality as false equality and (by the same token) put forward *race* as a false *in*equality. From that standpoint, there could be no mistaking the implication that for the winning side, *racial inequality* was a double negative. Writing after World War II, Horkheimer and Adorno commented skeptically on the deceptive equality offered by the surplus production of the "culture industry."[71] In relation to the discourse of responsibility discussed in this chapter, one might consider that in the 1990s it was surplus consumption that was (and continues to be) discursively key; the haunting question of a deceptive equality remains. As Congress deliberates the possibility of chartering new responsibilities, it is timely to look back—if only to escape the sense that all possible language is already claimed for partisan purposes.[72] Indeed, it is not; this, too, one can hope, is part of the value of listening sidelong across the laced and forked trails of discourse, for echoes that lessen the distraction (though not necessarily the disappointment) of announced destinations.

PART II

Responsibility, Risk, and Insurance

CHAPTER 4

Whereas, and Other Etymologies of Responsibility

Eric Wertheimer

The Lives of Assets

Whereas. In looking for a conceptual and linguistic source of "responsibility," one could do worse than the word "whereas." This is especially so when "whereas" is used as the introduction to a policy or proclamation. The *Oxford English Dictionary* tells us that the word began with its contrastive connotation, as an "illative or adversative conjunction," and subsequently emerged as a signal of due attention paid to prior contingencies—"in view or consideration of the fact that." It then underwent a rather sudden and swift identification with contractual legalese in the 1790s, becoming the first word of many contracts. It even came to stand as a satirical metonym for such discourse, as in the following from F. L. Holt in 1804: "I am as long-winded as the *Whereas* of a proclamation." And there it stayed.

Meanwhile, in the seventeenth and eighteenth centuries a particular kind of text, the insurance policy, capitalized on the specialized power of "whereas" to make the world outside a seemingly closed system of codified warranties even *more* dependent upon whereas's causational signifying. In other words, insurance intensified whereas's importance as a beginning, loading it with rhetorical intentions and conditioning methods. Primed by their powerful first word, insurance policies thereby transformed the way all texts might obligate us as human beings, inventing a form of responsibility we still recognize and, truth be told, are intimidated by; we tend to leave the instructions and consequences of such words to experts. Nonetheless, that intimidating transformation remade modern subjects. The marketplace for such insuring texts made available new access to these individual and collective responsibilities by economically valuing the virtues of personal precaution. Insurance's concepts renamed and restructured the silent field of conditions that precede every insurance contract's "whereas" and that demand our consent, tacit or verbal.

The word "responsibility" nicely parallels "whereas" in its genealogy, inasmuch as its major accent change is timed to the emergent individualist political economies of the latter part of the eighteenth century, especially the 1790s. Here is a usage from the *OED* that, if one is alert to it, speaks to the insinuating common structures of "whereas" and "responsible."

> 1787 HAMILTON *Federalist* No. 63 II. 193 Responsibility in order to be reasonable must be limited to objects within the power of the responsible party.

Hamilton's application here is clearly within the contexts of national statecraft and citizenship, but the methods and rhetoric of legal finance are not far away. Hamilton, the chief architect of modern American instruments of fiduciary money, embeds "responsibility" in the legal discourse that measured risks "reasonably," the very linguistic and event-filled territory that "whereas" enforced. Later, in the early nineteenth century, we have Robert Southey correlating responsibility to the question of risk quite directly. In this case, however, risk occurs within the situation of war:

> 1827 SOUTHEY *Hist. Penins. War* II. 746 He was made to understand that any risk which he incurred would be upon his own responsibility.

Writing about the Napoleonic Wars in peninsular Spain, Southey describes the warning—for all intents and purposes a warranty—put to one who opts out of the "whereas/responsibility" discipline. No matter the context, the two words share a rhetorical pivot for critical modern maneuvers.

Another way to think about this rhetorical function is that insurance (and the responsible whereas-ing of contracted experience) managed a vital nexus of private and public interests. It proceeded to call the marketplace of its availability—formally structured as Lloyds of London or the Insurance Company of North America, to name only two of the more influential varieties—both necessary and wise for individual and society. Individual and society launched each other into new orders of mutual recognition—Lloyd's underwriters were (and *still* are) known somewhat tellingly as "Names." Indeed, such amplified nomenclatures and totalizing textual innovations figured forth what I would call the "socialized individual"—in a slight departure from J. G. A. Pocock's or C. B. MacPherson's elaborations on the history of the modern "social individual." While the social individual achieves virtue by balancing her prudent measure of individual interests, obligations, and risks against collective forces, the social*ized* individual merges individual and collective, redistributing one's interests and risk into the capitalized pool of the collective.[1]

This new person was related conceptually to the possessive individual of C. B. MacPherson's Lockean discourse—one might even plausibly say that they were one and the same. But they had different faces. The socialized individual understood his singularity—by contrast with the in-taking possessive individual—as entailing risks that could be mitigated by the outward marketability of trust. The great nineteenth-century philologist Archibald Sayce was only half right when he wrote in the *Principles of Comparative Philology* (1874): "In a beehive community morality is impossible, much less a worship of one God. It is only when the conception of the individual has been reached that the idea of responsibility begins."[2] To view beehives and individuals as mutually exclusive is to miss the mutuality of singular interests and bundled welfare. Morality, as we have come to understand it, only becomes possible in beehive communities of individuals—commonwealths. Money and credit, the final innovative and necessary signifiers in this genealogy of responsibility, enabled an individual to acquire and then conserve by assuring outcomes through beehive-like networks of compensation and contractability.[3] The fences of each became home to all others.

Thus the socialized individual used insurance to administer the crisis of loss. And of course, as I have said, it went beyond such practicalities. It was also intended as a status display, both self-centered and civically oriented, a way for property owners to purchase a commodity that would reflect the virtues of a broader responsibility to the commons; at the same time, such a reflection would be securely and manifestly lodged within an individual's public identity. The florid and specialized way in which the policies named and announced their contracted subjects and objects were indications of the precise negotiations such texts made with individual obligation and public consent. As iconic and even artful documents of address and technical precision, insurance contracts exemplify the meeting place of artifice and cultural constructions of personal assurance. They render the world securely walled, fenced, circumscribed, and attributed—perfect scripts to help the eye avoid the (perhaps troubling) absence that is all around the documents.

What made the insuring text even more remarkable was in its helping to move modern society away from both religious totems of ethical social behavior and theistic ordinations about the events that occur within human lives. It substituted for these theologized assurances with secularized, scientific, and corporeal accounts of what the future might hold and, indeed, why the future may hold it. It did this with the nascent discipline of statistical probability and practical applications like actuarial science.[4] So too, insurance underwriting enabled socialized individuals to call on a new (both larger and more articulated) universe of ethical choice and action. By creating original circuits of understanding causation—circuits that bypassed ancient notions of natural misfortune, characterological tragedy, cosmic fate, and biblical determinism—the market for insurance policies thereby set the full injunction for action and prevention before each and every economic actor.

Indeed, it became *required* of economic actors if they were to be properly "economic" at all—recall again the possessive individual, but adduce the socializing of his private interests. As insurance began to obviate the terms of religious agency and passivity before greater forces, it began as well to signal a new kind of virtue, a virtue that arose out of, and thus assured, financial solvency as well as communal trust. Ravit Reichman, in her essay documenting the cautious imagination of early twentieth-century modernism, demonstrates just how thoroughgoing and enduring this effect on the imagination has proven. Purchasing an insurance policy, whether marine, fire, or life, assured a community of the similarly vested that the consumer cared (or shared a commensurate anxiety) about the fate of property. Buyers had many names for the objects that they purchased; property was linked to the socialized human individual by one of two names—"owner" or "slave."

That quality that property imparts to the legal discourse of insurable ownership is the touchstone of this essay. It still haunts the methods of responsibility that derive from such underwritings. Insurance, both as a historical and representational artifact and as an object of historical research, teaches us how slippery the idea of responsibility can be. The history of insurance demonstrates that responsibility's sources are tough to exhume and hard to disentangle; whatever its genesis and current incarnation, responsibility is difficult to fulfill. I argue, nonetheless, that this elusiveness is a product of the tensions built into the figure of the "socialized individual," whose every decision involved calculations and calibrations related to the various and obsessive measurements of inward gain and outward protection. Finally, these tensions come to rest in a core paradox generated by the need to represent property in multiple forms (insurance policies, slave registries, Web sites, novels). As a result, individual responsibility is continually rendered incoherent—indeed mute, amnesiac, and ineffectual—by the opposition between the commons and the corporate individual. In that lesson, this essay connects with the historical, legal, and political complexities of responsibility that are elucidated by the other essays in this volume. Its form is a set of descriptive narratives about the various ways that insurance, abolitionism, and slavery have driven the historical paradox of the socialized individual, and it ends by asking us to consider the critical archivist as a possible answer to the problems posed.

One of the primary reasons for insurance's odd relation to responsibility is in its emergence alongside abolitionism. Abolitionism's rhetoric of personal liberation and communal salvation elicited friction with the legal regime of personal care and commercial probity called upon by the underwritten world. The co-emergence of insurance underwriting and abolitionism seems more than coincidental. Both insurance and abolitionism call on similar relationships between individual and group, but in sometimes opposing ways. With the discourse of liberation come (it admittedly sounds a little ridiculous to say) the twinned discourses of property insurance (a broad construal of marine insurance, for our purposes) and life insurance. Abolitionism and merchant capitalism cultivated an anxious proximity because of their shared sense of responsibility—one a responsibility entailed by a transcendent notion of human freedom and the other by the obligations of contracts. That entwined history offers the spectacle of kidnapping, ransom, mass murder, and slave insurance becoming grotesque emblems in modern commercial life—leaving to us in the present deeply "irresponsible" texts masquerading as moral contracts. These spectacles tendered a complex jealousy concerning the terms of property and its (financially) responsible parties.

That jealousy led to some fascinating legal impasses in the history of the trade in human beings. Ian Baucom, in *Specters of the Atlantic*, has recently written on precisely this, offering a definitive critical analysis of what has come to be called the *Zong* incident or *Zong* disaster of 1781.[5] The episode became an abolitionist cause célèbre because of its circulation among middle-class British subjects, and it also became a landmark case in the history of insurance and property law. It involved a slave ship called the *Zong*, which, during its voyage from Africa to Jamaica carrying 440 slaves, was beset by a deadly outbreak of disease. The ship's skipper, Captain Luke Collingwood, determined that the slaves who were sick but not yet dead should be thrown overboard, since it would increase the odds of the healthy surviving and would enable the recovery of full insurance reimbursement for the already valueless (lost) cargo.

The case turned on the question of what was "necessary" as opposed to what was "natural," a contest that arose out of a clever decision made by Captain Collingwood. Collingwood had taken advantage of a warranty that allowed for marine insurance reimbursement in the case of loss that occurred out of "necessity"—natural losses, outside the bounds of Collingwood's executive decision making, were excluded. The underwriters, sensing a perverse dodge, refused to pay. As a result, the ship's owners sued their insurance underwriters in 1783 to recover the "value" of their "lost" slaves. The suit was initially decided in the owners' favor but was reversed on appeal.

The *Zong* case cut the idea of responsibility for property to its core. It disordered and then reordered the seemingly well-defined boundaries between what is human and what is an asset. And while the muddle may have furthered the cause of slave traders in their legal quibble, the questions it entailed gave a new public vocabulary to the substantive arguments of abolitionism: To whom does one owe primary responsibility? Can human beings truly be property if they are not "replaceable"? To what extent does society have an obligation to impose moral limits on the possessive individual? As Baucom puts it, the argument involving drowned slaves "might" be a matter of individual property rights, apart from humanist legalisms: they might "have convinced the Lords Commissioners that the matter was none of their business, nor, in any important sense, that of the empires's."[6] Privatizing at the level of morality while socializing at the level of individual virtue, the *Zong*'s slave owners attempted to maintain their tense accounts at the expense of a legal humanism that abolitionists and ultimately the presiding magistrate Lord Mansfield would make hard to ignore.

The *Zong* case urges us to consider responsibility's hybrid family tree. Such a genealogy traces the reproduction of responsibility into the modern individual, with bloodlines descending from categories of human bondage. Dictated by the supposition that we are, in the end, subjects (slaves even?) to chance, the individual must struggle in manifold ways for freedom, no matter the explanatory belief accounting for it. The roots run deep, but the historical manifestations—abolitionism, women's rights, indeed, the full panoply of human rights—are relatively new blown. It goes without saying that the relationship between property and human rights was new and unresolved. But things got tricky in this relationship when abolitionism demanded that the slave owner forego primary responsibility to property and recall that, whereas all humans are self-possessed, his first responsibility is to inalienable freedom. Property rights versus liberty—the tension is among the first in a procession of conflicts at the heart of bourgeois democratic history. Can one be free in a society that demands profound allegiances to property?

Property's problematic claim on us as responsible socialized individuals is manifest in less horrific historical sites, such as the insurance office. The subtle trace of the terms of modern bondage is audible in a famous passage from Ralph Waldo Emerson's "Self-Reliance":

> The civilized man has built a coach, but has lost the use of his feet. He is supported on crutches, but lacks so much support of muscle. . . . His notebooks impair his memory; his libraries overload his wit; the insurance office increases the number of accidents; and it may be a question whether machinery does not encumber; whether we have not lost by refinement some energy, by a Christianity entrenched in establishments and forms, some vigor of wild virtue.[7]

Emerson's bemoaning the loss of some "wild virtue" at the expense of this new regime of textuality—from the libraries demanding our obedience as readers and students to the insurance offices naming and thereby "inventing" accidents—diagnoses a problem at the heart of the terms of modern responsibility. In particular, Emerson speaks for a range of nineteenth-century critiques of property when he describes how unnervingly responsibility translates into the requirements and purported virtues of property ownership, especially as that translation affords either slavery or freedom. The beehive morality of a community of property owners fails to make free individuals with its mandatory ethics of responsibility.

But a prior question is called for, before we determine the importance of the binary of slave and owner. Who exactly was a "property owner"—who in the new world of carefully commercialized texts would acknowledge the word "whereas"? Perhaps the safest and most apposite answer to all of these questions is the following: such people, or groups of people, that are responsible for the life of an asset. There is, of course, a devilishly legalistic yet metaphorically powerful term imbedded in that answer—"the life of an asset." To what extent do objects *live*, and to what extent can lives be objectified (if at all)? The answer to *those* questions may be most profitably found in Susanna Blumenthal's fascinating essay on the legal questions at the heart of human/animal agency; it is a set of questions that has occupied theorists of property from the eighteenth century until the present day. But what I hope is becoming clear in this essay is that the very texts that worry about the longevity of assets are themselves subject to some odd historical lifelines.[8]

Citizens and Consumers

In the context of responsibility, answers to the question of the longevity of assets—indeed, their *alive*-ness—only make the situation more complex. When that property was human—as in the biological term designated in life insurance, or the ongoing ambiguity of the term "life of the contract,"[9] or when marine insurance named slaves in the terms—it signals a responsibility that cuts both ways, asking only whose interest motivates the investment. The interests of a party involve inherently narrative-driven, historical questions. Determining the nature of responsibility for the insured becomes a matter of locating the origins of the identified parties. Indeed, it is insurance policies that are often the most reliable documents when reconstructing the facts of slavery that have been lost or deliberately erased. A good example is James Madison's plantation, Montpelier. Historians used a surviving fire-insurance policy in order to reconstruct the slave quarters that had been disappeared from Montpelier's grounds. The archival policy thereby became central to the obligations of identity and the fluctuations of meaning that property imparts to objects and people. And the pursuit of the archives of slavery has engaged not only academic researchers but political classes.

The state of California has recently pioneered the attempt to assess responsibility in the accounting for slavery in the history of modern insurance companies, but this has not been an unproblematic task. The barriers to transparency include categorical imprecision, bad record keeping, corporate change, and legal wariness. The archive of liability that descends legally from *Zong* is still with us. As the California Department of Insurance (CDI) Web site puts it:

> In August 2000 the California legislature found that "[I]nsurance policies from the slavery era have been discovered in the archives of several insurance companies, documenting insurance coverage for slaveholders for damage to or death of their slaves, issued by a predecessor insurance firm.

> These documents provide the first evidence of ill-gotten profits from slavery, which profits in part capitalized insurers whose successors remain in existence today." (SB2199 Sec. 1(a))[10]

The California state legislature proceeded to craft and pass a statute (Representative Tom Hayden was its chief supporter) that would enable state entities to identify the sources of "ill-gotten profits" and thereby (perhaps) assume responsibility by disinvestment. (Illinois followed California with a nearly identical piece of legislation in 2003, which provided, as might be expected, almost identical research results.) Governor Gray Davis signed the bill into law in September 2000, and it took effect on January 1, 2001. As the California Code of Regulations, title 10, sections 2393–2398, implements the statute, there are four principles at stake:

> §13810 The Commissioner shall request and obtain information from insurers licensed and doing business in this state regarding any records of slaveholder insurance policies issued by any predecessor corporation during the slavery era.

> §13811 The Commissioner shall obtain the names of any slaveholders or slaves described in those insurance records, and shall make the information available to the public and the Legislature.

> §13812 Each insurer licensed and doing business in this state shall research and report to the Commissioner with respect to any records within the insurer's possession or knowledge relating to insurance policies issued to slaveholders that provided coverage for damage to or death of their slaves.

> §13813 Descendants of slaves, whose ancestors were defined as private property, dehumanized, divided from their families, forced to perform labor without appropriate compensation or benefits, and whose ancestors' owners were compensated for damages by insurers, are entitled to full disclosure.

Once the implementation process began, public hearings were held and then letters sent out to all 1,357 life, property, and casualty insurance companies doing business in California. The letters notified the companies of their required compliance with the statute. As of the latest Web site data, the compliance rate has been 92 percent. Whether this means that compliance is complete is unclear; what is clear is that noncompliance results from "the insurer fail[ing] to describe the research it did to determine whether or not it has documents related to slavery era insurance, or failed to report as to predecessor companies." Reporting that research has been attempted is all that is needed.

Nonetheless, the reports on behalf of the insurance companies are fascinating for both what they offer and what they seem to withhold. I am skeptical of their completeness, though I admit that I cannot prove that they are hiding anything. My skepticism arises from the research impedimenta I encountered in my work on *Underwriting* (I'll return to this in a moment) taken in hand with the otherwise proud habit of disclosure evident in the insurance industry's love of corporate history.[11] Indeed, giant insurance conglomerates, with two-centuries-old histories (the statute refers to their "family trees")—companies such as the American International Group (branded as AIG)—find precious little that betrays guilt in regard to the California legislation. It should be noted as well that the statute is explicit in asking for a research rubric that would ensure proper accounting for, and responsibility with regard to, the historical past. But again, one is left wondering about the efficacy of such rubrics, given the ability of corporations to truncate their histories in ways that benefit their potential exposure. The Department of Insurance report on the insurers' responses is similarly wry in its skepticism:

> The vast majority of responses indicated, in some fashion, that as the insurer had been incorporated sometime after the end of the defined slavery era and since there was no predecessor company that existed during the applicable period, that the insurer had nothing to report.
>
> The Department also received a few responses indicating that the company or its predecessor was doing business during the applicable period, and conducted a thorough search of its archives and records, but was unable to find responsive information or documents. A variation of this response was that the insurer routinely destroyed documents beyond a certain age and therefore, had no way of knowing whether or not a slavery era predecessor existed. A permutation of this response was that a slavery era predecessor existed, as evidenced by other corporate archives, but that responsive documents had been lost or destroyed.

At a certain distance, the formal and statistical specifics of the insurer responses are illuminated. Eight of the companies are identified as having provided "substantive" responses. Of all the companies that could potentially take responsibility for holding slavery-era policies, given the potential market loss in the present that such an acknowledgment might mean, the New York Life Insurance Company seems the most forthcoming. It would seem that, for the CDI, a response was tantamount to "responsibility" itself. A typical line of information in the registry reads as follows:

Slaveholder Last, First Name: Archer, Richard
County (or Parish), State: Chesterfield County, VA

Slave Name: Reuben
County (or Parish), State: Same
Other Identifying Information: Miner at the Mines-Chesterfield Policy
   Number(s) 1107
Submitted By: New York Life Insurance Company

Perceptible here is what Baucom, in examining the *Zong* documents of two centuries ago, refers to so accurately as a "mincing bureaucratese"; in the clerical rhetoric of this rearchiving, there is a noticeable bookkeeping flatness to the historical experience of bondage. In the wake of property protocols like slavery, the socialized individual was relentlessly included as a statistic or record; he or she was lost, in the manner of Emerson's plaint, as a full human being.

It is worth taking a more careful assessment of the procedures that the companies used in fulfilling their responsibilities for research and disclosure. For instance, ACE, a major insurance company that is the descendant of both the Insurance Company of North America (the oldest insurance company in North America) and Aetna Fire, hired lawyers before doing anything else. (The Illinois registry report identifies the lawyers as belonging to Wolf, Block, Schorr and Solis-Cohen, LLP, Philadelphia, Pennsylvania.) Of course, "lawyering up" is not an unwise or incriminating move necessarily, but it is interesting given the results of the research. It was the lawyers who then delegated and directed the research of select archivists and historians. Here is the "Research Methodology" section of the CDI:

> ACE reported that in order to comply with the regulation, it retained a law firm to assist in its efforts to identify and compile all of the records and information related to slavery era insurance policies. ACE said that, through counsel, it contacted archivists and historians from several universities and historical societies and obtained insights on how they might most fully identify any responsive data located in its archives.
>
> To assist in its search, ACE acquired a database of information about the transatlantic slave trade that contains the records of 27,233 transatlantic slave ship voyages made between 1595 and 1866.[12] ACE reported that it also reviewed the historical records that it received from its predecessor corporations.
>
> ACE reported that it found a copy of a slave policy written in 1855 by Aetna Life, and that even though this was after its separation from Aetna Fire, in the interests of full disclosure it was submitting the document. This policy insured the life a slave named Peter, identified as a laborer, and was issued in Mississippi.

The singular nature of that lone extant policy stands as ACE's act of regretful integrity. Full disclosure offers a slave named Peter, from Mississippi, but we learn of him only after he has been rhetorically distanced within a series of exculpating qualifying clauses.

Identifying such categories is no small thing in the work of historical accounting. Definition becomes all important, and not just for legal reasons—that linguistic precision enacts a kind of reversal of the warranty section of the insurance contract, retroactively naming a new form of responsibility. We would do well to be alert to that discourse: the socialized individual, product of the insuring property regime of the early modern period, has assumed a new voice here; the people of California demand to know their fiduciary responsibilities, as they generate a new form of textual property, now defined and registered for public attention.[13] The registry does not, interestingly, mandate any action regarding what is revealed—the socialized individual hovers about its results and is invited to take any action deemed ethically and morally appropriate. Again, naming and defining take precedence here, as it does in so many other instances of witnessing after historical atrocities. The statute's definitions of slaves and slaveholders reverses the historical contracts that originally named the properties in question—the public is now, in effect, ordaining the "whereas" of historical wrongs that must be respected.

California's responsibility was dependent upon the same documents of insurable sociability that make the need for responsibility so urgent. As the California standards for reporting under the Slavery-Era Insurance Policies statute describe the related categories at their core, it becomes quietly apparent that the very meaning of the term "slave" derived from the semiotic web of personalities and durations constructed by the policies and contracts of commercial slavery:

d. The term "slave" means a person wholly subject to the will of another, having no freedom of action and whose person and services were wholly under the control of another, and who was in a state of enforced compulsory service to another.

e. The term "slaveholder" means owners of slaves; owners of business enterprises using slaves; owners of slave-carrying vessels or other means of transporting slaves; merchants and/or financiers dealing in the purchase, sale, or financing of the business of slaves and slavery; slave dealers and slave brokers.

f. The term "slaveholder insurance policies" means policies issued to or for the benefit of slaveholders to insure them against the death of, or injury to, human property.

g. The term "slavery era" means prior to 1865.

In reading through these definitions, we begin to discern the problems that arise when research conducted into historical texts purports to make us responsible for what happens to people and things. Who is responsible for answering to these definitions? Once you have your definitions, what do you do with them? And in what sense is putting names to the categories a subject for responsible accounting in the first place?

The matter of responsibility, when seen as a textual process that redounded on the parties tied to property definitions, becomes uniquely difficult to fulfill. In what capacity the citizens of California should be reading the registry report is unclear—are they citizens or consumers? The CDI website was able to reverse the textual responsibilities for the public, but not without unintentionally revealing the ironies of socialized individuality: All the subheadings for the registry bear before the colon the tag "Consumers," producing such incongruities as "Consumers: Slave Names" and "Consumers: Slaveholders Names." In the textual methods of responsibility, the discourse of property continues to confuse those it seeks to name as owners or assets. What does one do with this information as a "consumer" or a citizen?

Longevity

When researching *Underwriting: The Poetics of Insurance in America*, I came across another kind of entanglement that plagues the methods of responsibility and speaks to why corporations might have held back from the California Registry. In working with one very old insurance corporation, the levels of legal suspicion that attended my attempt to gain access to eighteenth-century policies was at times astonishing, especially so given the welcoming disposition of most scholarly archives. While trying to obtain images of eighteenth-century policies that I might use as examples of the iconographic power of the documents, I was put through a series of legal holds in order to determine my intentions regarding the research I was conducting.

Apparently, their fear was precisely the goal of the California registry—that incriminating slave information might be revealed. In addition, there was worry about the privacy of the policyholders themselves, even those who died over two hundred years ago. About a year after the book was completed, I asked the corporate archivist that I had been working with if she would be willing to discuss with me the obstacles that I had encountered in my research. She was extremely reluctant to comment on the record about whether documents within their archives should be subject to corporate protection, citing a rather contentious professional atmosphere. That contentiousness presumably arises from competing allegiances within the world of archivists—allegiance to history academically conceived as against the interests of the corporations that employ them. For the archivist, professional organizations provide a public that consists of overlapping and contending factions, each with different obligations to historical guardianship. That contest is a version of the old postabolitionist dilemmas about the responsibility for property within new social arrangements. Slavery marks the line that extends from the origins of socializing individuality and continuously redraws different corporate publics.

Corporations, it would seem, call themselves "public" in peculiar ways. When companies sell themselves to shareholders it is commonly referred to as "going public." This term of art refers to a form of property distribution above all else, limiting the "public" to a particular kind of open call—investors—with sufficient capital to enter into an exclusive marketplace. It is, in short, a public appeal to private interests. But the word "public" and the means by which publicity is made, found, or claimed haunts the methods of public-ness. This is especially so in a democracy where some marketplaces are, as the California Registry makes clear with regard to insurance, genealogically related to the trade in slaves. This haunting, what Baucom calls "specters of the Atlantic," or what we might want to think of as the ghostly histories of the corporate present, is actually the *new* responsibility we find emerging so problematically from its past.

What scholarship can offer conventional political publics (such as the people of California) is its sustained attention. This does not necessarily mean it should speak in mass idioms but instead simply use forms of address that are recognizable beyond the classroom or symposium (legal and political commentary, blogs, journalism, art, etc.). This is a professional problem, but it is also one of temperament and anxiety, a lack of comfort with the possibility of nonprofessional criticism or suspicion of motives. I'd like to conclude by drawing on a literary example that might fortify us against discomfort and suspicion, offering an analogue for the critic and archivist who is obliged by the present and the past to chase both etymologies and their subjects.

It is the beginning of *Moby-Dick*, Herman Melville's great book about archives, schooling, and cargo.[14] Actually, my example comes from *before* the beginning. The prologue to the narrative is a kind of novelistic "whereas"—often overlooked—that infers, in some sense, the *ars poetica* of the text to follow. The novel is one of the great socializing forms of modernity, but this novel, perhaps more than any pre-Modernist novel that I can think of, asks us to be alert to the necessary failures of linguistic attribution and narrative control that come with the recollection and retrieval of commodities (mammalian or linguistic). It asks us as readers to own up to our eager failings.

Before Ishmael sails, we are in a library, where Melville launches his quasi-authorial skepticism, a moody and scholarly warranty about settled textual answers to the question of evil/whaleness. The reader is made aware of the collective inability of readers and collectors to, for better or worse, escape libraries and their undertow of etymologies, and so too, readers and archivists cannot hope to collect everything. The librarian is the antitype of the malevolent re-searching Ahab, but in this case, the librarian is somewhat heroic in his pathetic and hapless guise. He is uncomfortable. I quote at length.

ETYMOLOGY

(Supplied by a Late Consumptive Usher to a Grammar School)

The pale Usher—threadbare in coat, heart, body, and brain; I see him now. He was ever dusting his old lexicons and grammars, with a queer handkerchief, mockingly embellished with all the gay flags of all the known nations of the world. He loved to dust his old grammars; it somehow mildly reminded him of his mortality.

"While you take in hand to school others, and to teach them by what name a whale-fish is to be called in our tongue leaving out, through ignorance, the letter H, which almost alone maketh the signification of the word, you deliver that which is not true." HACKLUYT

"WHALE. * * * Sw. and Dan. hval. This animal is named from roundness or rolling; for in Dan. hvalt is arched or vaulted." WEBSTER'S DICTIONARY

"WHALE. * * * It is more immediately from the Dut. and Ger. Wallen; A.S. Walw-ian, to roll, to wallow." RICHARDSON'S DICTIONARY

KETOS, Greek. CETUS, Latin. WHOEL, Anglo-Saxon. HVALT, Danish. WAL, Dutch. HWAL, Swedish. WHALE, Icelandic. WHALE, English. BALEINE, French. BALLENA, Spanish. PEKEE-NUEE-NUEE, Fegee. PEKEE-NUEE-NUEE, Erromangoan.

EXTRACTS

(Supplied by a Sub-Sub-Librarian)

It will be seen that this mere painstaking burrower and grub-worm of a poor devil of a Sub-Sub appears to have gone through the long Vaticans and street-stalls of the earth, picking up whatever random allusions to whales he could anyways find in any book whatsoever, sacred or profane. Therefore you must not, in every case at least, take the higgledy-piggledy whale statements, however authentic, in these extracts, for veritable gospel cetology. Far from it. As touching the ancient authors generally, as well as the poets here appearing, these extracts are solely valuable or entertaining, as affording a glancing bird's eye view of what has been promiscuously said, thought, fancied, and sung of Leviathan, by many nations and generations, including our own.

So fare thee well, poor devil of a Sub-Sub, whose commentator I am. Thou belongest to that hopeless, sallow tribe. . . . Give it up, Sub-Subs! For by how much more pains ye take to please the world, by so much the more shall ye for ever go thankless! Would that I could clear out Hampton Court and the Tuileries for ye! But gulp down your tears and hie aloft to the royal-mast with your hearts; for your friends who have gone before are clearing out the seven-storied heavens, and making refugees of long pampered Gabriel, Michael, and Raphael, against your coming. Here ye strike but splintered hearts together—there, ye shall strike unsplinterable glasses![15]

Lest it appear that I am arguing in this essay for the angelic heroism of the critic—who would be me—I hasten to add that my main affinity is with the sub-sub-librarian, the comically afflicted "dork" in the books. And while dorkiness has its accidental, windblown virtues, it is important to remember (and I hope this essay has illustrated this) that, as Carol Greenhouse argues in her essay in this volume, the academic researcher is never alone, never not public; she is only one narrator away from publicity. Such figures are, more importantly, hard to kill—which, through some form of representational transference, makes the symbols and texts they guard over and pore through that much more alive themselves. Ultimately, it is the librarian or critic who is responsible for the life of an asset; he determines its longevity because his enterprise outlives even corporate narratives.

That longevity derives its endurance from textual deferral surmounting the hope of peaceful rest; there are no endpoints in the methods of responsibility, no property that can coherently be reconstructed or possessed.

There is, as well, nothing conclusively "veritable" about any of the consumptive librarian's archival collection—no final completeness or singularity of meaning or affiliation (public or private). Just as the California Department of Insurance's slave insurer registry can never fully satisfy the resolving lens of responsibility, neither can the extracts collected in the library afford the "WHALE," even in its herd of linguistic guises. Melville's mocking affection for this character, with whom he is tied as his "commentator," seems to take seriously the project but remains doubtful ("Far from it") of the satisfaction of a result. The librarian/scholar/novelist/ angel of history achieves a kind of responsibility for the objects merely by being amidst them, traveling through time, summoning things above and below—"sub sub."

There is a lesson here in the work of first insuring, then accounting for, and finally restoring historical splinters—shatterings of any sort, whether glass, wood, or bone. The work is worth something, even if the words and categories that would resurrect and reference the fragments offer no easy redemption. Scholars and archivists, in reminding us of this enduring attention to word and historical record, demonstrate the never-finished work of memory and obligation in contemporary political life. Such work is the only real insurance.

CHAPTER 5

"Death by His Own Hand":
Accounting for Suicide in Nineteenth-Century Life Insurance Litigation

Susanna L. Blumenthal

Under the headline "Melancholy Occurrence," newspapers in the Hudson River Valley and beyond regretfully reported the death of Hiram Comfort, a wealthy and respectable merchant of Catskill who "put a period to his existence" on June 25, 1839, by jumping from the steamboat *Erie* and perishing in the river. Comfort was accompanied on board by several friends, who ardently hoped the journey would cure the merchant of the "mental derangement" he appeared to suffer as a result of unspecified "business difficulties." But less than a mile into the trip, Comfort eluded the grasp of his companions and sprang overboard, disappearing into the depths of the Hudson and leaving behind a wife and several children. The case was adjudged a suicide in the popular press, though this verdict was announced without the expectation that any criminal proceedings would follow in the aftermath of this distressing event. The drowning was instead regarded with knowing compassion, in view of the "speculative mania" that had lately spread across the country, constituting both the cause and effect of the Panic of 1837, a financial crisis that pushed all too many businessmen to the brink of despair.[1]

The circumstances surrounding Comfort's death would be subject to greater scrutiny with the passage of a few years and the filing of a civil law suit. This suit pitted the administrator of the dead man's estate, Peter

Breasted, against the Farmers' Loan and Trust Company, which had issued a $5,000 insurance policy on Comfort's life several months before embarking upon the *Erie*. The policy contained a "saving" clause explicitly releasing the insurer from liability if the insured died "by his own hand." Determining this to be such a case, the insurance company refused to pay on the policy, which prompted Comfort's administrator to pursue his claim in state court, averring that the company remained liable because the insured was "of unsound mind, and wholly unconscious" when he drowned himself. To this, the company demurred, insisting that the fact of insanity was immaterial. The trial judge thought otherwise, construing the phrase in question—concededly "somewhat indefinite and equivocal"—to refer to "a criminal act of self-destruction," which could only be performed by one "in the possession and enjoyment of his mental faculties." The issue of Comfort's state of mind was then tried before court-appointed referees, who specially found that the insured "threw himself into the Hudson River . . . while insane, for the purpose of drowning himself, not being mentally capable at the time of distinguishing between right and wrong." The insurance company was accordingly ordered to make payment on the policy.[2]

Appealing this judgment, the insurer maintained that the clause encompassed any intentional act of self-destruction, even under circumstances where the actor was exempted from "all moral culpability." However, this argument proved unavailing, as a divided appellate panel affirmed the trial court ruling in 1853, by a vote of five to three. Writing for the majority, Judge Willard questioned the very idea that an insane person—or at least one who was "incapable of discerning between right and wrong"—could perform an intentional act. Because an insane person had "no mind" to either approve or oppose a course of action, the resulting consequences could not be attributed to him; they were, instead, "the offspring of the disease." So in Comfort's case it was mental disease that propelled him overboard, and thus the insurer was just as liable for his death as if it had occurred by accident or was the byproduct of duress. "Can a man be said to do an act prejudicial to the insurer when he is compelled to do it by irresistible coercion," Willard rhetorically asked, "and can it make any difference whether this coercion came from the hand of man or the visitation of Providence?"[3]

More or less dodging this question, the dissenting judges contended that this line of analogical reasoning was based upon faulty premises. For the factual record hardly established that Comfort's willpower had been so completely vanquished by his mental disease. To the contrary, on their reading of the referee's report, the merchant's self-destructive act was both voluntary and purposeful; he had intelligently decided to cast himself overboard, fully appreciating the physical—if not moral—nature and consequences of his act. If this was not "'dying by his own hand' within the spirit and intent of this clause of the policy," the dissenters submitted, "it is difficult to attach any legal significance to such language." In effect, Comfort's chosen manner of death was "a willful breach of contract," one that could not be excused on account of a "want of moral perception to distinguish between right and wrong." The policy was rendered invalid as a result of this "act of volition," regardless of whether the actor was a "responsible moral agent" at the time that he met his watery end.[4]

Breasted v. Farmers' Loan and Trust Company was a case of first impression in the United States, raising basic questions about the relationship between moral agency and responsibility, as a matter of law. What had initially been cast as the lamentable death of a salesman took on a more ambiguous aspect in the course of litigation. Had Comfort committed suicide in the legal sense of the word? Was this equivalent to dying "by his own hand" within the meaning of the policy that insured his life? Did his deranged state of mind render him morally and, therefore, legally unaccountable for his self-destructive act? Might he still be held to be the responsible agent even if he did not comprehend the moral significance of his action? And what, after all, was the moral significance of Comfort's act, to the extent that it could be intelligibly ascribed to him?

The difference of opinion exhibited by the members of the appellate bench in *Breasted* extended well beyond the jurisdiction of New York. As similar cases were litigated in other state and federal courts, nothing approaching a consensus emerged about the legal significance of suicide-exclusion clauses, the decisions of judges growing only longer and more conflicted as the century wore on. While juries were generally expected to favor plaintiffs in these civil suits, members of the bench appeared less easily swayed, with some expressing unease about the distorting effects of sympathy and error during the trial proceedings.[5] As committed as they commonly were to effectuating the intent of the parties, they diverged considerably in their interpretations of the state of mind that the insured had to be in to be deemed to have died "by his own hand" or have "committed suicide." To clarify their intended meaning, a number of insurance companies added the words "sane or insane," "felonious or otherwise," or "voluntarily or involuntarily" to the provisos about self-destruction. Even so, courts continued to find it necessary to consider the mental condition of the insured in order to distinguish self-destruction from wholly unintentional acts causing death, whether resulting from disease, mistake, or sheer accident.[6] Indeed, it seemed that no amount of careful redrafting on the part of insurers could completely insulate them from litigation that placed the mind of the insured in issue, ultimately presenting the question of what constituted the *self* in self-destruction.

While this doctrinal story has a certain intrinsic interest, it is recounted here in order to shed light on the subject of responsibility as it was understood by members of the bench in nineteenth-century America. Their conflicting judgments about the mental prerequisites of the suicidal actor are here viewed as part and parcel of broader cultural shifts in thinking about rational and responsible behavior as the fledgling life insurance industry marketed a new means of securing against the "fatal chances of life." In the boom-and-bust economy of the era, a man's fortune could be made or unmade by unpredictable forces well beyond his control, but still he might provide his family with "a certainty against their future want" through "the agency of a life policy." This was the main thrust of antebellum advertising campaigns, as insurers seeking to avoid any imputation that they were promoting "betting on lives" endeavored to convince the public at large that buying their product was not just a prudent measure but an ethical imperative. The head of family who failed to do so was more than merely foolish—he was "criminal in his neglect," exhibiting a degree of selfishness that was likely to elicit an even harsher rebuke when he was finally called to judgment before his Maker.[7] This promotional literature may have succeeded too well with men like Comfort, for they seemed to have taken the insurers' ethos of familial responsibility to its logical limit, apparently estimating that life was no longer worth living.

So chillingly calculated were these acts of self-destruction that they constituted grounds for doubting the sanity of the actors, for questioning whether they truly were the agents of their own demise. The hypothesis of insanity was presented most forcefully by the intended beneficiaries of the policy—most often, the dependents and creditors of white propertied men—who were seeking to prevent its forfeiture on account of suicide. This way of accounting for the death had often been seized upon by coroners' juries, in order to avoid a verdict of *felo de se* and the ignominious burial and property confiscation that accompanied such a ruling under the English common law.[8] Yet the plea of insanity took on a different cast when it was redeployed in nineteenth-century American insurance litigation. In these sorts of cases, the plea was intended to answer a charge that the alleged suicide had violated the terms of a contract rather than the criminal code. Moreover, the forfeiture here threatened redounded to the benefit of the insurer rather than the state. The task of construing the policy terms in such cases was further complicated by the fact that suicide had all but ceased to be a punishable offense in most American jurisdictions by midcentury, though there was in a few states a countervailing tendency in this same era to enact penal sanctions for attempted and assisted suicide.[9] Ambivalence about the suicidal actor was also evident in the social world beyond the courthouse. Although throughout the century prominent ministers and moralists continued to condemn self-murder as a mortal sin, alternative perspectives were provided by a host of medical men, statisticians, and social reformers who pointed to the biological and social roots of the self-destructive impulse.[10] In so doing, they sparked a wide-ranging public debate about the sanity of suicide, which often spilled over into the courtroom, mainly serving to intensify the problem of attribution repeatedly presented to the court in the cases that followed that of *Breasted*.

Living in an age when suicide was so often associated with "pecuniary embarrassment," nineteenth-century American judges were impaled on the horns of a dilemma. A ruling that the death was self-inflicted might reduce the intended beneficiaries to want or at least relative penury. But allowing compassion for the dependent family to decide the matter was problematic in its own right, and not only because the court's indulgence came at the expense of company stockholders and other innocent policyholders. To require payment on the disputed policy was arguably to facilitate a fraud on the insurer, essentially rewarding and thereby encouraging a rather monstrous form of financial planning. Such clashing considerations help account for the accumulating mass of inconsistent decisions in cases where the insurer's defense of suicide was met by the beneficiaries' plea of insanity.[11] In this maze of rulings it might be possible to discern the outlines of what one scholar has aptly described as "the order of equity, if not the equity of order."[12] Yet this begs the question of what it meant to do equity in the minds of the judges, implying greater uniformity of thought than was in fact expressed in their opinions. Upon closer inspection of the law reports published across the century, it becomes clear that the American judiciary remained deeply conflicted about how to allocate the burden of loss as between insurers and beneficiaries, never arriving at a settled consensus as to the applicable rules of responsibility in cases of self-destruction. In case after case, this essay will show, the alleged suicide had a destabilizing effect on the doctrinal landscape. Embodying market failure as well as moral hazard, this figure confounded conventional moral and legal categories.[13] Though he seemingly took charge of his own destiny, this self-sacrificing actor nonetheless appeared a rather crazed confidence man, so much so that he plausibly could be counted among the casualties of capitalism—a haunting emblem of an economic order in which most everything could be bought and sold.

It was precisely because the alleged suicide appeared both deliberate and deranged that judges struggled with the issue of liability, their clashing judgments revealing ambiguities and tensions at the core of the nineteenth-century ideal of the responsible provider.[14] In accounting for the death of a broken man like Comfort, members of the bench could hardly ignore evidence of careful planning seemingly motivated by a profound sense of duty to his family and creditors. Yet to credit the actor with such acts of self-sacrifice was, ironically, to dispossess him of the capacity to fulfill his obligations as a husband, father, and businessman. For the designated beneficiaries to recover under the life policy, the death had to be attributed to circumstances beyond the control of the erstwhile head of household. That is to say, it was only by denying that the insured had any choice about the time and manner of his death that courts could ensure that he met the expectations of his family, creditors, and the wider community of which he was a part. In so ruling, however, judges risked undermining this model of responsible manhood, as their decisions might well be read as inducements to suicide, fatally tempting those who had fallen on hard times to liquidate their sole remaining asset—life itself—rather than endure its trials with unflinching fortitude. Faced with this dilemma of decision, members of the bench betrayed doubts about the moral agency of the insured, though most tended to locate the source of the constraint within the diseased body or mind of the actor rather than the surrounding social circumstances. However, nineteenth-century courts were far from ruling out the possibility of sane suicide, few questioning the basic premise that suicides *could* be choosers. Indeed, the sane suicide appeared to be a nearly indispensable character in the jurisprudence of the era, his willful death serving to mark the moral limits of the enterprise of life insurance. Standing outside the bounds of coverage, this self-destructive figure ultimately provided a strange sort of assurance that human life could not be freely alienated like other commodity forms.

"To Whom Belongs the Property of Life?"

The specter of suicide was frequently conjured up in the popular press in the decades following American independence, often as a haunting symbol of the perils of untutored freedom in the young republic.[15] However extensive the rights and liberties secured to those living under the newly established government, self-killing was not generally understood to be among them. Defenders of suicide, both ancient and modern, were made known to the reading public mainly by way of their detractors, who selectively quoted from an array of biblical, classical, and Enlightenment texts to demonstrate that a man's life was not his for the taking.[16] Although human life was rightly regarded as "a species of property," its possessors were not free to dispose of it as they willed, for it was merely "a loan from our maker, which we are bound to protect and improve, and which we are at length to resign, with all its appendages, into the hand of him who gave it."[17] Conservative ministers were perhaps the most vocal and insistent on this score, their sermons expatiating on "the guilt, the folly, and the doom of the self-murderer," whose manifest failure "to stand against the Wiles of the Devil" constituted a sin against God, human nature, and society.[18] The severity of these decrees were nonetheless tempered by the ministers' recognition that the "madness" in the heart of such a sinner might arise from "mental derangement" of a sort that a physician could relieve, and they joined forces with secular reformers in establishing humane societies that were expressly committed to resuscitating would-be suicides, variously described as "horrid Criminals" and "victims of despair." While they figured themselves as benevolent rescuers and restorers of religious faith and hope, they were also motivated by a positive sense of their own rights and duties as Christian men and citizens of the new nation. As one reformer recalled explaining to an unwilling beneficiary of his aid: "I maintained that he had . . . attempted to commit a crime against society and to deprive it of one of its members; that his life was the property of society; and that as one of it I owed it as a duty, in common with every other individual, to prevent, as far as I had it in my power . . . the destruction of any of its members."[19]

Whether suicide did in fact constitute a crime, in the formal legal sense, was a considerably more complicated question in the several states, due in no small part to the variations in the penalty schemes enacted and enforced by English and colonial American authorities over the course of the preceding centuries. At common law, the self-destroyer was denominated a *felo de se*, his actions warranting the penalties of forfeiture and ignominious burial.[20] Yet, as was the case with any felony, the actor might be released from liability if he was shown to be *non compos mentis* at the moment when he took his own life or if the death was deemed to be an accident.[21] Moreover, not all colonial American jurisdictions matched the harshness of the traditional English law.[22] As early as 1641, Massachusetts prohibited the confiscation of the personal estates of suicides, though ignominious burial was subsequently imposed by way of a 1660 enactment directing that their corpses were to be buried in a highway with a cartload of stones laid upon the grave "as a brand of Infamy, and as a warning to others to beware of the like Damnable practice."[23] Pennsylvania likewise removed the penalty of forfeiture, doing so by way of a 1701 charter provision, which declared that "if any person, through Temptation or melancholy, shall Destroy himself, his Estate, Real & Personal, shall, notwithstanding, Descend to his wife and Children or Relations as if he had Died a natural death."[24] By contrast, the General Assembly of Providence Plantations (later to become the state of Rhode Island), explicitly incorporated the common-law rule of forfeiture in cases of suicide in 1647, imposing the forfeiture of goods and chattel on one who committed the "most unnatural" act of killing himself "out of a premeditated hatred against his own life or other humor."[25]

The prosecution and punishment of suicide was even more variable than these legal provisions suggest, given the vagaries of the practices of coroners and inquest jurors from one region to the next, shaped to differing degrees by the status and reputation of the accused and their families, the interplay between the economic and political interests of royal officials, religious authorities, and local communities, and the broader cultural interface between elite and popular cosmologies.[26] The fragmentary nature of the surviving court records further impedes the process of historical reconstruction, making it especially difficult to recover a sense of how and why coroners' juries distinguished felonious from excusable self-killings as they did.[27] However, these sources do rather clearly indicate that there was a pronounced increase in the proportion of *non compos mentis* verdicts in the early modern period, such that it became "the usual outcome" in both English and colonial American jurisdictions by the last decades of the eighteenth century.[28] This apparent trend toward leniency has long been interpreted by historians as a key indicator of the secularization of suicide, the jurors' verdicts standing as evidence of the gradual spread of more tolerant attitudes toward the act of self-killing, especially—but by no means exclusively—when performed by prosperous and respectable heads of household.[29] Yet it would seem that the jurors who returned these verdicts did so without much guidance or encouragement from medical experts and in the face of mounting criticism from members of the bench and bar and other concerned traditionalists.[30]

Typifying this negative reaction was the English jurist William Blackstone, who reaffirmed the criminality of suicide in no uncertain terms in his 1769 volume *Of Public Wrongs*, the fourth volume of his *Commentaries on the Law of England*. "Self-murder, the pretended heroism, but real cowardice of the Stoic philosophers," Blackstone began, "is wisely and religiously" prohibited under English law, ranking among the "highest crimes." Indeed, the suicide was held to be "guilty of a double-offense; one spiritual, in evading the prerogative of the Almighty, and rushing into his immediate presence uncalled for; the other temporal, against the king, who hath an interest in the preservation of all his subjects." Although Blackstone admitted criminal liability would be suspended if the actor was out of his senses when he killed himself, he maintained that "this excuse ought not to be strained to that length, which our coroners' juries are apt to carry it," prone as they were to take "the very act of suicide" to be "an evidence of insanity, as if every man, who acts contrary to reason had no reason at all." Such logic, he observed, might "prove every other criminal *non compos* as well as the self-murderer," but the criminal law more narrowly defined insanity, since "every melancholy or hypochondriac fit does not deprive a man of the capacity of discerning right from wrong." None of this was to deny the difficulty of punishing one who had withdrawn himself from the reach of human laws, and Blackstone in fact conceded that the existing penalty scheme "borders a little upon severity," though he hastened to add that the "power of mitigation is left in the breast of the sovereign" in appropriate circumstances. In all other cases, the full force of the law ought to be applied, the jurist believing the threat of such punishment was likely to deter the would-be suicide "from so desperate and wicked an act," out of "care for his own reputation, or the welfare of his family."[31]

The arguments for rigor helped sustain the traditional common law of suicide well into nineteenth-century England, with forfeiture provisions remaining in force until 1870[32] and religious penalties not entirely removed until 1882.[33] However, a different story unfolded on the other side of the Atlantic in the decades following the American Revolution, as leading statesmen took the opportunity afforded by independence to bring their criminal codes into conformity with "our republican form of government."[34] In proceeding with this work, law reformers sounded many of the notes of Enlightenment penal thought, pointedly renouncing the "cruel and sanguinary laws" of ages past, which had been shown to "defeat their own purposes by engaging the benevolence of mankind to withhold prosecutions, to smother testimony, or to listen to it with bias."[35] Drawing expressly and liberally from the Italian philosopher Cesare Beccaria's 1764 *Essays on Crimes and Punishments,* they renounced the existing penalties for suicide as unjust and inefficacious, essentially concurring with the philosopher's verdict that it was "in the power of God alone" to punish those who took their own lives.[36] The attempt on the part of the state to exact revenge upon the lifeless body of the offender was utterly "contemptible," and it was manifestly cruel to add to the suffering of his "innocent offspring" by confiscating his goods.[37] Nor could such harsh measures be justified on utilitarian grounds, for the offense was "so abhorrent to the feelings of mankind" and contrary to the "strong love of life which is implanted in the human heart" that it could never be "so frequently committed, as to become dangerous to society."[38] Moreover, any person who was "so destitute of affection for his family and regardless of the pleasures of life, as to wish to put an end to his existence" could hardly be expected to be "deterred by a consideration of their future subsistence."[39] To exit the world in this way was rarely defended as the right of the individual, but it was sometimes cast as a permanent sort of emigration, deemed to be less damaging to the state than relocation to another country, because the person departing this life left his property behind.[40] Since the threat of confiscation could make no impression upon one who was desperate enough "to make experiment of what is beyond the grave," and he was almost certain to be found *non compos mentis* by a jury of his peers in any case, American reformers insisted upon the abolition of this penalty scheme.[41]

The revision of the law of suicide in the early republic is often presented as a critical juncture, signaling broader cultural transformations in the treatment of the phenomenon of self-destruction, conventionally described in terms of decriminalization and medicalization.[42] While there is certainly a measure of truth to such accounts, they nonetheless obscure the disquiet and uncertainty as to the moral and legal standing of self-killers that continued to be registered by American politicians, lawyers, doctors, clerics, and laymen across the nineteenth century, an era that saw periodic moral panics about the "suicidal propensity." Even as states formally lifted penal sanctions as applied to accomplished suicides—a gradual and uneven process, not completely effected in some jurisdictions until the 1820s[43]—legislators and judges still recognized the criminality of the act itself insofar as they penalized those who attempted or assisted others in the commission of the offense.[44] Though utility and justice of punishing such offenders was a matter of some controversy, and prosecutions appear to have been relatively infrequent, the very existence of these prohibitions signaled that self-killing remained an offense against the state rather than the prerogative of any individual or a conclusive sign of mental unsoundness.[45] Mixed judgments were likewise rendered through the medium of the popular press, which provided the reading public with a steady stream of stories about suicides, both fictional and real, some of the latter disturbingly modeled after Goethe's all too well-known narrative *The Sorrows of Young Werther*.[46] These stories elicited moralistic responses from physicians as well as ministers and secular reformers, their writings collectively illustrating that sin and disease were not mutually exclusive categories when it came to thinking about the subject of suicide. Though the instigation of the devil did not figure prominently among the causes of self-killing enumerated by medical men, most resisted any easy equation of suicide and insanity, leaving conceptual space for the possibility of sane suicide and the moral culpability that went along with such a designation.[47]

The shifting ethical and legal significance of self-killing as it came under a scientific gaze was most clearly displayed in midcentury works of medical jurisprudence, which delineated "the anatomy of suicide" and offered prescriptions for its legal treatment. The earliest such texts were produced by medical specialists called alienists, who claimed insanity as a field of expertise, typically acquired while serving as superintendents of the insane asylums that increasingly dotted the American landscape in the first half of the nineteenth century.[48] Conceiving of medical and moral science as allied disciplines, they gathered and published "moral statistics" on suicide, which were intended to shed light on the mental and physical sources of this "fearful propensity," with the ultimate goal of prevention.[49] Upon the basis of data gathered from the popular press and institutional records, alienists were able to confirm that insanity was the most frequent cause of suicide, and they speculated that many of the other assigned causes—melancholy, pecuniary embarrassment, domestic trouble, disappointed love, intemperance, religious enthusiasm, fear of poverty, gambling, seduction, and desertion—"were probably attended with temporary derangement."[50] Alienists further noted a correlation between suicide and the commission of other crimes, particularly homicide and arson, which led some to think that all of these destructive impulses might be manifestations of an underlying mental disorder. Yet in calling attention to the environmental, biological, and hereditary factors contributing to the incidence of suicide, they were far from claiming the innocence of those who took their own lives or the impotency of their families, surrounding communities, and representatives of the state. To the contrary, the medical models carried with them the implication that the scourge of self-killing could both be contained by human means, and while most doctors hailed the removal of penal sanctions, they nonetheless urged the interposition of other sorts of restraints, both physical and moral, upon individuals who displayed self-destructive tendencies, whether rooted in depravity, despair, or disease.[51]

Suicide was thus placed within a complex causal network by midcentury alienists, their analyses rendering the question of responsibility newly ambiguous. Of course, the blameworthiness of the successful suicide was practically irrelevant, since most jurisdictions had removed the penal sanctions for the completed offense. Yet this did not entirely relieve judges of the task of determining the sanity of suicide, for litigants continued to press courts to consider self-destructive tendencies as evidence of mental incompetence in a variety of legal proceedings. On the criminal side of the docket, the plea of insanity might be raised to defend against a charge of attempted suicide, and the fact that a defendant attempted to kill himself after committing another crime was routinely offered to show that he was out of his mind at the time he committed the initial offense, thereby excusing him from responsibility.[52] A similar strategy was deployed in civil contests as a means of setting aside a disposition of property made shortly before the owner took his own life, the claim being that the instrument purporting to express his will was instead the offspring of a mental disease, such that it was invalid.[53] Support for these sorts of contentions were drawn from treatises on medical jurisprudence and the testimony of expert witnesses, but opposing counsel were usually able to counter with their own scientific authorities, particularly as most physicians held to the view that suicide was "sometimes an act of reason, sometimes an act of insanity." Indeed, parties on both sides of a given case might have recourse to the American alienist Isaac Ray's monumental 1838 *Treatise on the Medical Jurisprudence of Insanity*, which made a point of distinguishing "voluntary, imputable suicide" arising from "moral motives" from "maniacal, non-imputable suicide" resulting from "some pathological condition of the brain." Observing that "life was not the only nor perhaps the greatest gift we have received from the author of our being," the doctor submitted that "it ought not to appear strange that men should sometimes be willing to relinquish it for the sake of securing a good or avoiding an evil," particularly those who had suffered "reverses of fortune" or faced "the certain prospect of infamy and the world's scorn." And even in those cases where the suicide appeared to be guilty of foolishness or stupidity in choosing to terminate his existence, the doctor insisted that "we have no right to confound such error with unsoundness of mind." Though we might fairly presume "the mental disturbance is always great" in such instances, the same was surely true of those who committed crimes "under the excitement of strong passions," which ought not to be confused with "real pathological irritation."[54]

What, then, were the hallmarks of "suicidal mania" on the doctors' accounts, and to what extent were their expert opinions about the limits of responsibility relied upon by members of the bench? Alienists were the first to concede that the physical locus of this mental disorder was not always "appreciable to the senses," even when it was possible to conduct an autopsy, but they were nonetheless confident that the existence of insanity could be reliably determined in courtroom proceedings chiefly on the basis of behavioral symptoms. Recognizing that the act of suicide could not alone establish that the actor was insane and therefore irresponsible, medical writers delineated the telltale signs of mental derangement, commonly identifying two distinct "species" of suicidal mania. The first was marked by a "melancholic disposition," which ultimately ripened into a delusive state of mind, the sufferer adhering to false conceptions of his financial or spiritual condition or harboring groundless suspicions of those who were eminently deserving of his love and trust. In one possessed by "such a conviction of overwhelming and hopeless misery, the feeling naturally rises, of life being a burden, and this is succeeded by a determination to quit it."[55] By contrast, those afflicted with the second strain of the disorder had no apparent motive—real or imagined—for killing themselves, seemingly enjoying good health and surrounded with everything that could make life dear to them. Without warning or the slightest indication of mental distress, they impulsively killed themselves, sometimes prompted by nothing more than the sight of a deadly weapon or the mere mention of a prior case of suicide. The most unfortunate among them were tormented by a painful awareness of this dreadful propensity without any accompanying power to comprehend or counteract it, short of beseeching others to protect them from themselves.[56]

The suicidal maniacs depicted by midcentury alienists did not easily fit within the traditional common-law categories of persons *non compos mentis*, who were commonly said to suffer from a "total deprivation of reason," leaving them with no greater understanding than that of "an infant, a brute, or a wild beast."[57] The doctors' introduction of this novel type of mania was part and parcel of a broader effort on their part to encourage judges and legislators to revise the narrow, cognitive test of legal insanity to reflect the advances that had been lately made in the sciences of the mind.[58] More particularly, alienists urged courts to recognize partial forms of mental disease called "monomanias" that were understood to be circumscribed in their effects yet quite debilitating within their spheres of operation. A person might be found to labor under an insane delusion on a singular "topic," such as religion or even his family. Or he might be afflicted with a "lesion" of the will or some other sort of "moral insanity," unaccompanied by any discernible intellectual derangement. Working within this altered conceptual universe, alienists went on to name specific disorders, among which they included not only suicidal mania but also "homicidal mania," "kleptomania," "pyromania," "fanatico-mania," "politico-mania," and "erotomania." These disorders did not fall neatly on either side of the moral-intellectual divide, and their main symptoms seemed to track rather problematically many of the provisions of the criminal code, or so critics began to complain, sparking wide-ranging debate about the so-called insanity dodge, both among and between doctors, lawyers, and the public at large.[59]

The very fact that the doctors disagreed was considered by some American judges and jurists as reason enough to adhere to a cognitive test of criminal capacity, which was given its most influential restatement by a panel of English judges in 1843, after an acquittal was won in the celebrated McNaughtan trial. In what was clearly a rebuke to proponents of the medical theories of moral insanity, the famed McNaughtan Rules affirmed that criminal responsibility turned on the defendant's knowledge of the difference between right and wrong with respect to the charged offense.[60] This threshold of capacity was likewise adopted as the rule in most antebellum American jurisdictions, though members of the bench and bar remained conflicted about the status of those who lacked the moral power to avoid doing what they knew to be wrong, with a substantial minority of courts coming to recognize "irresistible impulse" as an excusing condition, even in the absence of any evidence of intellectual impairment.[61] However, the expansion of the legal definition of insanity did not necessarily make it any easier to establish mental incompetence on the basis of proof of a suicidal propensity. Indeed, antebellum judges displayed a certain wariness as they considered such pleas, their judgments clearly shaped by the abolition of penal sanctions for suicide, which lessened the pressure "to infer against the sanity in favor of innocence" or otherwise "warp the act itself beyond its legitimate influence from motives of humanity to the deceased's relatives."[62] In this altered doctrinal context, judges kept alive the notion of sane suicide, explicitly advising jurors that the act of self-destruction could not stand alone as conclusive evidence of insanity and further emphasizing that those afflicted with suicidal mania often retained the capacity to exercise "the usual discretion as to the management or disposition of property." Thus conveyed, these legal rules of capacity and responsibility served at once to safeguard the civil rights of suicidal actors without suggesting that an individual's prerogative to do what he willed with his own extended to the divine gift of life.[63]

So the legal relations between suicide and insanity were renegotiated as Americans made the transition from colony to nation. While suicide continued to be condemned as a "grave public wrong" by an array of clerics, moralists, doctors, and lawyers far into the nineteenth century, offenders escaped earthly punishment, both because of genuine doubts about their sanity and misgivings about traditional common-law sanctions, which seemed to impose undue hardship on surviving family members without serving as an effective deterrent against future acts of self-destruction. As these sanctions fell into disuse and were ultimately abolished in many American jurisdictions, suicide may have declined in significance on the criminal side of the docket, though those who assisted or attempted such an act were still at least potentially subject to prosecution and imprisonment or civil commitment. All the while, courts guarded against any automatic inference of civil incapacity from the mere fact of suicide or its attempt, consistently holding that suicide was not necessarily an indicator of insanity and that even the presence of suicidal mania did not rule out the possibility of legal competence where the management of property was concerned. The viability of this legal settlement would nonetheless be tested in the second half of the nineteenth century, as the expansion of the life insurance industry immeasurably complicated the question of what constituted a "good death," particularly in those cases in which it appeared that the insured had all too rationally calculated that the only way he could provide for his family was by killing himself.

A Premium for Self-Destruction

Almost from its inception in early modern Europe, the practice of insuring lives inspired charges of impiety, its detractors contending that it constituted an especially pernicious form of gambling. They figured the entire enterprise as an unholy mixture of sacred and profane, underwriters trading on the offensive notion that human life could be reduced to a pecuniary value, presumptuously and vainly attempting to anticipate "Heaven's Will." These criticisms were not entirely unwarranted, given the extent to which life insurance was used for purely speculative purposes, most obviously in the case of the policies taken out on the lives of public figures, such as the pope, which were essentially wagers as to when they would die. Betting on lives came to be regarded as all the more disreputable as disturbing stories surfaced about frauds perpetrated by insurers and policyholders alike; the former were often exposed as embezzlers, while the latter were shown to have misrepresented the age and health of the lives to be insured, sometimes even resorting to murder in order to collect on their policies. Such scandals prompted government officials to impose ever stricter regulations upon the insurance trade, which continental jurists reinforced by invoking the Roman law precept that *hominis liberi nulla estimatio*. As a result of their combined efforts, life insurance was effectively outlawed in nearly every country in Europe by 1700. The great exception to this rule was Britain, where moral objections to life insurance were "always comparatively muted" and the legal culture correspondingly more permissive. Yet even the British government came to see the need for official oversight and other forms of regulation, through which they endeavored to distinguish legitimate from "malign speculation." This was accomplished most comprehensively with the passage of the Gambling Act of 1774, which was intended to limit the universe of legally eligible policyholders to those who had "an interest in the life of the persons insured"—an interest that would be rather liberally construed by English courts, leaving unclear the extent to which the law allowed people's lives to be claimed as property and made the object of commerce.[64]

Although there were no more substantial legal impediments to the establishment of the life insurance business in postrevolutionary America,[65] the market for policies developed more slowly than it did in England. Enterprising insurance men called attention to this national difference as a means of boosting sales, circulating brochures provocatively asking: could it really be true that "an American loves his family less than an Englishman?" Despite such appeals, policies were not sold with much success in the United States until the 1840s, and it was only in the 1870s that the industry reached maturity, having found its best customers among members of the emergent middle class, "whose income depended upon their lives."[66] The modest growth of life insurance in the first half of the century was attributable to a host of economic, political, technological, and ideological factors, but the ones most often commented upon by industry leaders and more objective observers of the day related to the want of reliable statistics on mortality rates and the persistence of popular prejudices and general ignorance about the enterprise as a whole. Even industry boosters acknowledged the inherent difficulty of setting "just and accurate" rates of insurance "on scales measuring truly the probabilities and value of life, in its various stages of existence, in different climates, different employments, and in the vicissitudes of action to which it is subject"—a problem that only began to be redressed with the creation of the first comprehensive American experience table of mortality in 1868. No less formidable was the array of ministers and moralists who insisted upon the impiety of insuring life, which was "a gift of God, and when taken away was His resumption." They also raised more secular concerns about the speculative nature of life insurance and the other moral hazards introduced with its provision. From their standpoint, insurance agents were essentially peddling the "anodyne of security," thereby encouraging reliance "upon something beside economy and industry," which would "lead accordingly to the relaxation and decay of those cardinal virtues of society." Worse still, the policies gave designated beneficiaries reason to look forward to the death of the insured, tempting them to act unlawfully to bring this event about for the purpose of securing the premium. To give credence to their claims, critics were able to point to sensational accounts in American newspapers, colorfully chronicling the train of public scandals that accompanied the spread of insurance in England, often with the clear implication that a man might indeed "shorten his life by insuring it."[67]

Insurance entrepreneurs were quick to respond to these attacks, and they launched a counteroffensive in the form of an aggressive—and seemingly effective—public relations campaign intended to prove that their product was "advantageous, safe, and patriotic," promising their consumers "pecuniary independence from the risk of death." Company heads and their surrogates flooded the popular press with articles and advertisements elaborating the principles and operations of life insurance and averring that its benefits were "as various and numerous as the fluctuations of unstable fortune."[68] Those with reservations about the ethical character of these institutions were assured of the "charitable and philanthropic" purposes of their founders, who aimed to instill "habits of prudence in individuals by enabling them to make provisions for their families." Turning the tables on their opponents, insurance promoters averred it to be the Christian duty of every husband and parent to purchase a life policy for the comfort and security of the dependents that would be left behind with his death, a simple corollary of the principle that "Providence helps he who helps himself." Properly understood, then, life insurance was a "handmaiden" to religion and social welfare. Resting upon divine law, this beneficent institution operated to relieve Americans of anxieties about their financial state, thereby producing "an inward state of mind prompting to the correct life" while providing "life-saving household cement . . . that shall hold the broken family together" and guarantee the "subsistence of millions that would otherwise be left powerless and penniless, to constitute the scum of society."[69]

These professions of piety and public spirit were obviously not sufficient to contain the threat of abuse, fraud, and even homicide so luridly reported in the popular press. This was clearly a point of some sensitivity among insurers, and they endeavored to downplay the significance of the problem in promotional literature, categorically stating that there was "no analogy to be drawn between . . . the British and American Life Insurance impositions, and certainly nothing whatever to create alarm or uneasiness on the part of policy holders in these noble institutions." Yet despite these denials, or perhaps to back up such claims, insurers engaged in concerted efforts to insulate themselves from bad risks, well aware that their ability to distinguish "good lives" from "defective ones" might make the difference between the financial soundness or bankruptcy of their businesses.[70] Proceeding in the spirit of the much vaunted "moral science" of the statisticians, insurers built their enterprises on the assumption that "the past contains the grounds of expectation for the future," confident that this held true "of moral as well as physical phenomena"—even those events that appeared to be "the result of the freest volition."[71] But being at the same time cognizant of the shortcomings of the "life tables" at their disposal, insurers developed a range of supplemental means of "rationalizing mortality." They compensated for the want of statistics by requiring that prospective policyholders fill out elaborate applications, probing "every topic which can affect the probability of life,"[72] and they often deputized agents and physicians to conduct personal interviews and medical examinations. Such men were sent out into the field armed with manuals delineating the character traits borne by the most (and least) desirable applicants, clearly aimed to weed out those who were in poor mental or physical health, habitually intemperate, licentious, or otherwise prone to be reckless in their daily affairs or likely to behave dishonestly in their dealings with the company.[73]

To further safeguard the integrity of their enterprise, American insurers carefully crafted the terms and conditions of their policies so as to avoid providing "a premium for carelessness or roguery."[74] In their efforts, they were guided by the judicial doctrine of insurable interest, originally elaborated by English courts.[75] While the nature of this interest remained notoriously indistinct, and the applicability of the doctrine in the several states subject to doubt,[76] American insurers nonetheless invoked the general idea as a basis for denying applications, and they also incorporated it into individual policies, insofar as they required those taking out insurance on the life of another to sign a declaration affirming that the interest they had in such life was "equal to the sum assured."[77] In addition, these policies typically contained exclusion clauses that simultaneously policed the behavior of policyholders and designated beneficiaries while securing the financial and moral standing of the insurance companies. Under these provisions, policies were declared to be null and void in the event that the assured died as a result of intemperance, as the consequence of a duel, by his own hand, at the hands of justice, or in the known violation of the law. Finally, insurers reserved the right to terminate coverage upon the discovery of any sort of fraud, misrepresentation, or concealment in the original application for insurance.[78]

In thus limiting their responsibility for the ultimate loss of death, American insurers revived the threat of forfeiture, through which they sought to deter a number of misdeeds, only some of which were actual crimes.[79] However, companies were far from eager to impose such a penalty, particularly if this entailed going to court, where they were likely to face a less than sympathetic jury. And even if they were to prevail, insurers fully appreciated the risk of negative publicity accompanying such a victory, it being all too easy to imagine what might happen to their customer base if they were to be made the subject of a headline reading "Heartless Injustice to the Widow and Orphan by a Life Insurance Company."[80] The insurers' predicament was incisively presented in an 1869 edition of the *Insurance Monitor*:

> Fraud and incompetency have done their work. What recourse has the company? The law, say you? No sir; juries believe that corporations have no souls, and the direct cost and indirect damage done a company's general business by litigation fully balances all the probabilities of gain by evoking the aid of the law. Some companies make a virtue of necessity and largely advertise the fact that they *never contested a claim*.[81]

Doubtless the writer here indulges in a bit of hyperbole, but still he captures something of the dilemma that insurance companies faced as competition within the industry grew fierce in the second half of the century. Ever balancing the exigencies of the marketplace against the imperatives of conventional morality, insurers were truly caught in a bind. While their responsibility to policyholders—and the many wives and children whose money they held in trust—dictated a strict enforcement of contractual provisions, company leaders could not afford to disregard the hazards that lay on the pathway to the courthouse, knowing full well that a reputation for litigiousness would be judged more harshly by public opinion than a failure to penalize those who shortened their own lives.[82] Such considerations moved many companies to simply pay or negotiate a settlement when faced with doubtful claims, unless the fraud was so blatant as to nearly guarantee a favorable jury verdict.[83] But the cases involving suicidal breadwinners like Hiram Comfort presented a uniquely difficult challenge, even where the desperate act was evidently a premeditated one. This was because the man who appeared to have sacrificed his life so that others could live free from want could be conceived as the ultimate exemplar of the ideal of self-denial extolled in the insurers' own promotional literature. Indeed, he arguably bore a certain resemblance to the "pelican in her piety" that graced one insurance company's seal—a religious symbol based upon the creature's reputed propensity to pierce her own breast in times of famine to feed her young with her blood. Beneath this arresting insignia, the firm's motto was inscribed: "I live and die for those I love."[84]

Suicide for the Benefit of Others

Whether it was with the welfare of his wife and children in view that Hiram Comfort plunged into the Hudson cannot be known with certitude. Nor is it possible to know exactly why the insurer of his life chose to run the risk of litigation rather than settling the case out of court. The local press coverage of the apparent suicide was certainly sympathetic enough to militate in favor of the latter approach, but the short time that elapsed between the purchase of the policy and the fatal event may have cut in the other direction. The unprecedented nature of the case, from a legal standpoint, likely tipped the balance in favor of litigation as company officers considered their options. And there was good reason for optimism on their part, as they followed jurisprudential developments on the other side of the Atlantic, where English courts were just then grappling with two similar contests, *Borradaile v. Hunter* (1843) and *Clift v. Schwabe* (1846), each of which generated a split decision in favor of the insurer. The seriatim opinions issued by the English judges were readily mined by the opposing parties in the *Breasted* case, which likewise divided members of New York's highest court, though the majority in this instance held that the insured had the better part of the argument. This want of unanimity

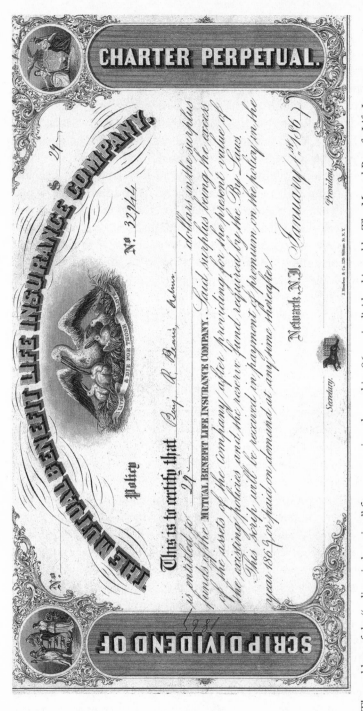

The emblem of the "pelican in her piety" figures prominently on this 1867 scrip dividend issued by The Mutual Benefit Life Insurance Company, along with the motto "I live & die for those I love," exemplifying the general tendency on the part of midcentury insurers to cast their business as beneficent operations upholding the ideal of self-sacrifice and promoting the end of family protection. (Courtesy of Hersh Stern, www.immediateannuities.com)

about what it meant for the insured to "die by his own hands" or to "commit suicide" within the meaning of a life policy continued to characterize the decisional law across American jurisdictions to the end of the century, the question possessing "a fascination which the judicial mind is unable to resist."[85] In elaborating their differences of opinion, members of the bench registered confusion about the moral culpability of those who took their own lives in the throes of pecuniary distress, particularly where this peculiar form of property crime benefited the perpetrator's family and creditors. Actuated by an altruism that tested the limits of sanity, these self-destructive men at once exemplified and called into question the concept of voluntary death, their actions exposing latent uncertainties and contradictions in the rules of responsibility that were supposed to resolve these vexing cases.

The moral and legal quandaries resulting from the alleged suicide of the insured were first introduced most fully before the English judges in *Borradaile* and *Clift*, decisions widely reported on both sides of the Atlantic, setting the terms of the debate in American courtrooms and legislatures in the decades that followed.[86] Although the manner of death in *Borradaile* differed from that in *Clift*—by drowning in the former, poisoning in the latter—the two cases presented the same basic problem of attribution: could an insane person cause his own death within the meaning of the exclusion clauses in standard life insurance policies? The English judges considered this question against the backdrop of a criminal code that still punished suicide and while they were in the midst of formulating the McNaughtan Rules, announced shortly after *Borradaile* was finally decided. Within this legal context, felonious suicide was sometimes said to be a risk excluded by implication where the policy was silent, lest it provide encouragement to crime, but such statements came in the form of *dicta*, there being no direct adjudication of the matter. Thus there was considerable room for interpretation as the English judges considered whether explicit policy language—"die by his own hands" in *Borradaile* and "commit suicide" in *Clift*—was to be read to encompass both felonious and nonfelonious acts of self-destruction, regardless of whether the assured was capable of distinguishing right from wrong when he performed the fatal deed.[87]

This expansive construction of the policy language was adopted by a majority of the court in each case, upon the basis of their consideration of ordinary usage, the objects of insurance, and the probable intention of the parties. Surveying popular dictionaries and encyclopedias as well as legal treatises, it was observed that the words at issue were commonly used to refer to self-destructive acts that did not entail any guilt or moral responsibility on the part of the actor. Nor was a criminal intent necessarily implied by the placement of the clause in the contract alongside exclusions in the event of death by dueling or sentence of the law, for surely the policy would not have been kept alive by showing that the insured had never planned to actually shoot his opponent or was in fact innocent of the crime for which he was executed. The manifest purpose of the proviso regarding self-destruction was to guard against the acceleration of the time for payment on the policy by the voluntary act of the party interested in the money. With this end in view, it made no difference whether the insured "was sane or under some delusion as to the moral quality of the act done," so long as he possessed "sufficient powers of mind and reason to understand the physical nature and consequences of such act, and . . . a purpose and intention to cause his own death by that act." This conclusion was further reinforced by drawing reference to the current state of the actuarial sciences, for while the probabilities of death from bodily diseases might be made "the fair subjects of calculation," the same could not be said of "the consequences of mental disorder, whether produced by bodily disease, by external circumstances, or by corrupted principle," all of which were "equally beyond the reach of any reasonable estimate." Thinking primarily from the insurers' perspective, the judges supplied still other reasons for construing the proviso to include both sane and insane suicides. Since the mentally ill were known to be swayed by "their affection for others" even "where fear of death or of personal suffering" had no influence upon their conduct, the threat of forfeiture might have been held out as a means of encouraging the insured (or those charged with his care) to keep his suicidal tendencies in check. Company officers might also have understandably sought to remove "the topic of criminality" from the deliberations of jurors, whose "compassion for a distressed family struggling with a large and wealthy body" would "prevent any calm appreciation of the evidence" in most cases, all too predictably yielding a verdict for the plaintiff.[88]

Taking the insurers at their words, the dissenting judges arrived at nearly the opposite conclusion, averring that the policy provisos had to be taken to refer to felonious self-destruction performed by a morally responsible agent capable of distinguishing right from wrong. This the dissenters took to be the necessary implication of "commits suicide," a phrase manifestly carrying with it the connotation of "a criminal taking away of one's own life." The same sense was also drawn from the figurative language, "die by his own hands," especially in view of the placement of the clause in the company of others relating to death resulting from dueling and state execution. These readings were reinforced by summoning up many of the same popular and legal texts referenced in the majority opinions, the dissenting judges contending that any lingering ambiguity about the insurers' chosen locution ought to be resolved against them, this rule of construction applying with particular force where the threat of forfeiture loomed on the horizon. One needed only consider the matter from the standpoint of the average purchaser to see why this was so. "A man anxious to provide for his family" would naturally desire insurance against the broadest possible array of risks, and as he contemplated "the calamities of life that might terminate it," he was sure to "anticipate madness as one." It could hardly be imagined that such a man would leave his surviving dependents unprotected against the risk of death by "insane suicide," where he retained but a "glimmering of reason" but was otherwise "lost to all moral sense, and for any other act or crime a complete madman." If the insurers wanted to exclude coverage in such cases, the dissenters thought it incumbent upon them to redraft the exclusion clauses to explicitly say so.[89]

Yet another layer of complexity must be here introduced, for there were intimations in the dissenters' opinions that "insane suicide" was itself something of a contradiction in terms, as they took the word suicide to imply a kind of moral agency that persons *non compos mentis* by definition lacked. Clearly perceiving a larger principle at stake, Chief Baron Pollock insistently probed the issue during the course of the proceedings in *Clift*. The defendant having acknowledged that the policy would have covered a self-killing committed in a state of delirium as well as one occurring by accident, Pollock pressed him to explain why the same treatment was not accorded to other forms of mental illness, particularly those robbing the sufferer of the ability to distinguish right from wrong. The judge's pointed interjections essentially reducing to a single, fundamental question, transcending all doctrinal categories: "If the party is not a responsible moral agent, can the act be his act?"[90] Readily responding in the affirmative, the defendant restated the majority rule in *Borradaile*, essentially holding that the act was rightly attributed to the actor so long as he retained sufficient mind to understand the physical character of his action and was not "incapable of volition."[91] However, Pollock remained unconvinced, his dissent casting serious doubt on the insurer's way of thinking about the subject of responsibility, civil as well as criminal. For if the policy protected an insanely deluded man who mistook "a deadly weapon for an instrument of music," the judge wondered, why should it not also cover one who "fancied himself an apostle, and that it became his duty to die the death of a martyr?" And why should it matter whether the death resulted from "physical blindness, in consequences of which the party insured walks into a well" or "intellectual or moral blindness, which . . . has deprived him of all judgment which should control and govern his acts and of all sense to perceive their moral consequences?" All the subtle distinctions that might be drawn between these various mental conditions were entirely out of place in the determination of cases such as the present, where "the peace, the happiness, and security of thousands of families" hung in the balance. A clearer, readily intelligible rule was in order, in this judge's estimation: "if the act be not the act of a sane responsible creature, but is the result of any delusion or perversion, whether physical, intellectual, or moral, it is not the act of the man." To hold otherwise seemed to him "a departure from the simplicity of the law," a ruling that was "repugnant to sound philosophy, which is the spirit of the law . . . on which all law ought to be founded."[92]

However appealing as a jurisprudential vision, Pollock's ideal of simplicity would prove elusive in American courtrooms. In most jurisdictions, suicide maintained a shadowy legal existence as a crime without a punishment, providing a rather ambiguous reference point as judges endeavored to make sense of the exclusion clauses that came before them. While state and federal courts were inclined to treat the phrases "dies by his own hand" and "commits suicide" as synonymous, there was hardly a common sense as to the meaning of these words, members of the bench dividing rather evenly between the two positions initially staked out by their English counterparts. Nor was this judicial conflict resolved by the insurers' redrafting of their disqualifying provisos to encompass any form of self-destruction—"sane or insane," "felonious or otherwise," "voluntary or involuntary." Still it remained for courts to characterize the self that acted destructively, so as to distinguish this excepted cause of death from those resulting from accident and mistake, which were indisputably covered by the policies. As they addressed the basic question of what made "the act of the man" *his* act, American judges exhibited a remarkable lack of consistency and coherence, manifestly struggling to identify the responsible party in the tragic circumstances of these cases. Indeed, it was with an unstable mixture of sympathy, horror, and incomprehension that members of the appellate bench reviewed the competing accounts of the manner in which the insured met his death, their decisions reflecting basic confusion about the constitution of the accountable agent beyond the formal confines of the criminal law.

The twists and turns of judicial reasoning may be traced through a series of leading cases handed down in two distinct waves, before and after insurers added the clarifying language with respect to the self-destroyer's mental condition. In the first wave of cases, brought in the 1860s and 1870s, the admissibility of evidence of insanity was the central bone of contention, effectively calling upon courts to determine what mental attributes a man had to possess—at a minimum—to be deemed the agent of his own undoing. Insurers attempted to relieve judges of this difficulty through their policy revisions, but they only managed to shift the interpretive battleground, encouraging another round of litigation about the relationship between consciousness and liability in the last quarter of the century. Ironically, these courtroom disputations descended still further into the realm of metaphysics, essentially pressing courts to determine whether an act of self-destruction entailed any sort of intentional state or mental awareness on the part of the insured—whether it could sensibly be performed by one suffering from "a total eclipse of the mind."

This doctrinal story begins with three cases decided in the wake of *Breasted*, which fairly reflect the range of meanings that American judges attached to the suicide-exclusion clauses in their initial, unmodified form. At one end of the spectrum was the 1862 Massachusetts case of *Dean v. American Mutual Insurance Company*, where the insured had died by cutting his throat with a razor, an action that the plaintiffs sought to prove was "the direct result of insanity," in the form of a "suicidal depression, impelling him to take his life." The evidence proffered on this score was, however, refused by the trial court, as it construed the policy's exclusion of death by the insured's "own hand" to apply "irrespective of the condition of his mind . . . at the time the act . . . was consummated." Since the proviso could not be taken literally, the court opined that this was the most reasonable construction, both in view of the juror bias against insurers and the nature of the moral hazard that the policy would otherwise have presented. Insisting that the temptation to commit suicide in order to fulfill obligations to family and creditors was a motive that might operate on a mind diseased as well as one sound, the *Dean* court submitted that it hardly made sense to limit the exception to "case[s] of criminal suicide, where the assured was in a condition to be held legally and morally responsible for his acts." This was not to say that the mental capacity of the insured was wholly irrelevant, for he certainly could not be held accountable if he took his life while in a state of "delirium or raving madness where the body acts only from frenzy or blind impulse" or "idiocy or the decay of mental power in which it acts only from the promptings of the lower animal instincts." Yet admitting these exceptions to the exception only served to show how little mind this court thought to be necessary for a person to be deemed the cause of his own death, at least as a matter of insurance law. So long as the insured acted with the conscious purpose of terminating his life, it was immaterial that he was driven to his death by an insane delusion or a mental depression, even one potent enough to "overwhelm and destroy the due influence and control of the reason and judgment." That it was in the throes of such a mental mutiny that he slit his neck—falsely believing he was "coming to want" and had no other means of saving his family from "extreme poverty"—in no way diminished the responsibility of this would-be breadwinner, his last desperate movement terminating the policy as well as his life.[93]

This model of accountable agency was expressly challenged by Maine's highest court in the 1866 case of *Eastabrook v. Union Mutual Life Insurance Company*, in which the plaintiff sued on a policy he had taken out on the life of his son,[94] who had committed suicide in what was alleged to have been "a fit of insanity." Evidence was admitted on this score at trial, and the jury was instructed to find in the plaintiff's favor "if the insured was governed by an irresistible or blind impulse in committing the act of suicide." A verdict was returned to this effect, the jury specially finding that the impulse was one "over which the will had no control" and that "the self destruction was not an act of volition." On appeal, the appellate panel voted by a margin of six to one to affirm this judgment,[95] the majority opining that the defendants had the benefit of a jury instruction far more favorable than these judges would have allowed. Distinguishing themselves from the *Dean* court, they sweepingly declared that suicide committed under the influence of insanity—whether partial or total—ought to be classed as a "death by disease" no different from that resulting from fever or consumption. "If the act be not the act of a responsible being, but is the result of any delusion or perversion, whether physical, intellectual or moral," the Maine judges insisted, "it is not the act of the man." Neither moral responsibility nor "legal blame" could attach in such a case, the insured's situation being analogous to "the individual who accidentally and unintentionally takes his own life," a contingency that certainly was covered by the policy before the court. The majority maintained this interpretation even as they recognized the peril presented by overly sympathetic jurors prone to infer insanity from the very fact of suicide. At best, this was an argument against trial by jury, and a rather weak one at that, for the jurors' inference was no doubt rightly drawn in the vast majority of such cases. Given these odds, the policy proviso appeared to be aimed at a phantom risk, so far as these judges could see, as they found it hard to imagine an insane man coherently calculating the money value of his life and even more difficult to believe that anyone in his right mind would go to the length of killing himself to provide for the financial welfare of his dependents and creditors. "Suicide for the benefit of others is rare, exceptional and Quixotic," came the pronouncement from the bench, with the assurance that the human "love of life, the strongest sentiment of our nature," afforded "reasonable security against a danger so remotely probable." And were this not enough, the judges hastened to add, insurers also had the comfort of knowing that the mortality tables used to set policy premiums already effectively insulated them from this hazard.[96]

So while *Dean* affirmed the ability of an insane person to "die by his own hands" within the meaning of the insurer's policy, *Eastabrook* defended the reverse proposition, nearly ruling out the possibility of sane suicide—or at least that of the altruistic sort. In their divergent constructions of clauses at issue, those who sat in judgment were confounded by the ponderous practical, equitable, and metaphysical considerations that weighed upon them. Determining which causes of death were within the coverage of the policy proved challenging indeed in an era when the moral agency of the suicidal actor had become such a contestable matter. Though ostensibly focused on the parties' intent, American judges nonetheless took note of evolving medical and lay understandings of the relationship between suicide and insanity, selectively incorporating them into their rulings in ways that often begged the question before the court. The interpretive impasse thus reached can be viewed with particular clarity in the 1869 Kentucky case of *St. Louis Mutual Life Insurance Company v. Graves*, in which the appellate bench evenly split as to whether "moral insanity" was a diseased condition that might disable the insured from killing himself in the sense of the policy or was instead a mere cover for precisely the sort of depraved conduct that insurers sought to discourage with the threat of forfeiture.

The man in question, Leslie C. Graves, was a quite prosperous livestock dealer who had taken out a $5,000 policy on his life that excluded the risk of death "by his own hand," as well as that resulting from "delirium tremens or the use of opium." The policy was purchased for the benefit of his "loved and loving young wife" just a few days after their marriage in January 1867. Some four months later, Graves was found one evening lying dead and alone in the darkness of his livery stable, a pistol nearby, which he had apparently used to shoot himself in the head. At trial, conflicting evidence was presented as to the circumstances surrounding his untimely end, the plaintiff offering lay and expert testimony going to show that shooting was "the offspring of moral *mania*" and the defendant countering with proof that the insured had imbibed "copious and solitary draughts of intoxicating liquors" for several hours before firing the pistol, the drinking deliberately done "to raise his animal courage to an adequate degree for the act." Though no clear motive was identified, several witnesses made mention of a rumor that Graves had set fire to his brother's rival livery stable the night before he had shot himself, with the implication that he had killed himself to escape "the agony of overwhelming disgrace." The charge to the jury directed them to find for the defendant if Graves had "intentionally" destroyed his life, though this was not entirely satisfied by proof that he did so while his intellect remained unimpaired, with the knowledge that "it was forbidden by both moral and human law." For if it appeared "at the instant of the commission of the act" that "his will was subordinated by an uncontrollable passion or emotion causing him to do the act, it was an act of moral insanity," in which case the plaintiff was entitled to a full recovery under the policy.[97]

So instructed, the jury returned a verdict for the plaintiff, but the appellate panel found itself to be deadlocked two for, two against as they reviewed the charge, the grounds of their disagreement elaborately stated in two separate opinions issued by the court. As they rehearsed the now familiar rationales for construing the exclusion clause in more or less expansive terms, the judges interlaced their opinions with critical remarks about testifying experts and works of medical jurisprudence, from which they drew differing conclusions about "the doctrine of moral insanity" and its application to the case at bar. Appearing side by side in the state law reports, these divergent analyses showed the Kentucky court to be conflicted about the difference between right and wrong where suicide was concerned and over the extent to which moral agency figured in the assessment of civil responsibility.

In this regard, consider first the opinion delivered by Judge Robertson, who affirmed that the policy remained in effect if the insured was "morally dead" when he shot himself. The metaphysical assumptions upon which this judgment was based were made apparent at the outset, Robertson starting from the proposition that "the mind is the man" and further suggesting that he could not be held accountable for his conduct unless he possessed "a rational mind" and "a presiding will." It was "as a free moral agent" that Graves consented to the policy terms, impliedly undertaking as he did "to abstain from any act jeopardizing his life beyond the ordinary accidents to which it was liable without his fault." Although this might have been an argument for construing the exceptions clause to encompass self-destructive acts for which the insured was not to blame, this judge took the contrary view, narrowly limiting it to instances of "death as a natural consequence of some *voluntary* act of the assured which he had some moral power to avoid . . . and not by accident or the merely mechanical hand of the maniac." What was contemplated here, he insisted, was an "avoidable death," as might result from "voluntary and habitual" use of opium or alcohol or from other causes that could have been prevented "by prudent and proper conduct." Without admitting the possibility that insanity might be brought about by self-neglect, the judge summarily placed insane suicide in the category of "death by disease," an eventuality "indisputably insured against." This did not, however, resolve the question of where *moral* insanity fit into the jurisprudential scheme of things, a point on which Robertson dwelled somewhat longer, mainly to show that the weight of "modern" medicolegal authority supported the existence of this circumscribed disorder, in which "the affections may be perverted, or the moral sentiments unhinged in such a degree as to subjugate the *will* to some morbid appetite or ungovernable passion" strong enough on its own account to precipitate "insane but *conscious* wrong." Yet the judge took care to disassociate himself from those experts who claimed that suicide was "necessarily an insane act," for there were prominent historical counterexamples of "reasoning suicide" voluntarily performed by believers as well as nonbelievers in "a future state of retribution." Self-destruction was nonetheless "so rare and awful, as, in itself and by itself, to imply insanity, in the absence of proof of motive or predisposing causes." For this reason, the burden was rightly cast upon the insurer to overcome the presumption that the insured's death was an *"inevitable* suicide."[98]

The very ease with which insanity was inferred from the act of self-destruction "in a Christian country" pointed toward a very different line of analysis in the second opinion, authored by Judge Williams. Given such widespread perceptions of suicidal actors as mentally unsound, Williams submitted, the jury charge effectively stood as an invitation to nullify the exclusion clause, and it was made all the more objectionable by its embrace of moral insanity, a doctrine that the judge made a point of denouncing before addressing the particulars of the case before him. "In all the vague, uncertain, intangible, and undefined theories of the most impracticable metaphysician," he fulminated, "no court of last resort in England or

America, so far as has been brought to our knowledge, ever before announced such a startling, irresponsible, and dangerous proposition of law." One needed only think of the implications of this doctrine for the criminal law to see why it had to be rejected, for it would spell the end of "responsibility for homicide, unless it be perpetrated in [a] calm, cool, considerate condition of mind," logically dictating that "the more violent the passion and desperate the deed the more secure from punishment will be the perpetrator" of this or any other offense. As he spun out this nightmare scenario, Williams curiously ignored a conflicting 1864 Kentucky ruling cited (and actually written) by Robertson, in which a unanimous court reversed a murder conviction on account of the trial judge's failure to acknowledge moral insanity as a distinct basis for exemption from criminal responsibility.[99] Proceeding as if this decision had not been made, Williams contended that Graves would not have been released from criminal liability if he had killed another rather than himself under the circumstances as they appeared in the trial record, particularly since the act itself appeared to be the only evidence of moral insanity. It could hardly be imagined that the doctrine had any greater power to exonerate the man in "a civil suit, founded upon a civil contract," the terms of which made the mental soundness of the self-destructive actor practically irrelevant. Of course, "the refined metaphysician" might insist that one "mentally or morally insane" could not "die by his own hand," but this "theorist" could not then offer the act of self-destruction as "evidence in *itself* of such moral insanity" without reducing the contested clause to "a mere *brutum fulmen*, a senseless, imbecile provision." There was, however, no need to further explore this "mazy, dark, and limitless region" of human psychology, for "a more practical solution" readily presented itself, one that was at once "within the comprehension" of the "plain, sensible men" who made contracts and sat on juries and consistent with "the true philosophy of the proviso and its reasons for insertion" in life policies. When faced with such a clause, this judge concluded, the most rational course a court could follow was to presume "the sanity of suicide" and hold the insurer blameless unless the plaintiff met the burden of proving that the death was not "the result of the will, or intention" of the party insured but instead "of blind impulse, of mistake or accident, or of other circumstances which the will can exercise no control."[100]

In the dueling opinions of this Kentucky court, we are thus presented with rival conceptions of the self in self-destruction, each standing as a plausible yet problematic reading of the policy proviso. For Robertson, it referred to a mode of dying that required a moral agent, one with an understanding of the wrongfulness of suicide and the freedom to choose whether to be or not to be. Yet this same judge strongly implied that suicide was seldom committed by anyone with a "sane and controlling mind," allowing a self-inflicted gunshot to stand as presumptive evidence to the contrary, which rendered it almost certain that the insurer would be held responsible for the death. The alternative construction offered by Williams was no doubt closer to the intended meaning of the policy drafter, and it can also be said that he more accurately captured the dubious reputation of moral insanity in most other state courts. But so thin was his description of "an act of volition" that it was difficult to see what remained of the actor as a choosing person. Nor was it obvious how an insured whose will was "subordinated" by an "uncontrollable passion or emotion" was to be distinguished from one driven to the same end by a "blind impulse" or why the life policy should extend to the latter case but not the former. Though both judges were wary of entering very deeply into the labyrinth of human psychology, "this occult subject" could not be entirely avoided as they struggled to construe a clause that neither thought could be taken literally and each understood to be limited to "voluntary" acts of self-destruction—a word that their own divergent analyses revealed to be without a settled meaning "in its legal sense." Even as they endeavored to convince their audience otherwise, the members of the *Graves* court only underscored the moral and legal ambiguities that continued to swirl around the suicidal impulse, and they themselves operated with diametrically opposed presumptions about the heart and mind of the former head of household at the center of this case.[101]

As state courts appeared irreconcilably split as to the significance of the suicide proviso, jurists, medical men, insurers, and journalists looked on with varying degrees of bemusement and concern. This "metaphysical legal question" occupied ever more space in legal literature, commentators judging it to be necessary to draw long excerpts from leading decisions to convey the state of the law, often peppered with editorial asides indicative of the consternation that these trials were occasioning across jurisdictions.[102] "We suspect that before this problem is settled," *The Albany Law Journal* acidly predicted, "many of the judges, if not themselves driven to self-destruction by the profundity of the arguments, may heartily wish that the ingenious counsel would take themselves off."[103] The issue also sparked controversy within the medical profession, as practicing alienists questioned whether suicide ought to be taken as "*prima facie* evidence of insanity" and lamented the readiness of nonspecialists to testify in support of such an inference, thereby perpetuating popular misconceptions at the insurers' expense and throwing open the doors to "materialism and irreligion." Indeed, it was from the alienists' ranks that came some of the most pointed reminders of suicides performed by undoubtedly sane and arguably honorable men, one medical writer going so far as to suggest that the rationality of self-destruction ultimately depended upon one's "theoretical views of life and death."[104] Of course, it was precisely these sorts of medicolegal quandaries that insurers insisted that they had meant to avoid in the drafting of their policies, particularly given the propensity of jurors to return *non compos mentis* verdicts no matter what they were told about the sanity of suicide. To allow such verdicts to stand, they contended, was manifestly unfair to those whose money the companies held in trust, and such rulings were also positively damaging to "the morals of the community," perversely encouraging the "mercenary motives" that insurers had sought to suppress by means of the clause at issue.[105] Yet the very notion that men might thus be led to engage in "such extraordinary speculation" on their own lives was pronounced "absurd" by more than a few editorials circulated in both the popular and professional presses, the writers emphasizing the equitable and economic reasons that insurers had for quietly settling with the suicide's survivors outside of court.[106] However, others strenuously objected to this mode of resolution, as it effectively compelled insurers "to administer uncovenanted charity to widows and orphans who happen to be needy," regardless of the interests of other policyholders. "If this be the law as distilled through the brains of judges," one editorialist archly opined, "then it is quite time that either the law or the brains were thoroughly reformed."[107]

In this volatile climate of public opinion, many looked expectantly to the U.S. Supreme Court, which stepped into the breach with their 1872 decision in *Mutual Life Insurance Company v. Terry*.[108] The outlines of the case took what had become the usual form: the plaintiff sued for recovery on a $2,000 policy issued to her husband for her benefit nearly two years before he died by poisoning himself, allegedly while insane, so as not to amount to a death "by his own hand." At trial, conflicting lay and expert testimony was presented on the subject of mental soundness, witnesses describing the husband, George Terry, as a man "highly excited and distressed" by rumors circulating about "his wife's fidelity"; he was given to strange bursts of laughter as he related his suspicions to friends, and he had made sure that the arsenic he purported to be purchasing to exterminate mice with "was enough to kill a man."[109] In the charge to the jury, Justice Miller advised that no inferences could be drawn about Terry's state of mind from the act of self-destruction alone; it was the plaintiff's burden to prove that the insured's death was "the consequence of insanity" of such a degree as to have disabled him from "using a rational judgment in regard to the act he was committing" or from resisting an "insane impulse" to kill himself. A verdict was returned for the plaintiff, and the defendant contended on appeal for an instruction more in conformity with *Borradaile* and its progeny.[110]

Writing for the court,[111] Justice Hunt roundly rejected this argument, declaring the proffered precedents to be "in hostility to the tests of liability or responsibility adopted by English courts in other cases from Coke and Hale onwards." In determining whether a given act—be it a contract, will, or crime—was attributable to the actor, courts had always admitted the plea of insanity, Hunt observed, and he could see no reason why "a similar principle" ought not to apply when it came to the alleged suicide of the insured. This was to ignore the areas of strict liability that had long existed or, more recently, had come to mark the law of the land and to gloss over substantial variations in the applicable standards of legal capacity, both across doctrinal fields and historical time.[112] Without acknowledging the contestation surrounding the jurisprudence of insanity at the precise moment he was writing, Hunt integrated bits and pieces of the works of medicolegal authorities as he formulated a rule of responsibility that spoke more directly to the relevance of moral capacity than had the lower court:

> If the assured, being in possession of his ordinary reasoning faculties, from anger, pride, jealousy, or a desire to escape from the ills of life, intentionally takes his own life, the proviso attaches, and there can be no recovery. If the death is caused by the voluntary act of the assured, he knowing and intending that his death shall be the result of his act, but when his reasoning faculties are so far impaired that he is not able to understand the moral character, the general nature, consequences, and effect of the act he is about to commit, or when he is impelled thereto by an insane impulse, which he has not the power to resist, such death is not within the contemplation of the parties to the contract, and the insurer is liable.[113]

This rule left considerable room for sane suicide, though it was a category that Hunt took to be limited to those who were moral agents, capable not only of understanding the difference between right and wrong but also adhering to the former and avoiding the latter. The person who acted without this set of moral and intellectual capacities "remained the form of a man only" in the estimation of the court. Since "the reflecting, responsible being" no longer inhabited the body of the insured when he took the fatal dose of arsenic, the insurer was obliged to pay on the policy, just as if the man's death occurred by accident or while endeavoring to escape from engulfing flames or some other life-threatening situation.[114]

With this rendering of manly responsibility and its limits, the court reaffirmed the importance of the element of moral fault in the adjudication of this question of civil liability, though the burden of proving a want of moral agency on the part of the alleged suicide was squarely placed on those who stood to benefit under the policy. While pronounced with an air of definitiveness, *Terry* did not produce the hoped for "uniformity in the rules of law upon this increasingly important subject,"[115] as the court's opinion was subjected to all manner of parsing by judges in the several states, where it did not constitute binding authority in any event. No case better exhibits this judicial tendency than *Van Zandt v. Mutual Benefit Life Insurance Company*, issued by New York's highest court just months after *Terry*, in which the appellate panel took critical aim at Justice Hunt's rule of responsibility, in the process all but overruling its own holding in *Breasted*. While allowing that "the loss of moral sense" so severe as to render the insured unable to distinguish right from wrong would certainly be an important factor in determining whether he had "voluntarily and intentionally" killed himself, the *Van Zandt* court did not consider such moral incapacity to be sufficient, in and of itself, to excuse the insured and make the insurer liable for his death. Whether one whose mind was "so impaired as to be incapable of appreciating the moral obliquity of the crime of suicide" was therefore unable to formulate and carry out such a plot was adjudged to be "rather a scientific than a legal question"—one that was too "speculative and difficult of solution" to be utilized "in the practical administration of justice." This was a remarkable statement, since knowledge of right and wrong was, at the time, the critical determinant of criminal responsibility within this jurisdiction. Saying nothing of this discrepancy, the New York court embraced the *Borradaile* rule of responsibility, now understood to be composed of a volitional and a cognitive prong, effectively recognizing "irresistible impulse" as an excusing condition in this realm of civil litigation. This judicial move was also in considerable tension with the criminal jurisprudence of the state, as the same court had earlier in the year barred such a claim when offered on behalf of a criminal defendant on trial for killing his wife, the judges then and there staunchly refusing to acknowledge the existence of a volitional disorder so easily mistaken for the mere "indulgence in evil passions," it being "'the object of the law to compel people to control these influences.'"[116]

Restraining the temptation to suicide was, of course, the insurers' stated rationale for policy exclusion, but company officers saw they could not depend upon the courts for consistent enforcement of this provision, at least as it had been written. A few insurers reacted to this situation by simply eliminating the penal clause, perhaps wagering that this might give them a comparative advantage as the scramble for business intensified in the Gilded Age—a period punctuated by financial panic, company failures, accompanying allegations of fraud and mismanagement, and calls for legislative redress, all of which generated negative publicity that no doubt made the policies harder to sell.[117] The more common response within this embattled industry, however, was to go back to the drafting table, with most firms adopting one of two policy revisions. Some retained the general proviso against suicide but agreed to either pay the reserve of the policy or return the premiums paid if the act was committed while the insured was in a state of insanity, though typically only if the policy had been in effect for at least six months prior to the death. Others sought to get out of the business of reading minds altogether by adding clarifying language to existing provisos explicitly excluding all forms of self-destruction from coverage, whether "sane or insane," "voluntary or involuntary," or "felonious, or otherwise," though usually with the promise to pay something short of the face value of the policy.[118]

Although courts uniformly declared these policy modifications perfectly lawful, new ambiguities surfaced as they proceeded to pass on their meaning, the U.S. Supreme Court taking the lead in its 1876 decision in *Bigelow v. Berkshire Life Insurance Company*.[119] The enforceability of the clause at issue—excluding coverage in cases of "suicide, sane or insane"— was readily confirmed in the Supreme Court's opinion, Justice Davis reasoning that if insurers were "at liberty to stipulate against hazardous occupations, unhealthy climates, or death by the hands of the law, or in consequence of injuries received when intoxicated, surely it is competent for them to stipulate against intentional self-destruction, whether it be the voluntary act of an accountable moral agent or not."[120] The qualifying words "sane or insane" were thus understood to apply to any act of self-destruction where the insured "was conscious of the physical nature of his act, and intended by it to cause his death, although, at the time, he was incapable of judging between right and wrong, and of understanding the moral consequences of what he was doing." Yet this construal of the clause did not appear to embrace the more severe case of mental incapacity presented by the plaintiffs, who claimed that the insured was "so unsound of mind" when he fatally shot himself as to be "wholly unconscious" of the act he was committing. Assuming the truth of this proposition, Davis nonetheless released the insurer from liability for the death, as he took these words to confess that the insured "intentionally took his own life," understanding the physical nature and consequences of turning a loaded pistol upon himself, remaining unconscious only of "the great crime he was committing" due to the fact that "his darkened mind did not enable him to appreciate the moral character of his act." In reaching this conclusion, Justice Davis confused as much as he clarified about the boundaries of the category of "insane suicide," as his opinion expressly reserved judgment on the question of whether there might be some forms of mental unsoundness debilitating enough to render the death an accident as a matter of law.[121]

Thus the very words that insurers inserted into their policies to remove the "shadowy and difficult" subject of mental soundness "from the domain of controversy"[122] provoked a further round of litigation, in turn generating another set of conflicting decisions about what distinguished an "insane," "nonfelonious," or "involuntary" suicide from an "accidental death." As they confronted this new definitional borderland, plaintiffs seeking to recover deftly shifted their forensic tactics, tending to pursue one of two strategies. The first was to flatly deny that a suicide had occurred at all—to maintain that the death was a naturally occurring, wholly inadvertent, or essentially mysterious event, thereby leaving it to insurers to overcome the common law's twin presumptions in favor of sanity and against suicide, "which the law recognizes as arising out of the instincts of nature, one of which is the love of life."[123] But where the defending company was able to summon up substantial evidence to the contrary—most often in the form of a suicide note or a coroner's report—a different tack was often taken, the plaintiff insisting that appearances of "a death self-inflicted" were deceiving, because the fatal act was in fact the product of mental illness rather than the conscious will of the insured: it was "the result of an accident in an insane person that resulted from the disease." This claim was not easily distinguished from an invitation to nullify the exclusion clause, or so defense counsel sought to convince the court, sometimes finding it expedient to emphasize the correlation between insanity and suicide, making the most of any known eccentricities of the insured in order to fortify the conclusion that he had indeed committed the "unnatural" act.[124] Yet in so doing, insurers risked overplaying their hand, for they only prompted plaintiffs to posit ever more extreme diseases of the mind, ones that had completely vanquished the insured's mental and moral faculties. It was rather difficult to see what was left of the concept of individual agency in a situation where the putative actor was conceded to be "wholly bereft of reason and without the power to control his will."[125] Holding such a man legally responsible for the consequences of his action both deviated from the norms of "civilized" jurisprudence as plaintiffs understood them and strayed from the insurers' own deterrence-based justification for the suicide proviso, premised as it was upon the capacity of the insured to respond to the threat of forfeiture.[126]

The credibility of this threat, of course, continued to depend in no small measure upon the willingness of courts to carry it out, which proved no easier to gauge under the modified clauses. While sympathy for plaintiffs remained as pronounced as ever in the jury box, members of the bench were considerably less resolute and unified in their interpretations of clarifying language. In those jurisdictions following the *Terry* rule, the new qualifiers were most often understood to relieve insurers of the burden of proving the *moral* capacity of the alleged suicide, though they were still required to establish that the suicide had understood the *physical* consequences of his self-destructive act. But where this construction was already given to *un*qualified clauses, opinions splintered as to the significance of the "superadded words." The main lines of judicial conflict were most elaborately aired in the New York contest of *De Gogorza v. Knickerbocker Life Insurance Company*, in which a divided bench addressed the ultimate boundary case left unresolved by the *Bigelow* court: an insured "wholly bereft of reason" at the moment he discharged the contents of a pistol into his mouth, "so that the mere act of self-destruction was wholly involuntary."[127]

In the judgment of a bare majority of the five-member panel, the mental condition of the insured was wholly immaterial under the terms of the policy, which was rendered void by the fatal act. The only way to give "legal effect" to the phrase "sane or insane," they reasoned, was to exclude all evidence pertaining to the insured's state of mind, thereby relieving the insurer from liability for death resulting from "any physical movement of the hand or body of the assured proceeding from partial or total eclipse of the mind," even where he could be shown to be "to the very last degree mad or insane." Though it was concededly somewhat incongruous to hold "that a totally insane man may take his own life," the judges in the majority would not be distracted by what they took to be a matter of mere semantics. For it was apparent to them that the clause was intended to insulate the insurers from "death by insanity," a contingency that they held to be importantly distinguishable from a "pure accident," the latter having "no reference to the condition of mind of the party so dying."[128] The coherence of this line of analysis was, however, sharply challenged by the two dissenting judges, who maintained that the death of an insured "by his own hand, sane or insane" necessarily entailed the existence of an intentional actor capable of designing and carrying out this final act. Any person wanting the mental power to comprehend or control his behavior in such a basic sense could "no more be said to act than an automaton," nor was it clear why "an unintentional death of an insane man by his own hand" should be treated any differently from that of one who was sane. It being admitted on all hands that the policy covered the latter case, it hardly seemed just to deny recovery where the party in question labored "under the delusion" that the poison he imbibed was a harmless cordial or that the body of water into which he threw himself was an inviting flowerbed. Death under such circumstances "would properly be classified with accidents," on this analysis, as the fatality was "fairly attributable to disease" rather than to the insured himself. If the insurer wanted to be excused from liability "in case the brain of the assured became so diseased and his mind so disordered that he should unconsciously or unintentionally, or from an irresistible impulse, take his own life," then, the dissenters suggested, the policy ought to explicitly say so.[129]

Judicial advice of this sort was greeted with more than a little consternation on the part of insurers and their advocates, who had by now come to doubt it much mattered how the suicide proviso was phrased, cynically surmising that the true basis of decision was an "unwritten law of 'hardship'" slanted in the beneficiary's favor.[130] Jurists surveying the legal landscape from a somewhat more objective standpoint lent a measure of credence to such assessments. With an air of resignation, they pronounced that "the various decisions of the English, Federal and State courts, cannot, by any process of mental legerdemain be twisted into even the semblance of uniformity."[131] Yet these professional observers confirmed the general propensity of American judges to "sail round" the exclusion clause in order to find for plaintiffs "if any shadow of a rule of law can be found to support the ruling."[132] Worn down by and too often beaten in these legal contests, insurance offices increasingly came to the conclusion that the suicide clause was quite literally more trouble than it was worth, particularly as competitive pressures within the industry mounted in the last decades of the century. In these years, companies aggressively vied for customers by relaxing policy conditions, mindful that a "reputation for illiberality" was likely to prove self-defeating. An 1885 survey of the industry revealed that most companies offered policies that either made no mention of suicide or merely excluded it for an initial period after purchase ranging from one month to five years.[133] Moreover, a significant number of insurers self-reported their general tendency to make full payment on policies in cases of suicide unless there was unmistakable evidence of fraud.[134] The fact that this was now their customary practice was something that companies endeavored to publicize in a variety of ways, most boldly in the form of newspaper advertisements that sought to drum up business with boasts such as "no claims in dispute" and "not a case litigated."[135] This approach was effectively compelled by law as the century came to a close, with the passage of proconsumer legislation in several states barring the defense of suicide in insurance litigation save where it could be shown "that the insured contemplated suicide at the time he made his application for the policy."[136] However, it remained far from clear in other jurisdictions whether recovery could be had in the event of intentional self-destruction in situations where the policy made no mention of this manner of death. The liberalizing impulse among insurers thus pressed to the fore a question that had always lurked uncomfortably on the margins of the legal discourse: was sane suicide an insurable risk?

The fullest answer to this question would be provided by the U.S. Supreme Court in the 1898 case of *Ritter v. Mutual Life Insurance Company of New York*, concerning an apparently prosperous Philadelphia businessman by the name William M. Runk. This man had enjoyed a sterling reputation before fatally shooting himself in October 1892, nearly a year after he had purchased $75,000 in life insurance from the defendant, the policies at issue containing no express exclusions with respect to suicide.[137] News of the shooting was initially greeted with shock and incomprehension among those who knew him well, but a motive for his action soon emerged. As it turned out, Runk had been living something of a double life, having fallen into desperate financial straits over the preceding five years, the result of heavy speculation in the stock market, mainly using funds embezzled or otherwise obtained under false pretenses from the dry-goods firm of which he was a member, as well as from a local charity and a wealthy aunt. As his losses multiplied, he took out additional policies on his life, and he had a half million dollars of insurance by the time of his death. At trial, the presiding judge took the law of the case to deny recovery to the estate of the dead man if he killed himself intentionally, understanding the moral character and physical consequences of the act "as a sane man would." In an attempt to prove the contrary, the plaintiff elicited testimony from intimate friends and relations of the insured, who described him as uncharacteristically "nervous" in the last days of his life, upon the basis of which they opined that his mind was "unbalanced." However, on cross-examination, these witnesses were compelled to admit that their convictions about his mental condition were only formed after his death, and the jury charge all but ruled out the hypothesis of insanity, strongly suggesting that "the natural worry and distress occasioned by his unfortunate circumstances, and the contemplation of self-destruction as a means of relief" was sufficient to account for his unusual behavior and appearance. Perhaps even more decisive in securing a verdict for the defendant were the suicide notes entered into the record, painstakingly written by Runk in his final hours with the intent that they be delivered after his death to his executor, aunt, and several associates at his firm. Evidently seeking to avoid meeting with disgrace in his lifetime, the self-condemned man acknowledged his misdeeds in these melancholy missives, avowing as he did to fulfill his financial obligations by killing himself. As he most poignantly put it to his business partner: "This is a sad ending of a promising life, but I deserve all the punishment I may get. Only I feel my debts must be paid. This sacrifice will do it, and only this. I was faithful until two years ago. Forgive me. Don't publish this."[138]

On appeal, these words were likewise read as evidence of a man "entirely at himself" by the members of the Supreme Court, who readily confirmed that the jury had been properly instructed on the subject of insanity and fully warranted in concluding that the insured suffered from no such impairment at the time he took his life. The more vexing legal question presented was whether sane suicide was indeed a defense to liability under a life policy containing no exclusion clause to this effect. Answering in the affirmative for a unanimous bench, Justice Harlan advanced two distinct rationales, one grounded in the principles of contract law and the other based upon public policy. As a starting point, he looked to "the nature and object of life insurance," a business arrangement constructed upon the basis of experience tables "showing at any age the probable duration of life." Was it not, then, an implied condition of any life insurance contract that the insured "will leave the event of his death to depend upon some other cause than willful, deliberate self-destruction?" A similar condition was regularly implied in the case of both fire and marine insurance, and the grounds for doing so seemed only stronger where life rather than property was intentionally destroyed by the insured. "To hold otherwise," Harlan submitted, "is to say that the occurrence of an event upon the happening of which the company undertook to pay was intended to be left to his option. That view is against the very essence of the contract." Justice Harlan further provided that had the parties actually entered into such an agreement, one expressly covering the risk of deliberately self-inflicted death, it would have been deemed unenforceable by any court of justice, "in that it tempted or encouraged the assured to commit suicide in order to make provision for those dependent upon him, or to whom he was indebted," thereby constituting a threat to public welfare. Underscoring the dangerous consequences of removing the restraint against crime and fraud provided by the penalty of forfeiture, Harlan concluded that a policy that was silent on the subject of suicide had to be read to exclude coverage in such cases of self-sacrifice as that of *Ritter*.[139]

As for the fate of others who took their lives for the benefit of those they loved or counted as creditors, the judicial record remained quite mixed. The rule announced in *Ritter* won far more critics than followers in state courts. "The history of insurance, makes difficult the argument that the exception is not now expressed because it is necessarily implied," a New Jersey judge observed in an especially pointed decision allowing recovery in a case of sane suicide.[140] Indeed, it was the experience of litigating this issue that convinced some insurers of the inadvisibility of expressly excluding coverage in the event of self-destruction—a risk of death, it was well to remember, that was incorporated into the experience tables that companies used to set their premiums. State judges likewise balked at "the supposed analogy" that Harlan drew between property and life insurance, pointing out that the latter was not a contract of indemnity but instead "an arbitrary agreement to pay a fixed sum upon the happening of an inevitable event, to wit, the death of the insured, without regard to the value of his life or the loss sustained by the assured." Nor was the implication of an exception for sane suicide necessary in order to prevent the insured from profiting from his own wrongful act. For suicide was not a punishable crime in any American jurisdiction, and even if one were to grant that the act *was* inherently wrong—"which is a matter for the moralist rather than the judge"—the deliberate self-destroyer was placed "equally beyond gain and loss," his death redounding to the benefit of those who were innocent of any crime. Moreover, it was far from obvious that public policy always dictated the discouragement of suicide in a country where "the paternal theory of government" did not prevail. Though a democratic polity surely had an interest in the preservation of the lives of all its citizens, this interest was not rightly regarded as paramount over all others, and it was difficult to see why the state ought to be "more concerned to prolong a life that may be worthless to the public than to secure to creditors their just demands, or to afford a maintenance to wife and children." To allow recovery where the suicide risk had not been expressly excluded from coverage was therefore hardly the threat to communal welfare that Harlan made it out to be, especially in the estimation of those members of the bench who took there to be "no public policy more useful than that which holds contractors to performance."[141]

This allocation of risk and responsibility—and the exchange of money for life thereby authorized—occasioned even more spirited debate in the world beyond the courtroom in the decades straddling 1900, a period in which "the increase of suicide" was painstakingly documented by a new generation of moral statisticians, who viewed this social trend as the unavoidable concomitant of "the modern strenuous life," a telling indicator of the "deteriorating influences inseparable from what we call 'civilization.'" Although alarms to this effect had been periodically sounded over the course of the nineteenth century, they gained greater credibility and prominence with the publication of several full-length studies of self-destruction in the last decades of the century by prominent physicians and lawyers. Considering the phenomena to be "partly social, partly medical," the authors of these works were clearly influenced by the evolutionary sciences of the day, commonly speaking of suicide as "the effect of the struggle for existence" even as they reached divergent conclusions as to both the efficacy and propriety of human efforts to counteract these natural processes through such means as moral exhortation, legal restraints, psychiatric treatment, and "artificial selection." In so doing, they at once mirrored and contributed to the polarization of public opinion about "the justifiability of suicide" in *fin de siècle* America—a time when staunch defenders of a "right to die" at the time of one's own choosing were met by no less adamant calls for the reinvigoration of the traditional common law prohibitions against self-murder. Yet these extreme proposals won more attention than adherents in the popular press, most commentators registering a more tentative stance as they observed the mounting number of "victims of suicide,"[142] a choice of words indicative of the ethical disorientation many experienced as they confronted "the stern reality" of the statisticians' findings. As they tallied the numbers, it appeared this "social evil" had infiltrated "our upper classes" and was now attracting recruits "from the honest, law-abiding, respectable members of society." Were the lives thus taken to be simply accepted as part and parcel of "the eliminative processes of natural selection"? Or did these vital statistics constitute a more disturbing sign of the times, going to show that "the American system of living at 'high pressure'" was effectively promoting "the survival of the unfittest"?[143]

In such a nation of strivers, perhaps the fullest embodiment of this dilemma was the "heavily insured" businessman who found himself "involved in financial failure" and "committed suicide as a result." This figure stood apart from other world-weary men of his class who cravenly deserted their earthly posts—who chose death as a means of breaking an "engagement with Mr. Want and Miss Misery," heedless of the consequences of an untimely departure for the creditors and "dependent kindred" who survived them. For it was with a painful awareness of his duties and obligations to others and a desperate conviction that he was worth more to his family dead than alive that the suicidal insured finally liquidated his life. Many in the middle classes found it easy to sympathize with the predicament of the overextended merchant yet impossible to condone self-killing under any circumstances; adamantly insisting that human beings were but the trustees of their own lives, they contended that those who fell upon hard times had a responsibility—to society as well as to his family—to confront life's difficulties with courage and faith, never allowing pride to preclude him from accepting "temporary help" and always holding fast to the belief that those "of capacity and good habits" would eventually meet with success in the moral testing ground that was the marketplace. Others, speaking for and from the ranks of the workingmen, were markedly less sanguine about the correspondence between moral and material progress, especially in view of the structural inequities they perceived to be built into "the industrial system. They grimly estimated that the value of life was far more commonly questioned among those daily engaged in the struggle for subsistence "than the prosperous people of the country have any idea of."[144]

Still, for most, there was something distinctly unnerving about the suicides of heretofore "exemplary men" inspiring contradictory impulses to credit and excuse their self-sacrificing behavior, to lament and valorize what they had done to ensure their loved ones would live ever after in "comparative comfort." The moral valence of this mode of family provision was indeed left far from clear by those who editorialized on the subject. Some suggested that what might have been conceived as wrongdoing was mitigated by the exigent circumstances that the fallen businessman faced, likening his self-destructive act to that of "the mother who steals a loaf of bread to keep her starving child alive." However, others were inclined to view his mode of exit as a cowardly response to adversity, effectively forcing the insurer into the "paternal" role that the insured was supposed to assume, thereby proving him to be "unequal" to the "Napoleonic facing of destiny" required of the man of the house. However, more than a few who entered this judgment betrayed a grudging admiration for the sheer audaciousness of his attempt to die in "a state of solvency," whatever the costs in the world to come. Though this was a gamble no

Christian man should ever take, it was a risk he was encouraged to run by a host of all too willing accomplices, who were popularly indicted for aiding and abetting this offense. One needed to look no further than the law reports and statute books for evidence of the part that judges and legislators played in facilitating and legitimizing the monetization of life, pronouncing rules of law that ensured that "honest policy holders" would be the ones who ultimately suffered in the form of higher premiums. And the culpability of the insurers and their agents was even more obvious, as their own experience tables suggested the existence of a causal relationship between the purchase of life policies and the act of self-destruction, which their advertisements only served to reinforce, as they shamelessly bid for the business by touting ever more liberal policy terms, one even guaranteeing "in big black letters that 'suicide will not vitiate a policy.'" If there was nothing praiseworthy about the would-be provider who seized the main chance as he teetered on the edge of financial ruin, was he to be entirely blamed for accepting the "tempting offer" dangled before him in the form of the life policy?[145]

At once personifying the spirit of capitalism and its debasing effects, his was an especially arresting act of creative destruction, one that resisted definitive classification as a crime or misfortune in the divided minds of those Americans who were moved to ponder its significance in the Progressive Era. Although the trend toward liberality in insurance cases involving suicide continued into the twentieth century, expressions of discomfort about "the ease with which life may be thus converted into money" did as well, especially within the confines of the courtroom. Indeed, the law remained so unsettled that an editor of the *Harvard Law Review* was moved to offer these words of advice at the outset of an 1935 note on the subject of "Suicide and Insurance": "Before a ruined business man leaps from the sixty-second floor so that his family will live securely upon the proceeds of his life insurance, he might well pause to consider the legal confusion into which he is about to launch his dependents."[146] Surely this feature of the decisional law and its persistence across time can, to some extent, be accounted for by reference to the judges' mixed feelings about the insurance industry and their suspicions about the existence of unfair business practices on the part of insurers and their agents and outright fraud on the part of the insured in individual cases. Yet judicial opinions concerning insurers' liability cannot simply be read as rationalizations of preexisting biases and sympathies with respect to the parties or the larger enterprise of insuring lives. For in all the twists and turns of their doctrinal reasoning, judges also betrayed basic uncertainty about the status of suicide on the civil side of the docket, as the act ceased to be a punishable felony and increasingly was placed under the alienists' gaze. Did it necessarily describe an act of a morally responsible agent? How close was the connection between insanity and suicide? So close as to warrant some revision of the common law's twin presumptions in favor of sanity and against suicide? Who in his right mind would come to the conclusion that suicide was his only way out of an economic bind? Was one compelled to kill himself for this reason properly cast as the responsible agent, or was his death more justly treated as an accident of capitalism?

The ruined businessman who so chillingly calculated that his life was no longer worth living ultimately defied description within the established categories of the law and culture of the day. Though litigants saw good reason to present monocausal suicide stories, attributing the insured's death to mental disease *or* economic misfortune *or* moral bankruptcy, the facts in the record pointed toward a more complex reality, gradually bringing to light strains and ambiguities in prevailing models of self-made manhood and the conception of personal responsibility upon which they were founded. The very deliberateness with which these insured suicides seemed to orchestrate their own departures from this world, whether by drowning, shooting, hanging, poisoning, or slashing of the throat from ear to ear, was probably the most distressing aspect of all, at least from the standpoint of those who sat in judgment in these cases. As the story of the insured's shortened life was recounted in the courtroom—a narrative in which he was typically portrayed as the victim of financial reversal quite often traceable back to his own bad habits—it no doubt became easier to comprehend yet more unsettling to contemplate his ultimate act of self-sacrifice. Indeed, one suspects many judges could not help but identify with these desperate men even as they recoiled from their (almost) unthinkable acts. Those who perpetrated fraud in such a self-destructive way were not easily classed as ordinary criminals, but neither did they exactly fit the description of those whom the law called *non compos mentis* or victims of accidental death. And so while juries regularly returned verdicts for the plaintiff in such cases, judges could not so easily accept the hypothesis of insanity or accident as a way of avoiding forfeiture. Though they often let such verdicts stand, judges frequently expressed lingering misgivings about the commodity relations they were authorizing in and through their decisions, along with a deeper anxiety about the constraining effects of modern life, which threatened to drain the conjoined concepts of free will and moral hazard of all meaning. It was more than likely to stave off this nightmare vision that members of the bench took care to preserve a category of sane suicides who took out life policies with the calculated purpose of killing themselves, which rendered them guilty of fraud on the insurer, thereby marking the moral limits of this business enterprise and securing a certain space for the exercise of human freedom.

CHAPTER 6

Bonded and Insured:
The Cautious Imagination

Ravit Reichman

the art of losing's not too hard to master
though it may look like (*Write* it!) like disaster.

ELIZABETH BISHOP, "One Art"[1]

We are worried rather than frantic.

E. M. FORSTER, "Post-Munich"[2]

Introduction: Community and Compensation

In 1941, during the London Blitz, Winston Churchill instituted the Act to Provide War Damage Insurance, which aimed to distribute as widely as possible the loss of property due to the bombings. As Churchill explained in a public address, the measure was taken in the interest of those whose homes had been destroyed, "to reassure them that they have not lost all, because all will share their material loss."[3] Churchill's response to the attacks on London shifted the emphasis from "what" to "who," from thing to person. From the question of what had been lost—"they have not lost *all*"—he turned to the issue of who will take responsibility for the loss: "*all* will share their material loss." In moving from "all things" to "all people," Churchill takes what can be construed as property insurance and transforms it into an issue of tort law—into the principle of due care rather than financial compensation.

The Insurance Act marked a shift that had been some time in the making, one that insisted that individuals in wartime needed to cast their lot with their national community. Thus, in spite of economic criticism about the feasibility of such an insurance act, legal scholars were quick to point out that "the government is not concerned with the maintenance of a self-sustaining insurance fund but rather with community responsibility for individual war losses."[4] Initiated in a time of crisis, the British government's act points to the underlying—and underwritten—idealism in insurance. At its loftiest, insurance creates (or at the very least, fortifies) community when catastrophe threatens to turn a nation into a collection of individuals, each concerned only for his or her own well-being. Introducing insurance at this historical juncture thus not only spreads risk sharing and loss sharing as widely as possible; it also builds community out of compensation. As François Ewald observes:

> The paradigm of responsibility is the paradigm of insurance—it assumes the logic of loss compensation. The paradigm of solidarity is also a paradigm of insurance, of universal and indeterminate insurance, of social and compulsory insurance. It is not so much concerned with voluntary and contractual forms of compensation as with the institution of pools of all kinds. The paradigm linked to the precautionary principle will undoubtedly remain a paradigm of insurance, but in a new shape that will have to integrate new cultural boundary conditions.[5]

Yet the fact that the War Damage Insurance Act needed to be instituted at all suggests something more: not that war had unraveled a tightly knit society but that it had unveiled how tattered the fabric already was before the conflict began. E. M. Forster might certainly have seen it that way. In his essay "What I Believe"—written in the year before the Blitz and containing the famously Forsterian declaration "if I had to choose between betraying my country and betraying my friend, I hope I should have the guts to betray my country"—Forster addressed what he saw as the main condition for a just society:

> One must be fond of people and trust them if one is not to make a mess of life, and it is therefore essential that they should not let one down. They often do. The moral of which is that I must, myself, be as reliable as possible, and this I try to be. But reliability is not a matter of contract—that is the main difference between the world of personal relationships and the world of business relationships. It is a matter for the heart, which signs no documents. In other words, reliability is impossible unless there is a natural warmth. Most men possess this warmth, though they often have bad luck and get chilled.[6]

What might easily be taken for uninflected liberalism or an oversimplified social credo might also be read as a skeptical gloss on the prospects of Churchill's wartime insurance act. A national insurance plan in the wake of catastrophe may be fiscally sound, but it cannot produce a community of goodwill if none existed before. We can legislate compensation; emotions are another matter.

Today's insurance companies seem to be taking Forster's position to heart in their efforts to prove it wrong, fashioning a rhetoric of reliability by conflating the personal and the corporate. Reliability, they suggest—in marked contrast to Forster—is every bit a matter of contract, at least if one conjures a world of people where corporations ought to be. The slogans of many insurance companies—"Like a good neighbor, State Farm is there"; "You're in good hands with Allstate"; "New York Life. The Company You Keep"—warm up the cold comforts of business by projecting what transpires in the assessor's cubicle as the ethics of everyday life. From this perspective, the insurance company's dependability is just a larger, codified, and contractual version of ordinary, commonsense responsibility. As a Liberty Mutual customer states on the company's Web site: "Millions of us are guided by a sense of responsibility every day." The Liberty Mutual campaign, with its signature phrase "Responsibility. What's your policy?" thus suggests that an insurance policy is less a business contract than a more official version of our individual, de facto ethical "policies." It is not so much that corporations are anthropomorphized as that individuals are corporatized, each carrying his or her own personal "policy." Companies like Liberty Mutual only serve to make these "policies" official.

Both socially and personally, we invest a lot in insurance. But the question of whether its policies constitute or corrode responsibility remains a murky one. From the standpoint of public policy, the answer may seem clear. Through an actuarial lens, an insured person or institution is a responsible one. But the fictional imagination suggests an opposite tendency, in which insurance brings out the very worst in people. From the murder plots of noir films such as Billy Wilder's *Double Indemnity* and its reincarnation in the 1981 release *Body Heat* to the 1994 noir-influenced *The Last Seduction* and HBO's *The Sopranos*, insurance features as a source of scandal and intrigue—a policyholder's calculated pretext for a crime of passion. Indeed, the contemporary rise of insurance fraud suggests that the institution encourages unchecked irresponsibility in the form of criminality. So while it can be argued that insurance furthers responsibility by inducing us to imagine possible calamities and provide for their compensation, it can also be said that insurance compels us to imagine a world where compensation rather than responsibility forms the basis of justice. Seen in this light, one confronts a system of distributive justice supported by the legal fiction that all people and things are—in practice, if not in theory—fungible.

Elizabeth Bishop's "One Art," the last lines of which furnish the first epigraph to this chapter, suggests that writing both staves off and invokes disaster. The parenthetical command to "(*Write* it!)," after the speaker's many attempts to establish in suspiciously casual terms that "the art of losing isn't hard to master," offers a fitting depiction of underwriting's imaginative work. Writing disaster into life (the disaster that, as Bishop's lines remind us, takes such rhetorical pains to master), insurance companies promise to place such catastrophes out of mind while simultaneously asking us to imagine them. But the poem also suggests that writing and losing amount to the same thing—that they are, in other words, one art. In this sense, writing disaster into our lives in poetry or insurance constitutes not prudence or precaution so much as loss. In his own echo of Bishop's last lines, Maurice Blanchot in *The Writing of the Disaster* proposes (in the spirit of Hannah Arendt) that one of the most glaring losses in a bureaucratized world is individual responsibility:

> Responsible: this word generally qualifies—in a prosaic, bourgeois man-ner—a mature, lucid, conscientious man, who acts with circumspection, who takes into account all elements of a given situation, calculates and decides. The word "responsible" qualifies the successful man of action. But now responsibility—my responsibility for the other, for everyone, without reciprocity—is displaced.[7]

If, as François Ewald claims, "the paradigm of responsibility is the para-digm of insurance," Blanchot encourages us to ask what *kind* of responsi-bility this paradigm entails. While insurance companies would have us believe that individual and corporate responsibility differ merely in degree, Blanchot suggests that not only do they differ in kind but also that they are, quite disconcertingly, at odds. The calculated risks he ascribes to the "bourgeois manner" of responsibility call to mind the calibrations of the insurance agent, which Blanchot implies forces the need for individual responsibility out of the social picture, substituting for rather than com-plementing it.

What we lose when we insure is the concern of this essay, which begins with two simple questions: Does insurance make us more responsible or less responsible? When we insure our possessions or our lives, do we be-come more cautious or more reckless, more attentive or more indifferent? The answers, of course, depend on one's subject position, on whether one is the insurer or the insured and on what becomes of those who do not or cannot buy into insurance schemes. But I raise the rhetorical question of whether insurance makes us better or worse for the sake of opening up a range of subject positions, in order to consider how individuals figure in the transactions of insured communities.

As Eric Wertheimer and Susanna Blumenthal argue in different contexts in this volume, insurance turns out to be one of the best places from which to work out a cultural theory of responsibility. In thinking through how insurance invites us to regard the existence and the suffering of others, I propose to examine the relationship between insurance and responsibility through E. M. Forster's *Howards End* (1910). My reading of the novel situates insurance specifically within modernism. Thus, the argument takes up issues addressed by literary scholars of earlier periods but considers their twentieth-century implications.[8] For while connections between the respective histories of insurance and the novel point to changing ideas of ownership, labor, and commercialism in the eighteenth and nineteenth centuries, the twentieth century charts a different course for the insured imagination. The modernist itinerary draws its force from a changing sense of responsibility that coincides with the growth of tort law, a transformation that saw the development of the negligence doctrine as a way to adjudicate the rise in accidents associated with industrial growth. With negligence and its close relation, duty of care, individual agency took a new legal turn away from what one did to cause another's injury (formerly described as "trespass") to what one failed to do to avoid it. The ethical questions of agency raised by a modernist insurantial imaginary—the belief that some calamities simply cannot be prevented—have returned today with increasing intensity in the current growth of the "cat bond" (catastrophe bond) market. For if the rise of accidents in an industrializing world recast the notions of responsibility and agency a century ago, our own era of natural disasters promises to transform this paradigm once again. As Michael Lewis explained recently in the *New York Times*:

> An insurance company could function only if it was able to control its exposure to loss. Geico sells auto insurance to more than seven million Americans. No individual car accident can be foreseen, obviously, but the total number of accidents over a large population is amazingly predictable. The company knows from past experience what percentage of the drivers it insures will file claims and how much those claims will cost. The logic of catastrophe is very different: either no one is affected or vast numbers of people are.[9]

What becomes clear in the difference between a car accident and a hurricane is the need for the insurance industry to come up with new methods of valuing risk in the face of disaster. Thus the insurer's vantage, but what of the position of the insured—not of corporations but of individuals—in a world where accident insurance has given way to cat bonds? What social implications, in other words, arise in this kind of predictive and protective economic universe? In answering this question through Forster, I imply my own predilection for the literary imagination: to understand subjectivity in a world where individuals and companies are bonded and insured, we need to have a grasp of the narratives through which security, risk, and responsibility acquire shape and meaning. *Howards End* does more than take up these matters; it is consumed with and structured by them. At its heart is a concern with the mind that needs and acquires insurance: the cautious imagination that guards against the unpredictable and the emotional price of such policies. The novel's ethical preoccupation, moreover, is intertwined with its form, with characters built around a core of risk, events that feel more like accidents than incidents, and alliances formed in unguarded moments or avoided in guarded ones.

Most often read as a novel heralding the transition from Edwardian to modern England,[10] Forster's text depicts the ebbing of an old world of personal accountability against the rising tide of bureaucratized responsibility. At its heart is a concern with the shades of difference between the social and the business worlds and the tragic complexity of navigating the barely perceptible line between them. By taking up the issue of insurance in its literal incarnation, Forster opens a portal to the larger psychological and narrative consequences of an insured society. What does insurance ask us to imagine—and what does it absolve us from imagining? What risks does the insured imagination run?

Prose and Passion

E. M. Forster's fourth novel begins with an unexpected incident of social recklessness. Helen Schlegel writes to her sister, Margaret, with the news that she has fallen in love practically overnight with a man named Paul Wilcox, the younger son of a family that the Schlegel sisters have only just met. Margaret, older and more rational than her younger sister, determines to travel to the Wilcoxes' country home—the Howards End of the title—to deal with this sudden turn of events. Her aunt, Margaret's closest living relative, counsels her not to go unprepared. " 'But go with some plan,' said Mrs. Munt, admitting into her kindly voice a note of exasperation. 'Margaret, if I may interfere, don't be taken by surprise.' " Her niece, who admits to knowing nothing more than the spare contents of Helen's note, brushes off the advice: " 'I hate plans. I hate lines of action.' "[11]

Margaret's words issue a challenge subsequently taken up by the rest of the novel, whose narrative unfolds along two simultaneous and opposing trajectories of plans in their formal (read: legal) sense and in their murkier emotional one. The caution woven into the best-laid plans—insurance policies, wills—is undone through the unpredictability of friendship, fear, passion, and anger. Forster's famously aphoristic epigraph, "Only connect," thus expresses something beyond the surprising relationships that form over the course of *Howards End*, beginning with Helen and Paul's romance, broken off days later, and ending with the birth of Helen's illegitimate child, the progeny of the novel's tragic figure, Leonard Bast, who is killed shortly before the novel ends. The connections made in between these bookends are no less predictable: Margaret befriends Mrs. Wilcox in London; Mrs. Wilcox dies suddenly from an unspecified illness, leaving a note bequeathing Howards End to Margaret—a request that the bereaved and betrayed Wilcoxes summarily ignore. Margaret and Helen meet Leonard at a concert and take him on as their social charge; they learn from Mr. Wilcox that Leonard's company is at risk and urge him to take another job, which he does—only to lose this job soon afterward. Margaret eventually befriends the widowed Mr. Wilcox; he proposes marriage, and she accepts. Leonard's wife Jacky is discovered to have been Mr. Wilcox's mistress; Helen leaves England inexplicably; Margaret becomes the new Mrs. Wilcox; Helen's absence is explained when she returns pregnant with Leonard's illegitimate child; a falling bookcase kills Leonard. As the novel closes, Margaret, Helen, and Helen's baby have taken up residence at Howards End, which Margaret has inherited after all.

Passing from one connection to the next in Forster's narrative, one cannot help but feel a prevailing sense of the untamable and the arbitrary: only connect, indeed. Yet the links that this phrase demands amount to more than just unbridled, chance encounters. They are not collisions but connections forged through the painful *undoing* of longstanding discrepancies between thinking and feeling and between the letter of the law and its spirit. The temptation to view relationships and legal arrangements as competing frames of reference prompts Margaret to wonder aloud which, in the end, counts most. She muses to Helen:

> The truth is that there is a great outer life that you and I have never touched—a life in which telegrams and anger count. Personal relations, that we think supreme, are not supreme there. There love means marriage

settlements, death, death duties. So far I'm clear. But here my difficulty. This outer life, though obviously horrid, often seems the real one—there's grit in it. It does breed character. Do you think personal relations lead to sloppiness in the end? (28)

Margaret's difficulty issues from her sense that the life of "telegrams and anger" and that of human relationships parallel each other with no chance of intersecting. And it certainly does seem that some of Forster's characters live exclusively in one or the other of these worlds—Helen in the world of personal relations, Henry Wilcox in that of documents. But the novel ultimately seeks out the meeting points of such tendencies, the conditions under which the documented and the emotional life fuse into something more robust and genuine. It is in this fusion that Margaret ultimately finds her sense of purpose, and with it, the reiteration of the novel's epigraph: "Only connect! That was the whole of her sermon. Only connect the prose and the passion, and both will be exalted, and human love will be seen at its height. Live in fragments no longer" (195). The path that *Howards End* cuts between this prose and passion, I will suggest, offers a means of understanding the modern transit between policies and people: between the agents and agencies that insure the world and the individuals whose anxieties or assurances take shape in this bonded sphere.

The Character of Caution

If *Howards End* speaks to the problems of property, class, and inheritance in a changing England, it does so through the binding agents of caution and risk. In other words, if the novel's central metaphor is the country estate, the ties connecting it to both characters and plot are composed of the stuff of insurance. Indeed, the novel seems to consist of two kinds of characters: those who embrace risk and those who avoid it. Margaret, the strongest proponent of a risk-embracing paradigm in theory if not in practice (where she is surely outrisked by her scandalously pregnant sister), finds herself resisting time and again others' advice to proceed with caution. "She could not explain in so many words, but she felt that those who prepare themselves for all the emergencies of life beforehand may equip themselves at the expense of joy. It is necessary to prepare for an examination, or a dinner-party, or a possible fall in the price of stock: those who attempt human relations must adopt another method, or fail" (62). Her noble stance, however, is refigured in the novel less as a pronouncement than as a lingering question. It may well be the case that human relations cannot be insured like accidents or emergencies, but what provisions do we have to prevent unpredictable social ties from bringing us to ruin? In other words, why *not* insure, in some fashion, the social world? "'I hope to risk things all my life,'" (62) Margaret affirms, even as she acknowledges that her comfortable inheritance has made it easy not to take certain risks, and even as she agrees to marry a man who, many years her senior, is more a sound provider than an ardent lover. Without financial means to cushion life's blows, without a spouse or a family at one's side or a wealth of culture at one's disposal, how can we protect ourselves? And why would anyone run the risk of venturing into the social unknown?

Perhaps the surest argument that the novel, through Margaret, offers against thinking of social relations in terms of insurance comes to us in the guise of genre and in the idea that life's ordinary experiences cannot be built up into something resembling a well-plotted, purposeful story, whether tragic, comic, or picaresque:

> Looking back on the past six months, Margaret realized the chaotic nature of our daily life, and its difference from the orderly sequence that has been fabricated by historians. Actual life is full of false clues and sign-posts that lead nowhere. With infinite effort we nerve ourselves for a crisis that never comes. The most successful career must show a waste of strength that might have moved mountains, and the most unsuccessful is not that of the man who is taken unprepared, but of him who has prepared and is never taken. On a tragedy of that kind our national morality is duly silent. It assumes that preparation against danger is itself a good, and that men, like nations, are the better for staggering through life fully armed. The tragedy of preparedness has scarcely been handled, save by the Greeks. Life is indeed dangerous, but not in the way morality would have us believe. It is indeed unmanageable, but the essence of it is not a battle. It is unmanageable because it is a romance, and its essence is romantic beauty. (111)

In Margaret's reasoning, the mind guided by principles of insurance looks for narrative markers and finds them. But if "actual life is full of false clues and sign-posts that lead nowhere," actuarial life is not. In this sense, bracing oneself for worst-case scenarios only distracts from the events of the present, which unfold not as a plot but as something decidedly formless—that is, as experiences rather than designs. Art, beauty, and romance—which figure here as the forms that resist predictability and traffic in surprise—understand this; insurance does not. Insurance does not so much stave off disaster as create a false teleology or causation: disaster was avoided because one prepared for it. But Forster insinuates that to prepare in this manner is to construct one's life around a vacuum—to live *via nega-tiva*—lending artificial shape to events that cast a pall even when they never happen. It is living with one's fists clenched, without painting or writing or touching, only to open one's palms and discover that one is, in the end, empty handed.

Yet to unclench one's fist, even momentarily, may be the source of one's undoing. Thus, even as the novel seems to promote taking risks for art's sake, it undercuts this encouragement through Leonard Bast, the novel's tragic figure and the Schlegel sisters' cause célèbre, who stands at the opposite end of the risk spectrum from Margaret and Helen. He ekes out a meager living as a clerk at the Porphyrion Fire Insurance Company and, true to his profession, sees life as a risky business: "There had always been something to worry him ever since he could remember, always something that distracted him in the pursuit of beauty" (41). Determined not to be distracted from loftier pursuits by his mundane job, Leonard reads steadily and desperately, acquiring what culture he can after work in his dimly lit flat. On one ill-fated evening, the pursuit of beauty leads him to a Beethoven concert, where Helen mistakenly walks away with his umbrella. At Margaret's suggestion, Leonard—who at this point in the story has yet to be named—follows her home to retrieve it:

> This young man had been "had" in the past—badly, perhaps overwhelmingly—and now most of his energies went in defending himself against the unknown. But this afternoon—perhaps on account of music—he perceived that one must slack off occasionally, or what is the good of being alive? Wickham Place, W., though a risk, was as safe as most things, and he would risk it. (38)

What makes this moment difficult to parse is its voice, which seems to be a strange combination of Leonard's free indirect discourse, the omniscient narrator's irony, and Margaret's earnestness. Its chorus of voices suggests something about the collective nature of insurance: even (or especially) in its social incarnation, we cast our insured lot with a stranger, at least when that stranger seems to have reassuring credentials. As though anticipating Margaret's meditation on the unsuccessful man "who has prepared and is never taken," Leonard chooses to be taken at the risk of being had. Significantly, his decision comes out of the experience of a work of art. "Perhaps on account of the music," his normally stiff resolve slackens; he would venture into something unknown, pursue the romance rather than the battle. It is a risk that, in the wider scheme of the novel, will prove disastrous. The endgame of throwing caution to the wind, it seems, is thus not romance but tragedy.

From Prudence to Indifference

The risk-embracing or risk-averse personalities of *Howards End* take shape against a social backdrop guided by a steady actuarial hand, which determines what counts as a minor incident (or character) and what qualifies as a noteworthy event, a turning point, a tragedy. Forster's novel thus instantiates what is in fact a larger cultural shift in attitudes toward risk and responsibility. The rise of accident insurance serves as an index of this new trend that replaced personal accountability with corporate compensation: the Railway Passengers Assurance Company, established in 1848 to insure only against railway accidents, extended its coverage to include any kind of accident in 1891.[12] Even before this expansion, however, the company had been well aware of the potential for insurance to create anxiety rather than reassurance in passengers. Railway clerks who sold insurance along with tickets were therefore instructed not to encourage travelers to purchase insurance, lest the mere mention of potential accidents trigger undue anxiety in patrons.[13]

The Railway Passengers Assurance Company's 1892 prospectus explained the rationale of expanded coverage in the following terms:

> "Accidents will happen!" How then can any one be asked to insure against them? If it is meant to insure against the occurrence of an accident, *that* is hopeless. "Accidents will happen," whatever care be taken. But that is the very reason why a prudent man should insure against the pecuniary loss which an accident is certain to involve. An accident implies a Doctor's bill at least, and if a man's income depends on his work, it implies moreover a suspension of his income during his disability, and perhaps the loss of it altogether. With such a contingency hanging over him, common prudence would suggest to every man the duty of providing against it.[14]

Its heavy-handedness aside, what is striking about this language is the emphasis on the "duty of providing"; what would have once been construed purely in terms of duty of care now becomes a matter of economic foresight. The shift in register marks a turn away from the language of torts toward what might be described, however oddly, as cavalier futility:

"whatever care be taken," one cannot avoid accidents, but at the very least one can afford them.

Howards End sets itself squarely in the moment when prudence emerged as a fiscal rather than just a behavioral concern—when jurisprudence, in effect, was eclipsed by capitalist caution. Through its depiction of a series of small accidents, however, the novel suggests that the insured society is less cautious than indifferent; collisions, in this world, do little to dent an unflappable confidence in well-hewn policies. When Margaret and Mrs. Wilcox, in the flush of their new friendship, set out to visit Howards End and happen upon Mr. Wilcox and his daughter Evie at King's Cross station, their chance encounter turns out to be the outcome of an accident emblematic of the tensions of modern life. Mr. Wilcox's automobile had collided with a horse and cart, and to the father's and daughter's irritation, their trip was therefore cut short. "But as we've insured against third-party risks, it won't so much matter" (91), declares Mr. Wilcox. Dismissing the event as little more than an inconvenience, he feels no obligation to consider it further. There is no sense of the damage done, of the other person involved—that "third party" who might have been anyone. To say "it won't so much matter" is thus to act as though it did not happen at all.

The business of underwriting in the novel, we come to understand, is also that of overwriting, of overriding an accident and making it a non-event. Moments that might have mattered—to someone, at any rate—bear no consequence; people who might have connected, to take up Forster's central dictate, drive off in opposite directions with hardly an exchange of words. After Margaret becomes engaged to Henry Wilcox, she sets off with a group of his friends on a motor tour of the countryside. The caravan of automobiles comes to a stop at a scene that promises to end badly: "the door of a cottage opened, and a girl screamed wildly at them" (221). Charles, the eldest Wilcox son, who rarely appears without his arrogance or his motorcar, informs the party that they need not worry, since the car had only "touched a dog" but had not hurt him. When one of the women smugly insinuates that a small payment would set the matter right, Charles replies with all the confidence of a policyholder: "The insurance company will see to that" (222).

Moments later, the group learns that the animal was not a dog but a cat. "'It is all right, madam,'" the driver assures Margaret. "'What's all right? The cat?'" she asks. "'Yes, madam. The girl will receive compensation for it'" (223). The absurdity of the exchange finds its corollary in the logic of insurance, in which things (and pets) are fungible and compensation rights a wrong.[15] But even more critical is the effect of this replaceability on the imagination of those who pay for it: to Charles and his companions, the question of whether the victim is a dog or a cat makes no difference. In the economy of compensation—for the policyholder, at any rate—one is as good as the other.[16]

Given Forster's pervasive undermining of caution, insurance, and security throughout *Howards End*, it is no surprise that Leonard Bast's employer has little to offer by way of stability. If Forster traffics in subtlety in the novel's minor episodes, he leaves less to the imagination in the fate of the Porphyrion Fire Insurance Company, which as Henry Wilcox informs Margaret and Helen, is on the verge of bankruptcy:

> "I thought an insurance company never smashed," was Helen's contribution. "Don't the others always run in and save them?"
>
> "You're thinking of reinsurance," said Mr. Wilcox mildly. "It is exactly there that the Porphyrion is weak. It has tried to undercut, has been badly hit by a long series of small fires, and it hasn't been able to reinsure. I'm afraid that public companies don't save one another for love." (141)

Where previous exchanges were only inflected with matters of insurance, the issue surfaces here in broad daylight as a moment of explicit economic instruction. With the grim prediction laid clearly before them, Margaret and Helen convince Leonard to resign from his job, which he does—only to lose his next job when the bank that hires him reduces its staff.

What might seem a breach of Forster's typical light touch contains an additional turn: Mr. Wilcox's information was wrong, and the Porphyrion does not declare bankruptcy after all. Leonard, unemployed and destitute, would have been neither if not for this advice that seemed to guarantee his livelihood. Outraged and guilt-ridden, Helen takes up Leonard's case with Henry Wilcox, only to discover that he shares nothing of her sense of responsibility:

> "Oh, come, come!" he protested pleasantly. "You're not to blame. No one's to blame." . . . The poor are poor, and one's sorry for them, but there it is. A civilization moves forward, the shoe is bound to pinch in places, and it's absurd to pretend that anyone is personally responsible. Neither you, nor I, nor my informant, nor the man who informed him, nor the directors of the Porphyrion, are to blame for this clerk's loss of salary. It's just the shoe pinching—no one can help it; and it might easily have been worse." (199)

Laced as it is with a rhetoric that echoes an insurance company's resignation ("accidents will happen!"), Henry's impersonal narrative traces an economic community where accountability has no place. The fate of this particular man may be bleak, but as a rule—from the standpoint of socio-economic patterns and actuarial tables—he fits in perfectly. The poor will always exist, and the fact that this individual now counts among them is due to little more than chance. In the larger scope of events, like Henry's accident earlier, "it won't so much matter."

It is in this light of this belief in fungibility that we can read Margaret's comment to her sister about the decline of human relationships: "I believe that we shall come to care about people less and less, Helen. The more people one knows, the easier it becomes to replace them. It's one of the curses of London. I quite expect to end my life caring most for a place" (136). In a world where one poor man is the same as another, where a cat is identical to a dog and proper compensation writes harm out of the picture, one may well view care for people as meaningless. And in one sense, Margaret makes good on her premonition: at the close of the novel we find her at Howards End in the company of her husband, Helen, and Helen's illegitimate son. An outcast society of two women, an older man, and an illegitimate child, the Forsterian family has effectively written itself out of the wider economy of acceptable social life. But there is a prevailing sense in these last pages that the enclave at Howards End subsists less on the love for this old, vanishing English emblem than on a deeply rooted ethic of care. After Leonard's death, a catastrophe that no one predicted and no insurance policy covered, Margaret's recourse seems to be precisely the opposite of what she had anticipated. Contrary to her expectations, she cares about people more and more. And in so doing, she reintroduces a torts-oriented sense of responsibility—duty of care rather than duty of prudence—in an era when it seemed that the time of care had passed.

The form of responsibility championed in *Howards End* thus comes down to questions of attachment, making good on Forster's epigraph, "Only connect," by adopting the classic modernist posture of disconnection through self-imposed exile. Opting out of conventional life, the strange family unit of husband, wife, sister, and illegitimate son create a commune of sorts, one both progressive in its unconventionality and traditional in its return to the English country home. The connections that this exile from a modernizing England allows, however, exist only insofar as they remain uncompromised by policies that would purport to guarantee them. In other words, they are open to chance, unscripted rather than underwritten. Insurance, far from serving a mediating role in these relations and allowing them to flourish without fear of blame or compensation, interrupts them. For whether one opts in or out, insurance asks us to conceive of every person not as a possible source of compassion but as the personification of unmitigated greed. It is this world, where each encounter is potential lawsuit, that George Bernard Shaw inhabits when he writes in a letter in 1913:

> What is urgent—what you must have above all is insurance against "third party claims." If you get killed you are dead. If the car is smashed, *it* is dead. But if it runs into a motor bus or a beanfeast, everybody in it can take action against you, and even keep on taking actions against you until the end of their lives every time they have a fresh nervous symptom, and get enormous damages. You may have to support them and their children for ever. And you will have to buy a new bus for the company. Your salary will be attached; you will be reduced to beg on the streets. This always happens in the first 5 minutes with an uninsured car. And you must insure your driver. Otherwise he will sprain his thumb or knock out his eye, and live on you for the rest of his life.[17]

Simultaneously lampooning and taking seriously the near-paranoia of the uninsured, Shaw spins out a world fraught with accidents—a scenario that insurance companies would be quick to endorse—in which individuals without the good sense to buy a policy pay dearly for opting out. But it is insurance, of course, that gives him grist for his *reductio ad absurdum* in the first place. The worst-case scenario comes into play only in a world where the haves and have-nots become the insured and uninsured.

Forster's imagined community exists apart from this economy, without guarantees save that of human connection and the care such connection demands. No agent mediates these relations, and no one receives compensation if they fail. *Howards End* forces a reevaluation of Shaw's cautionary tale: if the responsible individual for Shaw buys an insurance policy, the responsible person for Forster refuses to live in a world where injuries matter if no policy covers them. Responsibility is still deeply personal in this model, resisting the bureaucratization that worries Blanchot by giving literary life to his articulation of personal accountability in *The Writing of the Disaster* as "my responsibility for the other, for everyone, without reciprocity" (25). Anticipating the sort of corporate responsibility of today's insurance companies—Liberty Mutual's "Responsibility. What's your policy?"—Forster writes against the policy, whether personal or corporate, of taking calculated risks, weighing the necessity of every action and reaction. It is at Howards End, imagined community and unlikely commune, that we find the surest yardstick against which to measure the social cost of insurance.

Reckless Futures

In the spirit of care rather than prudence, Forster writes nearly three decades later in a radically different context: not the transformation of England but the gradual descent into another world war. In his essay "Post-Munich," from which the second epigraph to this essay is drawn, Forster diagnoses the political climate after Prime Minister Chamberlain signed the Munich agreement of 1938, handing control of the Sudentenland to Nazi Germany. He detects in this moment a mixed state of the union, which consists "of being half-frightened and half-thinking about something else."[18] Echoing Margaret Schlegel with telling accuracy, he writes:

> "Prepare, prepare!" does not do for a slogan. No more does "Business as usual." . . . We are worried rather than frantic. But worry is terribly insidious; besides taking the joy out of life, it prevents the victim from being detached and from observing what is happening to the human experiment. (23–24)

As an antidote to this distraction and self-absorption, Forster rather surprisingly prescribes a steady diet of profligate spending:

> Those who have money should start spending it at once—spending quiets the nerves—and should spend it as if civilisation is permanent; buy books, go to concerts and plays. It is childish to save; thrift was only a virtue as long as it paid, which it has ceased to do. . . . Spending on art has this advantage, apart from the pleasure to be gained from it; it does maintain an artistic framework which may come in useful to the future; it is connected with a positive hope. (24)

It is not, however, connected with prudence. Notwithstanding its Keynesian emphasis on consumption, Forster's seemingly ironic advice appears to promote a troubling frivolity in decidedly unfrivolous times. But reading his pronouncement in earnest—through the lens of *Howards End* and his unswerving liberal commitments—we might conclude that excess has this benefit: it traffics in fiction rather than resignation, a fiction inherent in the advice to act "as if civilisation is permanent." For if the business of insurance begins in resignation, the fiction of insurance begins for Forster in recklessness. To live as if there were no end in sight, no disaster on the horizon, might justifiably be accused of gross denial and irresponsibility. But it might also preserve the feeling of hope with which a fictional future—though never an actuarial one—is invested.

INTRODUCTION

Andrew Parker, Austin Sarat, and Martha Merrill Umphrey

1. http://www.libertymutual.com (accessed July 24, 2009).

2. Hannah Arendt, *Eichmann in Jerusalem: A Report on the Banality of Evil* (New York: Penguin Books, 1963).

3. William Jefferson Clinton, "First Inaugural Address." http://en .wikisource.org/wiki/Bill_Clinton%27s_First_Inaugural_Address.

4. See Glen Johnson and Dan Sewell, "Crowd Applauds Obama's Call for Personal Responsibility," *Chicago Sun Times* (July 15, 2008). http://www .suntimes.com/news/politics/obama/1055855,CST-NWS-obama15.article.

5. An important recent exception is Annika Thiem, *Unbecoming Subjects: Judith Butler, Moral Philosophy, and Critical Responsibility* (New York: Fordham University Press, 2008), which, as its title implies, seeks to bring poststructuralism and moral philosophy into dialogue with each other around the question of responsibility.

6. Andrew Eshelman, "Moral Responsibility," in *Stanford Encyclopedia of Philosophy*, revised August 14, 2004. http://plato.stanford.edu/entries/moral-responsibility (accessed July 24, 2009).

7. See Susan Sauvé Meyer, *Aristotle on Moral Responsibility: Character and Cause* (Oxford: Blackwell, 1993).

8. Bernard Williams, *Shame and Necessity* (Berkeley: University of California Press, 1993), 65. See also his "Voluntary Acts and Responsible Agents," in *Making Sense of Humanity and Other Philosophical Papers, 1982–1993* (Cambridge: Cambridge University Press, 1995), 22–34; and "Moral Responsibility and Political Freedom," *Cambridge Law Journal* 56 (March 1997): 96–102.

9. Williams, *Shame and Necessity*, 55.

10. Writing about the impact of the U.S. Constitution on the president and senators, John Jay writes: "With respect to their responsibility, it is difficult to conceive how it could be increased." See Alexander Hamilton, John Jay, and James Madison, *The Federalist: A Commentary on the Constitution of the United States* (New York: Modern Library, 1956), 422. See Richard McKeon, "The Development and Significance of the Concept of Responsibility," *Revue*

Internationale de Philosophie 11 (1957): 6, 23–24; and Thomas Haskell, *Objectivity Is Not Neutrality: Explanatory Schemes in History* (Baltimore, Md.: The Johns Hopkins University Press, 1998), 407n5. The French *responsabilité*, similarly coined with reference to the accountability of government officials, also dates from the late 1780s; see Jacques Henriot, "Note sur la date et le sense de l'apparition du mot 'responsabilité,'" *Archives de philosophie du droit* 22 (1977): 45–62. Max Weber's late nineteenth-century "ethic of responsibility" (*Verantwortungsethik*) seems in this respect to have developed from the eighteenth-century political notion; see "Politics as a Vocation," in *From Max Weber: Essays in Sociology*, ed. and trans. H. H. Gerth and C. Wright Mills (Oxford: Oxford University Press 1946), 77–128. For more on Weber, see Leonard Feldman's essay in this volume. On the German-language tradition more generally, see Kurt Bayertz, ed., *Verwantwortung: Prizip oder Problem?* (Darmstadt: Wissenschaftliche Buchgesellschaft, 1995).

11. Paul Ricoeur, "The Concept of Responsibility: An Essay in Semantic Analysis," in *The Just*, trans. David Pellauer (Chicago: University of Chicago Press, 1999), 11; and McKeon, "The Development," 6–7. Adjectival forms (such as "responsible") in English, French, and German preexisted the initial appearance of the abstract noun, often by centuries.

12. See Immanuel Kant, *The Metaphysics of Morals*, ed. and trans. Mary Gregor (Cambridge: Cambridge University Press, 1966), 16: "An action is called a *deed* insofar as it comes under obligatory laws and hence insofar as the subject, in doing it, is considered in terms of his freedom of choice. By such an action the agent is regarded as the *author* of its effect [*als* Urheber *der Wirkung*], and this, together with the action itself, can be *imputed* to him [*können ihm* zugerechnet *werden*], if one is previously acquainted with the law by virtue of which an obligation rests on these."

13. On moving beyond the Kantian and Humean parameters that have dominated moral philosophy's interest in responsibility, see especially Marion Smiley, *Moral Responsibility and the Boundaries of Community* (Chicago: University of Chicago Press, 1992).

14. The growing significance of responsibility can be measured by its flowering in nineteenth-century tort law. Here the person who failed to avoid a "reasonably foreseeable risk" could be held responsible for an injury resulting from his negligence. In criminal law, responsibility has traditionally been attributed to subjects whose guilty act was accompanied by *mens rea*, a guilty mind. A guilty mind is the mind of someone who purposefully, knowingly, or recklessly engages in prohibited conduct. See David J. Ibbetson, *A Historical Introduction to the Law of Obligations* (New York: Oxford University Press, 1999); and Paul Robinson, "Mens Rea," *Encyclopedia of Crime and Justice* (2002), 995 (http://ssrn.com/abstract=661161).

15. Lucien Lévy-Bruhl, *L'Idée de responsabilité* (Paris: Hachette 1884).

16. Hannah Arendt, "Collective Responsibility," in *Responsibility and Judgment*, ed. Jerome Kohn (New York: Schocken Books 2003), 147. For more on the distinction between individual and collective responsibility, see Joel Feinberg, *Doing and Deserving: Essays in the Theory of Responsibility* (Princeton, N.J.: Princeton University Press, 1970); and Larry May, *Sharing Responsibility* (Chicago: University of Chicago Press, 1992).

17. Ricoeur, "The Concept of Responsibility," 19, 11–12. On the global extension of the concept, see Winston Davis, ed., *Taking Responsibility: Comparative Perspectives* (Charlottesville: University Press of Virginia, 2001). Can (or ought) the term be extended to *fictional* worlds? "From the point of view of Art, the artist is responsible only to his work. From the point of view of Morality, to assume that 'it does not matter what one writes' is permissible only to the insane; the artist is responsible to the good of human life, in himself and in his fellow men." In Jacques Maritain, *The Responsibility of the Artist* (1960), trans. Georges and Christianne Brazzola. http://www2.nd.edu/Departments/Maritain/etext/resart.htm (accessed July 24, 2009).

18. See, for example, Susanna Blumenthal's essay in this volume.

19. Some contend that legal attributions of responsibility have kept pace with and in some cases exceeded their foundations in ordinary moral intuitions. See Lawrence M. Friedman, *Total Justice* (New York: Russell Sage Foundation, 1994).

20. Ricoeur is responding implicitly as well to Jean-Paul Sartre's suggestion that "I am responsible for everything, in fact, except for my very responsibility, for I am not the foundation of my being." *Being and Nothingness*, trans. Hazel E. Barnes (New York: Washington Square Press, 1956), 710.

21. Isaiah Berlin, *Liberty: Incorporating Four Essays on Liberty* (repr.; Oxford: Oxford University Press, 2002), 178.

22. See J. R. Lucas, *Responsibility* (Oxford: Clarendon Press, 1993), esp. chap. 2. Important work in this tradition includes Hilary Bok, *Freedom and Responsibility* (Princeton, N.J.: Princeton University Press, 1998); J. Angelo Corlett, *Responsibility and Punishment* (Boston: Kluwer Academic Publishers, 2001); H. L. A. Hart, *Punishment and Responsibility: Essays in the Philosophy of Law* (New York: Oxford University Press, 1968); Matt Matravers, *Responsibility and Justice* (Cambridge: Polity Press, 2007); T. M. Scanlon, *What We Owe to Each Other* (Cambridge, Mass.: Harvard University Press, 1998); Samuel Scheffler, *Boundaries and Allegiances: Problems of Justice and Responsibility in Liberal Thought* (Oxford: Oxford University Press, 2001); Peter Strawson, *Freedom and Resentment and Other Essays* (London: Methuen, 1974); and R. Jay Wallace, *Responsibility and the Moral Sentiments* (Cambridge, Mass.: Harvard University Press, 1994). Hans Jonas's landmark *The Imperative of Responsibility*

(Chicago: University of Chicago Press, 1984) asks whether collectivities can assume responsibility for their future acts. Bruce Robbins, *Upward Mobility and the Common Good: Toward a Literary History of the Welfare State* (Princeton, N.J.: Princeton University Press, 2007); and Iris Marion Young, *Global Challenges: War, Self-Determination, and Responsibility* (Cambridge: Polity Press, 2006) promote what might be termed left-wing theories of responsibility. François Raffoul's *The Origins of Responsibility* (Bloomington: University of Indiana Press, 2010) appeared after this volume went to press.

23. Sigmund Freud, *Totem and Taboo*, in *The Standard Edition of the Complete Psychological Works*, ed. and trans. James Strachey (London: The Hogarth Press, 1958), 13:87.

24. Jacques Derrida, "'Eating Well': An Interview," trans. Peter Connor and Avital Ronnell, in *Who Comes After the Subject?* ed. Eduardo Cadava, Peter Connor, and Jean-Luc Nancy (New York: Routledge, 1991), 109.

25. Martin Heidegger, *The Basic Problems of Phenomenology*, trans. Albert Hofstadter (Bloomington: Indiana University Press, 1982), 137. See also François Raffoul, "Heidegger and the Origins of Responsibility," in *Heidegger and Practical Philosophy*, ed. François Raffoul and David Pettigrew (Albany, N.Y.: SUNY Press, 2002), 205–218. Emmanuel Lévinas develops his idiosyncratic notion of responsibility in *Otherwise Than Being; or, Beyond Essence*, trans. Alphonso Lingis (The Hague: M. Nijhoff, 1981). See in this connection Judith Butler, *Giving an Account of Oneself* (New York: Fordham University Press, 2005); and Denis King Keenan, *Death and Responsibility: The "Work" of Lévinas* (Albany, N.Y.: SUNY Press, 1999).

26. Jacques Derrida, "Performative Powerlessness: A Response to Simon Critchley," *Constellations* 7 (2000): 468. Derrida's most concentrated analysis of responsibility is *The Gift of Death*, trans. David Wills (Chicago: University of Chicago Press, 1995). See also Thomas Keenan, *Fables of Responsibility: Aberrations and Predicaments in Ethics and Politics* (Stanford, Calif.: Stanford University Press, 1997); and Gayatri Chakravorty Spivak, "Responsibility—1922: Testing Theory in the Plains," in *Other Asias* (Oxford: Blackwell, 2008), 58–96.

27. Maurice Blanchot, *The Writing of the Disaster*, trans. Ann Smock (Lincoln: University of Nebraska Press, 1986), 25–27.

28. Friedrich Nietzsche, *The Genealogy of Morals*, ed. and trans. Walter Kaufman (New York: Vintage Books, 1967), 58–59.

29. François Ewald, "Insurance and Risk," in *The Foucault Effect: Studies in Governmentality*, ed. Graham Burchell, Colin Gordon, and Peter Miller (Chicago: University of Chicago Press, 1991), 203. See also "The Return of Descartes' Malicious Demon: An Outline of a Philosophy of Precaution," in *Embracing Risk: The Changing Culture of Insurance and Responsibility*, ed. Tom

Baker and Jonathan Simon (Chicago: University of Chicago Press, 2002), 273–301.

30. Jonathan Simon, "The Emergence of a Risk Society: Law, Insurance, and the State," *Socialist Review* 89 (1987): 61–89.

31. Malcolm Feeley and Jonathan Simon, "The New Penology: Notes on the Emerging Strategy of Corrections and Its Implications," *Criminology* 30 (1992): 458.

1. ASSUMING RESPONSIBILITY IN A STATE OF NECESSITY
Leonard C. Feldman

1. In common law, necessity is often distinguished from duress in one of several ways: first, Alan Wertheimer argues that a natural cause is often said to produce a situation of necessity while a human cause produces a situation of duress. Thus, for instance, a natural disaster requiring the violation of property laws would make available a necessity defense, while someone placing a gun to my head and demanding that I perpetrate a crime would constitute duress. See Alan Wertheimer, *Coercion* (Princeton, N.J.: Princeton University Press, 1987), 146. However, necessity and nature may also be distinguished from each other and opposed. See Eric Wertheimer, "Whereas, and Other Etymologies of Responsibility," in this volume. Alan Wertheimer argues in addition that necessity is often presented as a justification while duress is presented as an excuse. This leads to the final way of distinguishing the defenses: as a justification, necessity involves the assumption of some aspect of free will, because it involves the *choice* of a lesser evil. On the other hand, as an excuse, duress is a claim about the lack of free will. As Arlene Boxerman writes: "The duress defense is based on the theory that a person should not be held responsible for a criminal offense which was committed under pressure great enough to deprive an ordinary person of free will." Arlene D. Boxerman, "The Use of the Necessity Defense by Abortion Clinic Protesters," *Journal of Criminal Law and Criminology* 81, no. 3 (1990): 680.

2. Max Weber, "Politics as a Vocation," in *The Vocation Lectures*, trans. Rodney Livingstone, ed. David Owen and Tracy B. Strong (Indianapolis, Ind.: Hackett, 2004), 32–94.

3. Ibid., 84.

4. Michael Walzer, "Political Action: The Problem of Dirty Hands," *Philosophy and Public Affairs* 2, no. 2 (Winter 1973): 177.

5. Jean Bethke Elshtain, "Reflection on the Problem of 'Dirty Hands,'" in *Torture: A Collection*, ed. Sanford Levinson (Oxford: Oxford University Press, 2004), 81.

6. Ibid., 83–84. See also Oren Gross, "Are Torture Warrants Warranted? Pragmatic Absolutism and Official Disobedience," *Minnesota Law Review* 88.

7. Elshtain, "Reflection," 84.

8. Richard A. Posner, "Torture, Terrorism, and Interrogation," in *Torture: A Collection*, ed. Sanford Levinson (Oxford: Oxford University Press, 2004), 296, emphasis added.

9. The *Oxford English Dictionary* presents one definition of discretion as "the liberty or power of deciding, or of acting according to one's own judgement or as one thinks fit; uncontrolled power of disposal." Another definition of discretion is "the quality of being discreet," where discreet is an adjective describing a person who "can be silent when speech would be inconvenient."

10. Which is where she departs from Weber and aligns her approach with a "Catholic" tradition, also identified by Walzer in his reading of Camus, which focuses on the permanence of moral rules and demands that the rule breaker "in many situations, accept punishment or do penance" Elshtain, "Reflection," 82.

11. Ibid., 87.

12. In this sense also following Michael Walzer's preferred way of thinking about "dirty hands," which posits that when an official "commits a determinate crime, and he must pay a determinate penalty." Walzer, "Political Action," 178. However, whereas Walzer suggests that we may, at best, only be able to imagine a punishment for official extralegality, Gross develops legal-juridical and deliberative-democratic elements as a way to make the possibility of punishment real (at least within the confines of his model).

13. Elshtain hints at a broader public responsibility to judge official extralegalism when describing how state officials *may* be called to account for their actions, but this is not a developed aspect of her model.

14. Oren Gross, "Prohibition on Torture," in *Torture: A Collection*, ed. Sanford Levinson (Oxford: Oxford University Press, 2004), 240.

15. Ibid., 242.

16. Oren Gross, "Chaos and Rules: Should Responses to Violent Crises Always Be Constitutional?" *Yale Law Journal* 112 (2003): 1100.

17. Ibid.

18. Ibid., 1111.

19. See David Cole, "Judging the Next Emergency," *Michigan Law Review* 101 (August 2003): 2589.

20. See ibid.

21. Television shows such as *24*, which valorize the state agent who has the moral courage to "get his hands dirty" by, for instance, acting extralegally to torture a suspected terrorist, help to implant such an extralegal norm.

22. Elshtain, "Reflection," 81, 83, 87.

23. Oren Gross, "Torture and an Ethics of Responsibility," *Law, Culture, and the Humanities* 3 (2007): 44.

24. Ibid., 48, 46.

25. David Dyzenhaus, "The State of Emergency in Legal Theory," in *Global Anti-Terrorism Law and Policy*, ed. Victor Ramraj, Michael Hor, and Kent Roach (Cambridge: Cambridge University Press, 2005), 73, emphasis added.

26. Weber, "Politics as a Vocation," 54, emphasis in original.

27. David Dyzenhaus, *The Constitution of Law: Legality in a Time of Emergency* (Cambridge: Cambridge University Press, 2006), 52.

28. See Terrence Haliday and Bruce Caruthers, "The Recursivity of Law," *American Journal of Sociology* 112, no. 4 (January 2007): 1135–1202.

29. Drucilla Cornell, "The Relevance of Time to the Relationship Between the Philosophy of the Limit and Systems Theory," *Cardozo Law Review* 13 (1992): 1582.

30. Jay Bybee, "Memo: Jay S. Bybee to Alberto Gonzales," August 1, 2002. In Mark Danner, *Torture and Truth* (New York: New York Review Books, 2004), 115.

31. David Luban, "Liberalism, Torture, and the Ticking Bomb," in *The Torture Debate in America*, ed. Karen Greenberg (New York: Cambridge University Press, 2006), 58.

32. Bybee, "Memo," in Danner, *Torture and Truth*, 116.

33. Ibid., 142.

34. Ibid., 149.

35. Ibid.

36. See Ian Johnstone, "The Plea of 'Necessity' in International Legal Discourse: Humanitarian Intervention and Counter-terrorism," *Columbia Journal of Transnational Law* 43 (2005): 350.

37. Bybee, "Memo," in Danner, *Torture and Truth*, 150–151.

38. "Working Group Report on Detainee Interrogations in the Global War on Terrorism: Assessment of Legal, Historical, Policy and Operational Considerations" (March 6, 2003). Available from the Center for Constitutional Rights, at http://www.ccr-ny.org/v2/reports/report.asp?ObjID = oShrzgi8q7&Content = 385. Also reprinted in Karen J. Greenberg and Joshua L. Dratel, eds., *The Torture Papers: The Road to Abu Ghraib* (Cambridge: University of Cambridge Press, 2005), 286–359.

39. "Working Group Report," 24.

40. Ibid., 33, 52.

41. Jane Mayer, "The Memo," *New Yorker* (February 27, 2006).

42. See Jack Goldsmith, *The Terror Presidency: Law and Judgment Inside the Bush Administration* (New York: W.W. Norton, 2007).

43. "Press Briefing By White House Counsel Judge Alberto Gonzales." http://www.whitehouse.gov/news/releases/2004/06/20040622-14.html.

44. Daniel Levin, "Memo RE: Legal Standards Applicable Under 18 U.S.C. Sec. 2340–2340A," in *The Torture Debate in America*, ed. Karen Greenberg (New York: Cambridge University Press, 2006), 361–376.

45. Ibid., 367. However, as Luban ("Liberalism," 72) points out, the Levin memo does not substantially revise the definition, because all of the examples he discusses are "on the upper end of the scale of barbarism," leaving "torture lite" permissible through the memo's silence.

46. Levin, "Memo," 362.

47. Luban, "Liberalism," 72.

48. Levin, "Memo," 362.

49. See on this point Jinee Lokaneeta, "Authorization of Torture in the War on Terror: Governmentality or Sovereignty?" Paper presented at the Western Political Science Association Annual Meeting, Albuquerque, N.M., March 2006, p. 17.

50. Sanford Levinson, "Preserving Constitutional Norms in Times of Permanent Emergencies," *Constellations* 13, no. 1 (2006): 70.

51. Detainee Treatment Act of 2005. http://jurist.law.pitt.edu/gazette/2005/12/detainee-treatment-act -of-2005-white.php.

52. See Luban, "Liberalism," 55.

53. As ibid., 45, argues, several implausible dimensions of certainty are presupposed in the ticking-bomb hypothetical: certainty that the ticking bomb exists and certainty that the person responsible is in their custody.

54. See Goldsmith, *The Terror Presidency*, 81, for a fascinating discussion of Bush administration officials' negative reaction when Goldsmith mentioned a version of the extralegal-measures model and its requirement of candid confession of extralegal action.

55. Elshtain, "Reflection," 83.

56. Weber, "Politics as a Vocation," p. 85.

57. Ibid., 85.

58. Ibid., 84.

59. Simon Critchley, "Crypto-Schmittianism" (2004). http://www .newschool.edu/gf/centers/what/paper_critchley041110.pdf.

60. Elshtain, "Reflection," 83.

61. Bybee, "Memo," 151.

62. Wayne R. LaFave and Austin W. Scott Jr., *Substantive Criminal Law* (St. Paul, Minn.: West Publishing, 1986), 1:630.

63. See Dyzenhaus, *The Constitution of Law*.

64. I include my own work in this critique. See my "Judging Necessity: Democracy and Extra-legalism," *Political Theory* 36, no. 4 (August 2008): 550–577. For an insightful account of the disconnect between normative theory's backward-looking exemplars (and their all-too-simple inside/outside-the-law

dichotomies) and current developments in emergency law, see Kim Lane Scheppele, "Legal and Extralegal Emergencies," *Oxford Handbook of Law and Politics*, ed. Keith E. Wittington, R. Daniel Kelemen, and Gregory Caldeira (Oxford: Oxford University Press, 2008), 165–184.

65. William Scheuerman, "Survey Article: Emergency Powers and the Rule of Law After 9/11," *Journal of Political Philosophy* 14, no. 1 (2006): 79.

2. HOW TO DO RESPONSIBILITY: APOLOGY AND MEDICAL ERROR
S. Lochlann Jain

My thanks to Adam Sitze, Austin Sarat, Andy Parker, Martha Umphrey, Fordham University Press's anonymous reviewer, and the participants of the Responsibility Conference at Amherst College in 2008. I gave a version of this paper at Yale Law School, and I am indebted in particular to Maxine Kamari Clarke.

1. Julie Sevrens Lyons, "Medical Mistake May Have Killed Man," *Mercury News* (November 2, 2005).

2. And there are, of course, many dimensions to medical error. Consider, for example, the fact that the American insurance system means that people will have to change doctors fairly regularly, making it impossible to build the kind of relationship (and personal connection) necessary for high-quality care.

3. T. A. Brennan, L. L. Leape, L. M. Laird, et al., "Incidence of Adverse Events and Negligence in Hospitalized Patients: Results of the Harvard Medical Practice Study I," *New England Journal of Medicine* 324 (1991): 370–377 finds that fewer than 2 percent of patients receiving substandard care actually sue. Finding medical experts can be difficult, given the professional networks in medicine.

4. "Kaiser Hospital Is Cited After 2nd Death From Double Dose," *Los Angeles Times* (November 10, 2005).

5. Medical malpractice law developed in the United States as the way in which people who were injured through medical error would be able to both recover a part of the damages they suffered as a result of that injury and as a way to try to hold doctors accountable for their mistakes. In general, someone is entitled to a damage award if their physician's conduct falls below the standards of reasonable care. The profession generally determines what those standards will be, and in bringing a suit a plaintiff needs to find medical experts willing to testify that one of their colleagues gave substandard care. This can be difficult, for as Jerome Groopman has recently laid out in *How Doctors Think* (Boston: Houghton Mifflin, 2007), the process of diagnosis varies vastly and in many, many cases, there simply is no "standard of care." In any case, as Tom Baker reports in the *Medical Malpractice Myth* (Chicago: University of Chicago Press, 2005), patients have virtually no access to information on their

treatments, what errors may have been made, and the standards of care in similar situations—occasionally this leads a patient to make a medical malpractice claim just to have access to the records and procedures. Cases are stacked against the patient. The doctor writes and has access to the medical records and all of the expertise and social networks of the field; the patient has only his or her body as a relatively intangible form of evidence. One study, for example, found that only 30 percent of surgeons would be willing to testify against another surgeon who had removed the wrong kidney. Marc Franklin and Robert Rabin, *Tort Law and Alternatives: Cases and Materials*, 7th ed. (St. Paul, Minn.: West Publishing Company, 2001), 116. Occasionally a judge will intervene in this internally judged standard. One judge determined that although it was not standard practice to count the number of clamps after a surgery (and one had been left in the body of the patient), it "requires no expertise to count," even if it is not the usual practice. At best, then, at its most just, medical malpractice litigation offers a highly time-consuming, expensive, and labor intensive fault-based insurance system.

6. Between 1986 and 1994, the plaintiff win rate in medical malpractice is about 33 percent, compared to plaintiff win rates of about 50 percent in other categories of cases. Gary T. Schwartz, "Symposium: Medical Malpractice, Tort, Contract, and Managed Care," *University of Illinois Law Review* (1998): 893. Furthermore, since insurance attorneys are paid by the hour but plaintiffs attorneys are only paid out of winnings or settlement, insurance only very rarely settles before they hit the steps to the courthouse.

7. While the adage "do no harm" does a great deal of rhetorical work, in fact a great deal of harm has resulted from medical intervention. Estimates of the number of hospital patient that suffers negligent treatment resulting in death and disability range from 1 to 4 percent, and fewer than 30 percent of errors are disclosed. P. Weiler, H. Hiat, and J. Newhouse, et al., *A Measure of Malpractice* (Cambridge, Mass.: Harvard University Press, 1993). Considering as well the more institutionalized injuries of aggressive treatments such as surgeries or chemotherapy, the history of medicine also provides a history of the contested line between how tradeoffs between the injuries of disease and the risk of injuries from treatment are rendered logical and acceptable. Some of these contestations within the medical field have been made explicit. Cancer surgery provides a particularly gruesome example of extreme surgeries as the standard practice through the twentieth surgery, with virtually no proof of efficacy. For example, historians have analyzed the history of the Halsted radical mastectomy, which for decades removed muscles, bones, and lymph nodes, while other medical tradeoffs, such as the use of chemotherapy for solid tumors, remain embedded within institutional practices. See, for example, James Olson, *Bathsheba's Breast: Women, Cancer, and History* (Baltimore, Md.: The

John Hopkins University Press, 2002). Although the history of breast-cancer surgery throughout the twentieth century is one of the better documented in secondary literature, surgery for other cancers was equally as aggressive, operating (as it were) under the theory that all areas to which cancer may have spread should be removed. It is now understood that cancer metastasizes to distant organs. In the 1970s, the rise of the randomized control trial, comparing the survival rates of patients receiving lesser surgeries, led to a reduction in the removal of organs and other body parts, although the use of these trials was exceedingly controversial. See S. Lochlann Jain, "The Mortality Effect," *Public Culture* (Winter 2010).

8. See, for example, Sherwin B. Nuland, "Whoops!" *New York Review of Books* 49, no. 12 (July 18, 2002). Nuland celebrates this refreshing new voice of the surgeon willing to admit to having made mistakes but collaborates in the erasure of the patient and the question of responsibility in inevitable mistakes. It is enough, for Nuland, that the mistakes are acknowledged—albeit not to the patients.

9. Atul Gawande, *Complications* (New York: Picador, 2003), 77 (italics mine). Here is Gawande again: "There is . . . a central truth in medicine . . . all doctors make terrible mistakes." Ibid., 55.

10. The section on the "Liability of Physicians and Surgeons" reads: "When they put out a sign, it is to be presumed they consider themselves competent to prescribe, and perform operations; and the community, believing such to be the fact, feels a degree of security, in cases of emergency. But if they call upon them, and physicians and surgeons refuse to act, or they act unskillfully, the party employing them has a right to demand damages at a tribunal of justice." J. V. C. Smith, ed., *The Boston Medical and Surgical Journal* (Boston: David Clapp, 1853), 48:506.

11. Walter Channing, "A Medico-Legal Treatise on Malpractice and Medical Evidence—Review," *Boston Medical and Surgical Journal* 62, no. 12 (April 19, 1860): 304.

12. Four interviews with author, February–July 2005.

13. National Academy of Health Report, *To Err Is Human: Building a Safer Health System* (2000), 1, 3. On the ways in which physicians manage error internally, see Charles L. Bosk, *Forgive and Remember: Managing Medical Failure* (Chicago: University of Chicago Press, 1979). His illuminating study highlights that "however lamentable the fact, the patient is an exogenous variable falling outside of the system of control." Bosk, *Forgive*, 25.

14. One author reports the difference as from one in one thousand in 1960 to one in 240,000 in 2002. R. Voelker, "Anesthesia-Related Risks Have Plummeted," *Journal of the American Medical Association* 273 (1995): 445–446.

15. J. B. Cooper, R. S. Newbower, C. D. Long, and B. McPeek, "Preventable Anesthesia Mishaps: A Study of Human Factors," *Anesthesiology* 49, no. 6 (1978): 399–406.

16. S. Lochlann Jain, *Injury* (Princeton, N.J.: Princeton University Press, 2006), 9. In furthering Galison's analysis, I argue there that at a certain point the persons and things are in fact mutually constitutive—and thus, in showing how the legal framework that attempts to set them apart and set out blame and responsibility can only misread how commodities and technologies circulate through the culture, I ultimately disagree with Galison's nevertheless incredibly useful point.

17. A recent World Health Organization report ranked American mortality thirty-sixth in the world despite the United States having the most expensive system in the world. "Using five performance indicators to measure health systems in 191 member states, [the WHO study] finds that France provides the best overall health care followed among major countries by Italy, Spain, Oman, Austria and Japan. . . . The U.S. health system spends a higher portion of its gross domestic product than any other country but ranks 37 out of 191 countries according to its performance, the report finds." The reasons for the low performance can only partially be attributed to the large number of citizens who are un- and underinsured. http://www.who.int/whr/2000/media_centre/press_release/en/index.html.

18. Lucian Leape, "Understanding the Power of Apology: How Saying 'I'm Sorry' Helps Heal Patients and Caregivers," *Focus on Patient Safety: A Newsletter from the Patient Safety Foundation* 8, no. 4 (2005). See also A. Lazare, *On Apology* (Oxford: Oxford University Press, 2005); A. Lazare, "Apology in Medical Practice: An Emerging Clinical Skill," *Journal of the American Medical Association* 296, no. 11 (2006): 1401–1403; Thomas Gallagher et al., "Disclosing Harmful Medical Errors to Patients," *New England Journal of Medicine* 356, no. 26 (June 28, 2007): 2713–2717; Nicholas Tuvachis, *Mea Culpa: A Sociology of Apology and Reconciliation* (Stanford, Calif.: Stanford University Press, 1991).

19. Janna Thompson, "The Apology Paradox," *Philosophical Quarterly* 50, no. 201 (2000): 470–475; Deborah Cameron, *Working with Spoken Discourse* (London: Sage Publications, 2001); Lee Taft, "Apology Subverted: The Commodification of Apology," *Yale Law Journal* 109, no. 5 (2000): 1135–1160.

20. Rachel Zimmerman, "Medical Contrition: Doctor's New Tool to Fight Lawsuits," *Wall Street Journal* (May 18, 2004).

21. The safe haven for apologizers was introduced by a Massachusetts legislator whose daughter was killed by a driver when cycling. The driver never apologized. The safe-harbor statute provides: "Statements, writings or benevolent gestures expressing sympathy or a general sense of benevolence relating to the pain, suffering or death of a person involved in an accident and made to such a person or to the family of such a person shall be inadmissible as evidence of an admission of liability in a civil action." *Mass. Gen. Laws Ann.*

chap. 233, ss. 23D (West Supp. 1998). Cited in Taft, "Apology Subverted," 1151. One critical aspect of this legislation is that it differentiates an accident from a sequence of events, separating the emotions one might (or should) have from being in an agentive position in an event where someone is hurt from any legal responsibility for having caused this sequence of events.

22. Liz Kowalczyk, "Hospitals Study When to Apologize to Patients," *Boston Globe* (July 24, 2005).

23. Reni Gertner, "The Art of Apologizing Takes Hold in the Legal World," *St. Louis Daily Record* (December 22, 2005). Is there such a thing as a *possible* risk?

24. Kowalczyk, "Hospitals Study." These numbers pose complicated issues beyond the scope of this chapter. Many of these complications have to do with the politics of medical malpractice and the enormous amounts of money involved in a private healthcare system. Because of the cost for insurance companies of litigating these claims (may charge $300 to $500 per hour), many insurance companies have set up their own in-house legal departments. This enables them to take more cases all the way to court rather than settling, thus forcing, with the caps on damages, a situation in which it is simply not tenable to bring many legitimate claims to court (for example, if someone cannot claim a huge loss-of-income settlement).

25. In my essay "Dangerous Instrumentality (Bystander as Subject)," *Cultural Anthropology* (February 2004), I examined how the introduction of the automobile shifted how urban dwellers were understood in relation to cars—as owners, drivers, mothers, and so on. I argued that these positionings were integrally tied up with the distribution of car-based injuries.

26. Kevin Sack, "Doctors Say 'I'm Sorry' Before 'See You in Court,'" *New York Times* (May 18, 2008).

27. Taft, "Apology Subverted," 1140. Italics mine.

28. Zimmerman, "Medical Contrition."

29. Constantine D. Mavroudis, Keith Naunheim, and Robert Sade, "Should Surgical Errors Always Be Disclosed to the Patient?" *Annals of Thoracic Surgery* 80 (2005): 404.

3. RESPONSIBILITY AND THE BURDENS OF PROOF
Carol J. Greenhouse

My thanks to Austin Sarat and Andrew Porter for organizing a stimulating conference in Amherst and to all who participated in that memorable conversation—as well as to an anonymous reviewer for a constructive reading of this chapter in draft.

1. "New world order" was President Bush's coinage. George H. W. Bush, "Address Before a Joint Session of the Congress on the Persian Gulf Crisis

and the Federal Budget Deficit," September 11, 1990. http://bushlibrary
.tamu.edu/research/public_papers.php?id=221 7&year=1990 &month=9.

2. United States Senate, *Civil Rights Act of 1990. Hearing Before the Committee on Labor and Human Resources*, United States Senate, 101st Cong., 1st
sess. on S.2104, February 23, 27; March 1, 7, 1989 (Washington, D.C.: Government Printing Office, 1990) (hereafter Senate 1990); United States House
of Representatives, *Contract with America—Welfare Reform. Hearing Before the
Subcommittee on Human Resources of the Committee on Ways and Means*, 104th
Cong., 1st sess., January 13, 20, 23, 27, 30, 1995, part 1, serial 104–43 (Washington, D.C.: United States Government Printing Office, 1996) (hereafter
House of Representatives 1996, part 1); and United States House of Represen-
tatives, *Contract with America—Welfare Reform. Hearing Before the Subcommittee
on Human Resources of the Committee on Ways and Means*, 104th Cong., 1st sess.,
February 2, 1995, part 2, serial 104–44 (Washington, D.C.: United States
Government Printing Office, 1996) (hereafter House of Representatives 1996,
part 2); United States Senate, *Welfare Reform Wrap-Up. Hearing Before the
Committee on Finance*, 104th Cong., 1st sess., April 27, 1995 (Washington,
D.C.: United States Government Printing Office, 1995) (hereafter Senate
1995).

3. United States Congress, *Personal Responsibility and Work Opportunity Reconciliation Act of 1996*, 104th Cong., 2nd sess., H.R. 3734 (hereafter Welfare
Reform Act); United States Senate, *Civil Rights Act of 1990*, 101st Cong., 2nd
sess., S.2104 (hereafter CRA 1990).

4. The impact of the U.S. Supreme Court cases that proponents of the
Civil Rights Act of 1990 intended to reverse was a matter of debate in the
hearings for the bill, as discussed below. For contemporary assessments of
antidiscrimination law and the future role of law in relation to progressive
politics, see respectively Alan Freeman, "Antidiscrimination Law: The View
from 1989," and Cornel West, "The Role of Law in Progressive Politics,"
both in *The Politics of Law*, ed. David Kairys (New York: Pantheon, 1990).

5. Felicia Kornbluh, *The Battle for Welfare Rights: Politics and Poverty in
Modern America* (Philadelphia: University of Pennsylvania Press, 2007).

6. This shift was not limited to the United States. Anthropologists working
on the social effects of neoliberalism in other parts of the world note the
pervasive effects—filtered through the specificity of regional and even local
contexts—of the marketization of governance on the experience of citizenship.
See John L. Comaroff and Jean Comaroff, *Ethnicity, Inc.* (Chicago: University
of Chicago Press, 2009); James Ferguson, *Global Shadows: Africa in the Neoliberal World Order* (Durham, N.C.: Duke University Press, 2006); Carol J.
Greenhouse, ed., *Ethnographies of Neoliberalism* (Philadelphia: University of
Pennsylvania Press, 2009); Aihwa Ong, *Neoliberalism as Exception: Mutations in*

Citizenship and Sovereignty (Durham, N.C.: Duke University Press, 2006); Justin B. Richland, "On Neoliberalism and Other Social Diseases: The 2008 Sociocultural Anthropology Year in Review," *American Anthropologist* 111 (2009): 170.

7. The focus in what follows is the mutual embeddedness of responsibility and race as political symbols—*race* sometimes functioning as social description of individuals or communities and sometimes as a template of difference (i.e., encompassing gender). For a related discussion of the gendering of inequality in the context of the same hearings discussed here, see Carol J. Greenhouse, "Scale(s) of Justice," *Cambridge Anthropology*, in press.

8. Karl Polanyi, *The Great Transformation* (Boston: Beacon Press, 1957 [1944]).

9. Saskia Sassen, *The Mobility of Labor and Capital: A Study in International Investment and Labor Flow* (Cambridge: Cambridge University Press, 1988); and Saskia Sassen, *The Global City: New York, London, Tokyo* (Princeton, N.J.: Princeton University Press, 1991).

10. On downward mobility, see Katherine S. Newman, *Falling from Grace: Downward Mobility in the Age of Affluence* (Berkeley: University of California Press, 1999). On income gaps and loss of value, see Joel Handler, *The Poverty of Welfare Reform* (New Haven, Conn.: Yale University Press, 1995).

11. I use "keyword" in Raymond Williams' sense of a word made powerful by the nature of the social investment in its effects. Raymond Williams, *Keywords: A Vocabulary of Culture and Society* (New York: Oxford, 1983 [1976]).

12. See John Comaroff and Jean Comaroff, *Ethnography and the Historical Imagination* (Boulder, Colo.: Westview Press, 1992), chap. 1.

13. See Elizabeth Mertz, "Legal Language: Pragmatics, Poetics, and Social Power," *Annual Review of Anthropology* 23 (1994): 435.

14. On hegemony and legitimacy in relation to discourse, see Carol J. Greenhouse, "Fractured Discourse: Rethinking the Discursivity of States," in *Democracy: Anthropological Approaches*, ed. Julia Paley (Santa Fe, N.M.: School for Advanced Research Press, 2009), 193.

15. The divisions were evident throughout but were fully exposed in the Senate floor debate over the reconsideration of the bill after the president's veto. See note 40, *infra*.

16. David Harvey, *A Brief History of Neoliberalism* (Oxford: Oxford University Press, 2005).

17. United States Senate, *Civil Rights Act of 1991*, 102nd Cong., 1st sess., S.1745.

18. *Wards Cove Packing Company v. Atonio*, 490 US 642 (1989).

19. William T. Coleman counted 320 cases overturned as a consequence of *Wards Cove*. Senate 1990, 57.

20. Ibid., 1.

21. Ibid., 2.

22. Ibid., 4.

23. Ibid.

24. Ibid.

25. Ibid., 8–9. The reference to "turning back the clock" is an echo of *Brown v. Board of Education*'s prologue to overturning *Plessy v. Ferguson*. *Plessy v. Ferguson*, 163 U.S. 537 (1896); *Brown v. Board of Education*, 347 U.S. 483 (1954).

26. Senate 1990, 10.

27. Ibid., 30.

28. Ibid., 13.

29. Ibid., 77.

30. Loury is highly critical of so-called culture of poverty arguments and of social legislation that steepens the vulnerability of the poor. See Glenn C. Loury, "Politics, Race, and Poverty Research" in *Understanding Poverty*, ed. Sheldon H. Danziger and Robert H. Haveman (New York: Russell Sage Foundation; Cambridge, Mass.: Harvard University Press, 2001), 447–453.

31. *Griggs v. Duke Power Company*, 401 U.S. 424 (1971).

32. Senate 1990, 15.

33. Ibid., 66.

34. Ibid., 86.

35. Ibid., 86–87.

36. Ibid., 110.

37. Ibid., 87.

38. Hardening on key points discussed here is evident in the exchange between Senator Kennedy and Deputy Attorney General Donald B. Ayer; ibid., 114–117; see also Kennedy's statement in response to the president's veto message, implying that the administration had broken faith with a long-standing compromise. *Congressional Record* (October 24, 1990): S 33379.

39. Senate 1990, 87.

40. *Veto Message on S.2104—Message from the President, PM 152, Congressional Record* (October 22, 1990): S 31868.

41. These codings are most explicit in the Senate floor debate following the president's veto. After bitter debate, the Senate failed to override the president's veto. *Civil Rights Act of 1990—Veto. Congressional Record* (October 24, 1990), S 33379–33406.

42. See note 40, *supra*.

43. See note 37, *supra*.

44. "Republican Contract with America" (n.d.). http://www.house.gov/house/Contract/CONTRACT.htm.

45. See note 2, *supra*.

46. House of Representatives 1996, part 1, 128.

47. Ibid., 129.

48. Ibid., 163.

49. Ibid.

50. Ibid.

51. See, for example, ibid., 238.

52. Ibid., 163–164.

53. Ibid., 264.

54. House of Representatives 1996, part 2, 1092.

55. See, for example, the testimonies of Kate Michelman and Clifford Johnson, ibid.

56. Ibid., 1071.

57. House of Representatives 1996, part 1, 166.

58. Ibid., 173.

59. Senate 1995, 2.

60. House of Representatives 1996, part 1, 74.

61. Ibid., 157.

62. Ibid., 167.

63. Senate 1995, 16.

64. Senate 1995, 50.

65. House of Representatives 1996, part 1, 134; emphasis added.

66. Welfare Reform Act, 6.

67. Ibid., 8.

68. Gunnar Myrdal, *The American Dilemma: The Negro Problem and Modern Democracy* (London: Transaction, 1995 [1945]); United States Department of Labor, Office of Policy Planning and Research, "The Negro Family: The Case for National Action" (1965, popularly known as "the Moynihan Report"). http://www.dol.gov/oasam/programs/history/webid-meynihan.htm. Moynihan's misspelled name in the Web address is *sic*.

69. See Carol J. Greenhouse, "Hegemony and Hidden Transcripts," *American Anthropologist* 107, no. 3 (2005): 356. In this sense, the displacement from center to periphery noted by Kearney as a condition of postcoloniality was here strategically inverted in the process of establishing the hegemony of neoliberal reform: displacing identity- and rights-based social movements to the center, reworked as excessive costs. Michael Kearney, "The Local and the Global: The Anthropology of Transnationalism and Globalization," *Annual Review of Anthropology* 24 (1995): 547, 551.

70. Michael J. Sandel, *Democracy's Discontents: America in Search of a Public Philosophy* (Cambridge, Mass.: Harvard University Press, 1995), 3.

71. Max Horkheimer and Theodor Adorno, *The Dialectic of Enlightenment: Philosophical Fragments*, ed. Gunzelin Schmid Noerr, trans. Edmund Jephcott (Stanford, Calif.: Stanford University Press, 2002), 94–136.

72. The healthcare debate is ongoing as I write this.

4. WHEREAS, AND OTHER ETYMOLOGIES OF RESPONSIBILITY
Eric Wertheimer

1. See, for instance, J. G. A. Pocock, *The Machiavellian Moment: Florentine Political Thought and the Atlantic Republican Tradition* (Princeton, N.J.: Princeton University Press, 2003), esp. the chapter "Rome and Venice: Guicciardini's *Dialogo* and the Problem of Optimate Prudence"; and C. B. Macpherson, *The Political Theory of Possessive Individualism: Hobbes to Locke* (Oxford: Clarendon Press, 1963). It is worth noting that the republican tradition seemed to thrive conceptually in commercial environments such as Renaissance Florence, seventeenth-century London, or eighteenth-century Philadelphia—all centers of insurance underwriting.

2. Archibald Henry Sayce, *Principles of Comparative Philology* (Adamant Media Corporation, 2000), 290.

3. See Jennifer J. Baker, *Securing the Commonwealth: Debt, Speculation, and Writing in the Making of Early America* (Baltimore, Md.: The Johns Hopkins University Press, 2005).

4. See Ian Hacking, *The Emergence of Probability: A Philosophical Study of Early Ideas About Probability, Induction, and Statistical Inference* (Cambridge: Cambridge University Press, 1984).

5. See Ian Baucom, *Specters of the Atlantic: Finance Capital, Slavery, and the Philosophy of History* (Durham, N.C.: Duke University Press, 2005). The origins of the story as a public event lay in the narrative of Olaudah Equiano, who mentions the atrocity in *The Interesting Narrative of the Life of Olaudah Equiano, or Gustavus Vassa the African* (1789). The bicentennial of British abolition has occasioned renewed reflection on the *Zong* affair; see Tristram Hunt, "Special Report: Slavery: The Long Road to Our Historic Sorrow," *The Observer* (November 26, 2006).

6. Baucom, *Specters of the Atlantic*, 8.

7. Ralph Waldo Emerson, *Essays and Lectures*, ed. Joel Porte (New York: Library of America, 1983), 279–280.

8. See Barbara Johnson, *Persons and Things* (Cambridge, Mass.: Harvard University Press, 2008). See also Jonathan Lamb's work on "it-narratives" in the eighteenth century: "Modern Metamorphoses and Disgraceful Tales," *Critical Inquiry* 28, no. 1 (Fall 2001); and "The Crying of Lost Things," *English Literary History* 71, no. 4: 949–968.

9. See Ellen E. Schultz, "Companies Sue Union Retirees to Cut Promised Health Benefits," *Wall Street Journal* (November 10, 2004).

10. http://www.insurance.ca.gov/0100-consumers/0300-public-programs/0200-slavery-era-insur/.

11. For instance, see Prudential Insurance Company of America, *The Documentary History of Insurance: 1000 B.C.–1875 A.D.* (Newark, N.J.: Prudential Press, 1915); and Daniel Hawthorne, *The Hartford of Hartford: An Insurance Company's Part in a Century and a Half of American History* (New York: Random House, 1960). Lloyd's of London has a particularly rich historiographic bibliography: see, for instance, Hugh Cockerell, *Lloyd's of London: A Portrait* (Homewood, Ill.: Dow Jones–Irwin, 1984); and Antony Brown, *Hazard Unlimited: The Story of Lloyd's of London* (London: Peter Davies, 1973).

12. The database referred to in the text is *The Trans-Atlantic Slave Trade: A Database on CD-ROM*, ed. David Eltis, Stephen D. Behrendt, David Richardson, and Herbert S. Klein (Cambridge: Cambridge University Press, 1999).

13. And residing on the semipublic, shared domain that is the Internet.

14. Herman Melville, *Moby-Dick: or, The Whale* (New York: Modern Library, 2000).

15. This prologue, to my mind, also brilliantly anticipates Walter Benjamin's adaptation of Paul Klee's *Angelus Novus*. For Melville as for Benjamin, the historian/scholar is the angel of history, and with its characterization of "consumptive" "thanklessness," Melville's description rhetorically evokes Klee and Benjamin's trope of fragilely angelic exile and lofty Sisyphean refuge. (*Angelus Novus* even vaguely resembles the sperm whale, with its square head and splay eyes.) Benjamin's strange interpretive optimism, in the face of the ruinous archive of Western history, echoes Melville's comic "sub-sub" grammarian librarian. Benjamin's famous comment on the painting is descriptive and speculative: "There is a painting by Klee called *Angelus Novus*. It shows an angel who seems about to move away from something he stares at. His eyes are wide, his mouth is open, his wings are spread. This is how the angel of history must look. His face is turned toward the past. Where a chain of events appears before *us*, *he* sees one single catastrophe, which keeps piling wreckage upon wreckage and hurls it at his feet. The angel would like to stay, awaken the dead, and make whole what has been smashed. But a storm is blowing from Paradise and has got caught in his wings; it is so strong that the angel can no longer close them. This storm drives him irresistibly into the future to which his back is turned, while the pile of debris before him grows toward the sky. What we call progress is *this* storm." See Walter Benjamin, "On the Concept of History" (1940), *Gesammelte Schriften* (Frankfurt am Main: SuhrkampVerlag, 1974), 1:691–704. In translation: Walter Benjamin, *Selected Writings*, vol. 4: *1938–1940*, trans. Harry Zohn (Cambridge, Mass.: Harvard University Pres, 2003), 392–393.

5. "DEATH BY HIS OWN HAND": ACCOUNTING FOR SUICIDE IN
NINETEENTH-CENTURY LIFE INSURANCE LITIGATION
Susanna L. Blumenthal

I am grateful to Tom Baker, John Carson, Sally Gordon, Tom Green, Dirk
Hartog, Jill Hasday, Daniel Schwartz, Michael Tonry, and Barbara Welke for
their insights and comments on an earlier draft, as well as to the editors of this
volume and the participants at the Amherst conference for which this essay
was originally prepared.

1. *Hudson River Chronicle* (June 28, 1839); *The North American* (Philadelphia) 82 (June 28, 1839), col. D; *New-York Spectator* (Monday, July 1, 1839),
col. E.

2. *Breasted v. Farmers' Loan and Trust Co.*, 4 Hill 73 75 (1843); *Breasted v.
Farmers' Loan and Trust Co.*, 8 N.Y. (4 Seld.) 299 (1853).

3. *Breasted v. Farmers' Loan and Trust Co.*, 8 N.Y. (4 Seld.) 299–307 (1853).

4. Ibid., at 309–310.

5. See, e.g., *Mutual Life Ins. Co. of N.Y. v. Hayward*, 34 S.W. 801, 804
(1899); *Spruill v. Northwestern Mut. Life Ins. Co.*, 120 N.C. 141, 141 (1897).
Charges given at trial likewise reflected concerns about juror bias. See, e.g.,
Connecticut. Mut. Life Ins. Co. v. Groom, 86 Pa. 92, 93 (1878). The perception
that jurors (and courts more generally) favored plaintiffs in this sort of insurance litigation was also manifest in professional journals and popular literature. See, e.g., George Lawyer, "The Suicide Clause in Life Insurance
Contracts," *Central Law Journal* 52 (1901): 107, 111; C. L. Greene, *The Medical Examination for Life Insurance and Its Associated Clinical Methods* (Philadelphia: Blakiston's Son & Co., 1900), 357; F. H. Cooke, *The Law of Life Insurance*
(New York: Baker, Voorhis, & Co., 1891), 69; Charles Burke Elliott, "Suicide—Effect Upon a Life Insurance Policy," *Central Law Journal* 21 (1885):
378; J. B. Lewis, *Remarkable Stratagems and Conspiracies: An Authentic Record of
Surprising Attempts to Defraud Insurance Companies* (Baltimore, Md.: James H.
McClellan, 1878), 358–359. Unsurprisingly, the strongest misgivings about
"sympathetic juries" were expressed on the pages of insurance trade journals.
See, e.g., "Fractional Currency," *The Chronicle: A Weekly Journal, Devoted to
the Interests of Insurance, Manufacturers, and Real Estate* (1894): 306, 308; "The
Suicide Clause," *The Insurance Monitor* (March 1872): 216; "Suicide and Dueling," *The Insurance Monitor* (July 1869): 529; "Suicide and Insurance," *The
Insurance Monitor* (July 1869): 531. The extent to which these perceptions were
grounded in reality is more difficult to establish on the basis of surviving
sources, particularly given the murkiness surrounding the settlement practices
of insurance companies. The most that can be said with confidence is that the
vast majority of reported cases were appeals from verdicts favorable to
plaintiffs.

6. Modeled after similar provisions in British life policies, American insurance companies commonly inserted suicide clauses in the policies from the earliest years of their operation. They were often listed along with other policy restrictions relating to travel, occupation, habits (particularly relating to use of alcohol and other drugs), and manner of death. See Sharon Murphy, *Security in an Insecure World* (PhD diss., University of Virginia, 2004), 188; Tom Baker, "On the Genealogy of Moral Hazard," *Texas Law Review* 75 (1996): 237, 252–260. The redrafting of the clauses to include "sane or insane" was clearly done in response to court rulings such as *Breasted*. See, e.g., W. R. Vance, *Handbook of the Law of Life Insurance* (St. Paul: West Publishing, 1904), 522; F. H. Bacon, *A Treatise on the Law of Benefit Societies: And Incidentally of Life Insurance* (St. Louis: F. H. Thomas Law Book Co., 1888), 516–517; William M. Rockel, "Life Insurance—Suicide—Sane or Insane—Expert Evidence," *Central Law Journal* 25 (1887): 81–84; J. W. May, *The Law of Insurance* (Boston: Little, Brown & Co., 1873); G. Bliss, *The Law of Life Insurance* (New York: Baker, Voorhis & Co., 1872), 393–394.

7. See V. A. Rotman Zelizer, *Morals and Markets: The Development of Life Insurance in the United States* (New York: Columbia University Press, 1983); Murphy, *Security in an Insecure World*, 11–12, 262–274. On the broader legal and cultural conditions of success and failure in nineteenth-century America, see, for example, S. A. Sandage, *Born Losers: A History of Failure in America* (Cambridge, Mass.: Harvard University Press, 2005); J. Lears, *Something for Nothing: Luck in America* (New York: Penguin, 2003); B. H. Mann, *Republic of Debtors: Bankruptcy in the Age of American Independence* (Cambridge, Mass.: Harvard University Press, 2002); E. J. Balleisen, *Navigating Failure: Bankruptcy and Commercial Society in Antebellum America* (Chapel Hill: University of North Carolina Press, 2001); J. Hilkey, *Character Is Capital: Success Manuals and Manhood in Gilded Age America* (Chapel Hill: University of North Carolina Press, 1997).

8. See Michael MacDonald, "The Medicalization of Suicide in England: Laymen, Physicians, and Cultural Change, 1500–1870," *Milbank Quarterly* 67 (1989): 69–91.

9. See generally Thomas J. Marzen et al., "Suicide: A Constitutional Right?" *Duquesne Law Review* 24 (1985): 1, 98–100.

10. See Richard Bell, "Do Not Despair: The Cultural Significance of Suicide in America, 1780–1840" (diss., Harvard University, 2006); see also H. I. Kushner, *Self-Destruction in the Promised Land: A Psychocultural Biology of American Suicide* (New Brunswick, N.J.: Rutgers University Press, 1989), 13–61. While both Bell and Kushner speak in terms of the secularization (and accompanying medicalization and decriminalization) of suicide across the nineteenth century, the historical analysis offered in this essay is more closely aligned

with the recent work of historians of early modern and modern Europe, who have instead cast the process as one of "hybridization." On these accounts, "the moral explanation of suicide" was not wholly displaced by "a medical model, which explained suicide as the product of physical, often psychological problems," nor did the rise of the latter spell the end of state interest in regulating the phenomenon of self-killing. To the contrary, they show that these various approaches existed together to the end of the nineteenth century. See Róisín Healy, "Suicide in Early Modern and Modern Europe," *Historical Journal* 49 (2006): 903–919.

11. The number of litigated cases involving suicide clauses across the nineteenth century cannot be precisely determined, given how many were settled before reaching the court of last resort; the number of reported appellate cases approaches two hundred. However, it was not so much the volume of litigation as the "irreconcilable" nature of the judicial conflict that excited concern among members of the bench and bar, "the prospect of agreement" seemingly growing ever more unlikely as the century came to a close. Ward B. Coe, "The Suicide Clause in Life Policies," *Central Law Journal* 41 (1895): 272. For similar critical appraisals of the doctrinal landscape, see, e.g., "Suicide and Life Insurance," *Albany Law Journal* 4 (1871): 53–55; "Insanity and Suicide," *The Independent* 24 (June 9, 1881); J. F. Kelly, "The Effect of Self-Destruction in Life Insurance," *American Law Journal* 1 (1884): 324, 327; "Suicide of Insurance Policy-Holder," *Virginia Law Review* 13 (1889): 553, 556 (reprint from *New York Law Journal*); Lawyer, "The Suicide Clause," 107–108.

12. Morton Keller, "The Judicial System and the Law of Life Insurance, 1888–1910," *Business History Review* 35 (1961): 317, 335.

13. Here it is instructive to consider, by comparison, the figures of the (male) beggar, (female) prostitute, and (male) bankrupt, as drawn by legal professionals and reformers; while the first was cast as a moral failure, the second was more often treated as a victim of social and economic circumstances, and the third was likewise understood to have suffered from the ill effects of market failure rather than his own character flaws. On beggars and prostitutes, see A. D. Stanley, *From Bondage to Contract: Wage Labor, Marriage, and the Market in the Age of Slave Emancipation* (Cambridge: Cambridge University Press, 1998), 98–137, 218–263; on bankrupts, see John Fabian Witt, "Narrating Bankruptcy/Narrating Risk," *Northwestern Law Review* 98 (2003): 303.

14. See generally M. Grossberg, "Institutionalizing Masculinity: The Law as a Masculine Profession," in *Meanings for Manhood: Constructions of Masculinity in Victorian America*, ed. Mark C. Carnes and Clyde Griffin (Chicago: University of Chicago Press, 1990); see also E. A. Rotundo, *American Manhood: Transformations in Masculinity from the Revolution to the Modern Era* (New York: Basic Books, 1993), 178–185; Sandage, *Born Losers*; Balleisen, *Navigating Failure*; Hilkey, *Character Is Capital*.

15. For a comprehensive survey of this literature, construing these printed sources as evidence of "the unparalleled cultural currency of suicide in the early republic." See Bell, "Do Not Despair," 23, 53–124.

16. See, e.g., "On Suicide," *Worcester Magazine* (May 1786): 5, 61. On the history of arguments for and against suicide, see G. Minois, *History of Suicide: Voluntary Death in Western Culture*, trans. Lydia Cochrane (Baltimore, Md.: The John Hopkins University Press, 1999); O. Anderson, *Suicide in Victorian and Edwardian England* (Oxford: Oxford University Press, 1987); J. R. Watt, ed., *From Sin to Insanity: Suicide in Early Modern Europe* (Ithaca, N.Y.: Cornell University Press, 2004); A. Murray, *Suicide in the Middle Ages* (Oxford: Oxford University Press 1999, 2000). For works focusing on the peculiar contours of the debates throughout eighteenth-century Europe, see M. MacDonald and T. R. Murphy, *Sleepless Souls, Suicide in Early Modern Europe* (Oxford: Oxford University Press, 1990), 144–216; S. E. Sprott, *The English Debate on Suicide from Donne to Hume* (Chicago: Open Court Press, 1961); J. McManners, *Death and the Enlightenment: Changing Attitudes to Death Among Christians and Unbelievers in Eighteenth-Century France* (Oxford: Oxford University Press, 1981); Lester G. Crocker, "The Discussion of Suicide in the Eighteenth Century," *Journal of the History of Ideas* 13 (1952): 47–72.

17. "Suicide," *Weekly Recorder* (January 17, 1818): 4, 24.

18. S. Miller, *The Guilt, Folly, and Sources of Suicide: Two Discourses* (New York: T. & J. Swords, 1805).

19. Bell, "Do Not Despair," 53–124 (intriguingly describing this as an assertion of eminent domain over the bodies of would-be suicides).

20. Henri Bracton, *On the Laws and Customs of England*, trans. S. Thorne (1968), 2:423.

21. See, e.g., Edmund Wingate, *Justice Revived: Being the Whole Office of a Country Justice of the Peace* (1661), 61 (declaring "he is *felo de se* that doth destroy himself out of premeditated hatred against his own life, or out of a humour to destroy himself" and excluding idiots and lunatics from this class of persons). It is worth noting in this regard that penal sanctions were originally imposed only on sane suicides seeking to escape the forfeiture that accompanied criminal conviction in a given case; over time, this punishment scheme was extended to all sane suicides, and such a scheme appears to have been in place by the thirteenth century. See Roger D. Groot, "When Suicide Became a Felony," *Journal of Legal History* 21 (2000): 1–20; see also Gwen Seabourne and Alice Seabourne, "The Law on Suicide in Medieval England," *Journal of Legal History* 21 (2000): 21–48; Sara Butler, "Degrees of Culpability: Suicide Verdicts, Mercy, and the Jury in Medieval England," *Journal of Medieval and Early Modern Studies* 36 (2006): 263–290.

22. The history of the legal treatment of suicide in America has yet to be written; nothing comparable to the studies of early modern and modern England exists with respect to the British American colonies or the United States.

The two most extensive studies rely primarily on printed sources. See Burgess-Jackson, "The Legal Status of Suicide in Early America," 57, 60–66; Marzen et al., "Suicide: A Constitutional Right?" 1, 63–100. The only monograph devoted to the subject of suicide in America does analyze a limited set of coroners' inquests and draws additional evidence about the prosecution of suicide from diaries, sermons, and other manuscript sources. See Kushner, *Self-Destruction in the Promised Land*, 21–34. Moreover, the legal rules and practices in cases of suicide are treated in some depth in Roger Lane's valuable study *Violent Death and the City: Suicide, Accident, and Murder in Nineteenth-Century Philadelphia* (1999) and also throughout Richard Bell's very fine dissertation "Do Not Despair." Finally, it should be added that Terri Snyder is at work on a full-length study of the history of self-murder in the early British North American and Caribbean colonies; some of her preliminary findings with respect to colonial Virginia are presented in Terri Snyder, "What Historians Talk About When They Talk About Suicide: The View from Early Modern British North America," *History Compass* 5 (2007): 2.

23. *The Body of Liberties* (1641) and *Colonial Laws of Massachusetts*, both reprinted in John Noble, "Suicide in Massachusetts," *Proceedings of the Massachusetts Historical Society* 36 (December 1902): 524, 526. This penalty was applied even in cases of melancholy, which was considered "*prima facie* evidence of intention and thus of felony." See Kushner, *Self-Destruction in the Promised Land*, 25. Kushner suggests that Massachusetts was an outlier in this respect, as compared with other colonies as well as England.

24. John Cushing, ed., *The Earliest Printed Laws of Pennsylvania, 1681–1713* (Wilmington, Del., 1978), 206.

25. John Cushing, ed., *The Earliest Acts and Laws of the Colony of Rhode Island and Providence Plantations, 1647–1719* (Wilmington, Del.: 1977): 17, 59.

26. MacDonald and Murphy, *Sleepless Souls*; Sara M. Butler, "Cultures of Suicide? Suicide Verdicts and the 'Community' in Thirteenth- and Fourteenth-Century England," *Historian* 69 (2007): 427–449; Healy, "Suicide," 908–918; Snyder, "What Historians Talk About," 661–668.

27. On the nature and limitations of the sources, see Snyder, "What Historians Talk About," 660. The ambiguity of the verdicts of coroners' juries in suicide cases is especially well documented in Butler, "Degrees of Culpability," 271–277 (finding that medieval jurors were seemingly "very comfortable portraying a self-killing simultaneously as the outcome of both an insane and a criminal mind" and submitting that they "may have employed a complex understanding of insanity far different from what we might expect today"); cf. H. Brewer, *By Birth or Consent: Children, Law, and the Anglo-American Revolution in Authority* (Chapel Hill: University of North Carolina Press, 2005) (showing similar complexity in the treatment of age and criminal liability and

concluding that "intent had a different meaning and weight" in early modern England and America than it does today).

28. MacDonald and Murphy, *Sleepless Souls*, 109–143 (documenting change in proportion of *non compos mentis* verdicts over time, from under 8 percent in 1660 to over 90 percent by 1800); see also Bell, "Do Not Despair," 35–36 (discussing similar findings in a single American jurisdiction across the eighteenth and early nineteenth centuries); Snyder, "Talk About Suicide," 663–668 (same).

29. MacDonald and Murphy, *Sleepless Souls*, 114–132; cf. Anderson, *Suicide*, 220 (suggesting that the rarity of verdicts might have been "more of a side-effect of the defeat of the Crown by localism and private property than a consequence of altered religious or ethical attitudes towards the act of suicide" and that the man most likely to be judged guilty of this offense "was property-less or a stranger"); Snyder, "What Historians Talk About," 662–665 (noting disparities in punishments for suicide and observing that "at the same time that post-mortem punishments were declining among free populations, masters and overseers were remarkably quick to mutilate and display the corpses of their suicidal slaves"); Bell, "Do Not Despair," 201–203, 283–284 (providing evidence of the masters' punishments of suicidal slaves and documenting the relative ease with which jurors returned *felo de se* verdicts in cases where suicide occurred after commission of a homicide—familicide in particular—or while offender was imprisoned awaiting trial or execution).

30. See Michael MacDonald, "The Medicalization of Suicide," 85–86 (observing that physicians were "riding in the caboose of change, not driving its engine," as their ideas were most often pressed by laymen arguing for mercy in suicide cases); cf. MacDonald and Murphy, *Sleepless Souls*, 140 (revising this assessment insofar as medical men are now found "in seats near the front of the train," with lawyers "in the brake-van"). As noted above, the secularization thesis has been refined by more recent scholarship, which emphasizes the "protracted and contested" nature of turn toward leniency; these studies find greater ambivalence on the part of both clerical authorities and Enlightenment *philosophes* than previously recognized. Healy, "Suicide," 907–909.

31. William Blackstone, *Commentaries on the Laws of England* (1769), 4:189. In this, Blackstone was repeating the complaints of Matthew Hale. See Matthew Hale, *Historia Placitorum Coronae* (1700).

32. They were abolished by statute, along with those applying to treason and felony in general. Although it had by this time become "common for forfeited chattels to be returned by the Crown . . . forfeiture proceedings were not completely a dead letter." Anderson, *Suicide*, 220; cf. B. Gates, *Victorian Suicide: Mad Crimes and Sad Histories* (Princeton, N.J.: Princeton University Press, 1988), 6–7 (indicating that forfeiture was "generally waived by the

Crown in cases in which a suicide was not committed in order to avoid conviction for another felony, and temporary insanity was returned as a verdict far more often than *felo de se*").

33. By an 1823 enactment, Parliament outlawed ignominious burial but nonetheless required that the body of the suicide be buried privately in any churchyard or cemetery between the hours of nine and twelve at night without any religious rites. This remained the law until 1882, when Parliament removed such constraints on the burial of the suicide. Anderson, *Suicide*, 221.

34. On criminal law reform in post-revolutionary America, see Brewer, *By Birth or Consent*, 218–229; M. Meranze, *Laboratories of Virtue: Punishment, Revolution, and Authority in Philadelphia, 1760–1835* (Chapel Hill: University of North Carolina Press, 1996); L. P. Masur, *Rites of Execution: Capital Punishment and the Transformation of America* (Oxford: Oxford University Press, 1989), 54–72; S. Banner, *The Death Penalty: An American History* (Cambridge, Mass.: Harvard University Press, 2002), 88–111; Kathryn Preyer, "Crime, Criminal Law, and Reform in Post-Revolutionary Virginia," *Law and History Review* 1 (1983): 53–85; Christopher Adamson, "Wrath and Redemption: Protestant Theology and Penal Practice in the Early American Republic," *Criminal Justice History* 13 (1992): 75–111; on forfeiture in particular, see L. Levy, *A License to Steal: The Forfeiture of Property* (Chapel Hill: University of North Carolina Press, 1996).

35. Thomas Jefferson, "A Bill for Proportioning Crimes and Punishments in Cases Heretofore Capital," reprinted in Thomas Jefferson Randolph, ed., *Memoir, Correspondence, and Miscellanies: From the Papers of Thomas Jefferson* (Charlottesville, Va.: F. Carr & Co., 1829), 121–122.

36. Ibid. See also Zephaniah Swift, *A System of Laws of the State of Connecticut* (1796), 304; William Waller Hening, *The New Virginia Justice* (1820), 102, 312; Edward Livingston, *System of Penal Law for the United States of America* (1828), 121–122.

37. Swift, *System of Laws*, 304.

38. Ibid. Some confidently asserted that the "English malady" was unlikely to afflict Americans; perhaps the most famous such example was Thomas Jefferson's boast to the Comte de Volney in 1805: "it is our cloudless sky which has eradicated from our constitutions all disposition to hang ourselves, which we might otherwise have inherited from our English ancestors." See Bell, "Do Not Despair," 34–35, n. 64.

39. Swift, *System of Laws*, 304.

40. Jefferson, "Bill," 122. Here he was essentially paraphrasing Beccaria's *On Crime and Punishment*, though it should be noted that the Italian philosopher was not the first to draw such an analogy. See Minois, *History of Suicide*, 189 (referencing a 1695 treatise generally suggesting emigration and suicide

are indistinguishable). For an even stronger defense of suicide on this basis, see M. Dawes, *An Essay on Crimes and Punishments* (London, 1782), 70–74 (likening suicide to emigration and suggesting that the voluntary death offended neither divine nor human law, because "it is the Almighty that wills and suffers him to seek it by his own hands").

41. Jefferson, "Bill," 122.

42. Kushner, *Self-Destruction in the Promised Land*, 27–34; Snyder, "What Historians Talk About," 660.

43. Maryland and New Jersey did so by constitutional provision in 1776; North Carolina, New Hampshire, and Delaware followed in 1778, 1783, and 1792, respectively. Rhode Island accomplished the same by statute in 1798. Virginia abolished forfeiture for all felonies but suicide in 1789; only in 1811 was the sanction removed in the case of suicide, though the lag appears to have been the result of a technical oversight. Massachusetts reaffirmed the abolition of forfeiture in 1776 but did not abolish ignominious burial until 1825. Marzen et al., "Suicide: A Constitutional Right?" 148–242; Burgess-Jackson, "The Legal Status of Suicide in Early America," 63–67; Bell, "Do Not Despair", 30–32.

44. For a general overview of the doctrine as it stood in the middle of the nineteenth century, see Joel Bishop, *Commentaries on the Criminal Law* (Boston, 1856), 1:333 (observing that while the offense of suicide was "practically unknown in the United States . . . we recognize the act of self-destruction as criminal, when the opportunity of doing so indirectly arises"); ibid., 390–391 (tracing the outlines of accomplice liability); see also Joel Bishop, *Commentaries on the Criminal Law* (Boston, 1882), 2:665–666 (demonstrating the extent to which "there are with us collateral offences based on the idea that self-murder is a common-law felony" or otherwise established by statute, which impose liability for attempting suicide or assisting another in the same).

45. The imposition of liability in such cases required some twisting of logic and overcoming of technical difficulties on the part of the courts. See R. W. Withers, "Status of Suicide as a Crime," *Virginia Law Register* 19 (1914): 641. For a useful state-by-state survey of reported cases across the nineteenth century, see Marzen et al., "Suicide: A Constitutional Right?" 71–100, 148–242. The incidence and punishment of these offenses is difficult to reconstruct from surviving sources, though commentaries from the era suggest the laws were not stringently enforced. See, e.g., G. Styles, "Suicide and Its Increase," *American Journal of Insanity* 57 (1900): 97, 99.

46. See Bell, "Do Not Despair," 53–85 (documenting the "unprecedented popularity in *Werther* and its imitators" in the early republic as well as the anxiety it provoked on the part of moralists, who feared that the words and deeds would prove contagious).

47. On the decline of supernatural explanations for the incidence of insanity and suicide, see M. A. Jimenez, *Changing Faces of Madness: Early American Attitudes and Treatment of the Insane* (Hanover, N.H.: Brandeis University Press, 1987), 24–30; see also Kushner, *Self-Destruction*, 28–30, 38–39.

48. See D. Rothman, *The Discovery of the Asylum: Social Order and Disorder in the New Republic* (New Brunswick, N.J.: Rutgers University Press, 1979); G. Grob, *Mental Institutions in America: Social Policy to 1875* (New York: The Free Press, 1973); N. Dain, *Concepts of Insanity in the United States, 1789–1865* (New Brunswick, N.J.: Rutgers University Press, 1964).

49. Casting himself as a pioneer in this regard was the Victorian alienist Forbes Winslow, who presented his 1840 study *The Anatomy of Suicide* as "a branch of medical and moral philosophy" and aimed to show that "the disposition to commit self-destruction is, to a great extent, amenable to those principles which regulate our treatment of ordinary disease; and that, to a degree more than is generally supposed, it originates in the derangement of the brain and abdominal viscera." See F. Winslow, *The Anatomy of Suicide* (London, 1840), v–vii. For other midcentury contributions to this growing literature, see, e.g., C. H. Nichols, "Statistics of Suicides," *American Journal of Insanity* 4 (1848): 247–253; George Cook, "Statistics of Suicides," *American Journal of Insanity* 4 (1849): 303–310. For an overview of the emergence of the discipline of medical jurisprudence, see J. Mohr, *Doctors and the Law: Medical Jurisprudence in Nineteenth-Century America* (Oxford: Oxford University Press, 1993). On the development of a science of statistics, see T. Porter, *The Rise of Statistical Thinking, 1820–1900* (Princeton, N.J.: Princeton University Press, 1986); I. Hacking, *The Taming of Chance* (Cambridge: Cambridge University Press, 1990); L. J. Daston, "Rational Individuals Versus Laws of Society: From Probability to Statistics," in *The Probabilistic Revolution: Ideas in History*, ed. L. Krüger et al. (Cambridge, Mass.: The MIT Press, 1987): 1:295–304.

50. Cook, "Statistics," 308.

51. Winslow, *Anatomy*, 334–339. However, some alienists did advocate the imposition of criminal penalties for certain vices—most commonly gambling and drunkenness—with the expectation that this would diminish the number of suicides. Many also recommended legal restraints on the press, on the theory that explicit reports of suicide encouraged imitators. See Bell, *Do Not Despair*, 53–124, 376–453.

52. See, e.g., *State v. Stark*, 32 S.C.L. 479 (1847).

53. See, e.g., *Duffield v. Morris'Ex'r* 2 Harr. 375, 2 Del. 375 (1838); *McElwee v. Ferguson*, 43 Md. 479 (1876).

54. I. Ray, *The Medical Jurisprudence of Insanity* (1838), 372–385. For similar reasoning, see, e.g., Taylor, *Medical Jurisprudence*, 519 (observing that the apparent motives for suicide "appear insufficient to the minds of most men"

and questioning "what known motive" there was "sufficient to account for parricide, infanticide, or any other crime of a horrible nature"; concluding that "we must allow either that all crime is the offspring of insanity, or that suicide is occasionally the deliberate act of a sane person.")

55. F. Wharton and M. Stille, *A Treatise on Medical Jurisprudence* (Philadelphia: Kay & Brother, 1855) (quoting the Scottish physician/philosopher John Abercrombie); see also Ray, *Medical Jurisprudence*, 376–377.

56. Ray, *Medical Jurisprudence*, 377–378.

57. See J. Eigen, *Witnessing Insanity: Madness and Mad-Doctors in the English Court* (New Haven, Conn.: Yale University Press, 1995).

58. See Mohr, *Doctors and the Law*, 140–163.

59. Wharton and Stille, *Medical Jurisprudence*, 149; J. J. Elwell, *A Medico-Legal Treatise on Malpractice and Medical Evidence* (New York: J. S. Voorhies, 1860); see generally Susanna L. Blumenthal, "Mind of the Moral Agent: Scottish Common Sense and the Problem of Responsibility in Nineteenth-Century American Law," *Law and History Review* 26 (2008): 99–159. On parallel developments in nineteenth-century England, see R. Smith, *Trial by Medicine: Insanity and Responsibility in Victorian Trials* (Edinburgh: Edinburgh University Press, 1981); M. J. Wiener, *Reconstructing the Criminal: Culture, Law, and Policy in England, 1830–1914* (Cambridge: Cambridge University Press, 1990).

60. In jury charges, "good and evil" were "used interchangeably and synonymously" with "right and wrong." See Anthony Platt and Bernard L. Diamond, "The Origins of the 'Right and Wrong' Test of Criminal Responsibility in the United States: An Historical Survey," *California Law Review* 54 (1966): 1227, 1237. For a case history of *McNaughten*, see R. Moran, *Knowing Right from Wrong: The Insanity Defense of Daniel McNaughten* (New York: The Free Press, 1981).

61. See, e.g., *Andersen v. State*, 43 Conn. 514, 523 (1876).

62. *Duffield v. Morris' Ex'r*, 2 Harr. 375, 2 Del. 375, 382 (1838).

63. *Brooks v. Barrett*, 7 Pick. 94, 24 Mass. 94, 101 (1828); see also *Pettitt's Ex'rs v. Pettitt*, 23 Tenn. 191, 193 (TN 1843); see generally Henry F. Buswell, *The Law of Insanity* (Boston: Little, Brown & Co., 1885), 240.

64. G. Clark, *Betting on Lives: The Culture of Life Insurance in England, 1695–1775* (Manchester: Manchester University Press, 1999); see also Zelizer, *Morals and Markets*, 27–39, 69–72; Murphy, *Security in an Insecure World*, 146–150. Despite the passage of the Gambling Act, life policies were commonly auctioned to raise funds for old, infirm, and/or financially strapped policyholders. Moreover, insurers and courts came to regard the Gambling Act as requiring only that the insurable interest exist at the time the policy was issued and not limiting the ability of the policyholder to assign it to another party without any such interest. Murphy, *Security in an Insecure World*, 148–150.

65. The 1815 Massachusetts case of *Lord v. Dall* appears to be the first reported American decision addressing the question of whether "a policy of assurance upon a life" was an enforceable contract; answering in the affirmative, Judge Parker considered it "not a little singular" that the practice was outlawed in "commercial nations of Europe" such as France, reputedly on the grounds that "it is indecorous to set a price upon the life of man, and especially a *freeman*," even though "freedom has never been known to exist" in such places, while this concern had "never . . . been thought of in *England*, which for several centuries has been the country of established and regulated liberty." *Lord v. Dall*, 12 Mass. 115, 117 (1815). Antebellum courts split on the question of whether the purchaser of a policy had to demonstrate the existence of an "insurable interest" for the policy to be legally enforceable at common law, in the absence of any statutory prohibition. Compare *Ruse v. Mutual Ben. Life Ins. Co.*, 23 N.Y. 516, 526 (1861) (insurable interest required at common law on public policy grounds, the court opining that "policies without interest, upon lives, are more pernicious and dangerous than any other class of wager policies; because temptations to tamper with life are more mischievous than incitements to mere pecuniary frauds") with *Trenton Mut. Life & Fire Ins. Co. v. Johnson*, 24 N.J.L. 576, 584 (1854) (finding no such requirement at common law and insisting that "the danger, if any exists, would apply with great, although not with equal force, to policies where there is an interest, as well as to those where there is none"). Judicial disputations regarding the legality of "wagering life policies" were bound up with conflicts about whether to treat the agreements as contracts of indemnity or valued policies. See George D. Harris, "Insurable Interest in the Life of a Person," *Central Law Journal* 52 (1901): 381, 386. In the 1850s and 1860s, most states moved to enforce the insurable interest by statute. See Murphy, *Security in an Insecure World*, 154.

66. Sharon Murphy persuasively suggests that the supposed surge in the 1840s was not as sudden as previous historians have suggested and that the increase in sales was likely due to legislative reforms in the 1840s that made it easier for married women to purchase or otherwise benefit from life insurance policies on their own account. Like the wrongful-death statutes that John Witt has described, this legislation was primarily intended to ensure that widows and orphans were insulated against the loss of support accompanying the death of the husband/provider. The reformed statutes thus served to reflect and reinforce the broader cultural expectations documented by Witt, namely that "manly and upstanding men" were, by definition, self-reliant—that they did not look to their wives or children as sources of financial support. John Fabian Witt, "From Loss of Services to Loss of Support: The Wrongful Death Statutes, the Origins of Modern Tort Law, and the Making of the Nineteenth-Century Family," *Law and Social Inquiry* 25 (2000): 717–755. This

way of thinking about the responsible provider was also much in evidence in trade journals and the popular press concerning the insurance business; while "a money value" could and should be placed on "the lives of men in their capacities as husbands . . . because man is the money-getting power upon which the woman is dependent. . . . The husband who can deliberately set a money value upon his wife, is so far destitute not only of affection for her, but of respect for himself, has so much greed and so little manhood. . . . To him she is but a chattel . . . as such she is insured." The insurance of children was likewise considered objectionable, on account of the prevailing belief that "no manly man and no womanly woman should be ready to say that their infants have pecuniary value." In Zelizer, *Morals and Markets*, 62–63n.

67. See Zelizer, *Morals and Markets*, 73–77, 79–85; Murphy, *Security in an Insecure World*, 17–24, 82–84, 173–174, 268.

68. See *Hunt Merchant's Magazine* (February 1843): 1; *Hunt Merchant's Magazine* (March 1843): 11, 15.

69. Zelizer, *Morals and Markets*, 77–79, 94–101; see also O. J. Stalson, *Marketing Life Insurance* (Cambridge, Mass.: Harvard University Press, 1969), 3–216.

70. Murphy, *Security in an Insecure World*, 85–143.

71. Horace Binney's *Address, Centennial Meeting of the Philadelphia Contributorship for the Insurance of Houses from Loss by Fire* (Philadelphia, 1852), 58. On moral science and its practical applications in the nineteenth century, see Wiener, *Reconstructing the Criminal*, 163–164; see also Lorraine J. Daston, "Rational Individuals Versus Laws of Society: From Probability to Statistics," in *The Probabilistic Revolution: Ideas in History*, ed. L. Krüger et al. (Cambridge, Mass.: The MIT Press, 1987), 1:295–304; S. M. Stigler, *The History of Statistics: The Measurement of Uncertainty Before 1900* (Cambridge, Mass.: Harvard University Press, 1986); G. Gigerenzer et al., *The Empire of Chance: How Probability Changed Science and Everyday Life* (Cambridge University Press, 1989); I. Hacking, *The Emergence of Probability* (Cambridge: Cambridge University Press, 1975); I. Hacking, *The Taming of Chance* (Cambridge: Cambridge University Press, 1990); Porter, *The Rise of Statistical Thinking*; M. Norton Wise, ed., *The Values of Precision* (Princeton, N.J.: Princeton University Press, 1995).

72. W. Shrady, *The Law in Reference to Suicide and Intemperance in Life Insurance* (New York: C. C. Hine, 1869), 3.

73. Intimate friends and respectable community members were often questioned as well. Among the factors typically considered were climate, disease, environment of the home and places to which applicants intended to travel, occupation, gender, race, marital status, family and personal health history, susceptibility to disease, and alcohol consumption. Murphy, *Security in an Insecure World*, 85–143.

74. Quoted in Tom Baker, "Insuring Morality," *Economy and Society* 29 (2000): 559, 562. The quotation is from the 1867 edition of the Aetna Guide to Fire Insurance.

75. See Zelizer, *Morals and Markets*, 71–72. These rules were considerably relaxed in England by the mid-nineteenth century. Murphy, *Security in an Insecure World*, 145–148.

76. In particular, there was conflicting judicial authority on the question of whether the interest needed to be pecuniary or if it could be founded upon "dependence or natural affection." Guy C. H. Corliss, "Insurable Interest," *Albany Law Journal* 32 (1885): 385–387; see also Harris, "Insurable Interest," 381–384. The general trend in American jurisdictions, however, seemed to be in the direction of "increasing liberality," with courts gradually expanding the sorts of relationships giving rise to insurable interest. Harris, "Insurable Interest," 381–382; see also E. H. East, "Life Insurance Decisions," *Southern Law Review* o.s. 1 (1872): 595, 599; Murphy, *Security in an Insecure World*, 168–170. Moreover, it was undisputed that each individual had an insurable interest in his own life, and most jurisdictions held that he was free to take out and make a policy on his own life payable to anyone he chose. Corliss, "Insurable Interest," 388; but see Harris, "Insurable Interest," 384–386 (noting scattered rulings to the contrary); see generally Murphy, *Security in an Insecure World*, 170–172. At bottom, one commentator suggested, the reason to require an insurable interest was not because the insurance contract was one of indemnity but rather because insurers and courts wanted to "prevent its use for gambling purposes"—especially on the part of those who had no interest in the continuance of the life insured to counterbalance the interest in his death created by the contract. Erskine Hazard Dickson, "Insurable Interest in Life," *American Law Register* 44 (1896): 65, 78, 87.

77. Murphy, *Security in an Insecure World*, 151–156.

78. For a sample policy, see, e.g., C. C. Bonney, *A Summary of the Law of Marine, Fire, and Life Insurance* (Chicago: E. B. Meyers & Chandler, 1865); cf. C. D. Hughes, *A Treatise on the Law Relating to Insurance* (New York: O. Halsted, Collins and Hannay and Gould and Banks, 1833) (suggesting such exclusions were not typically found in policies taken out on the life of another).

79. For a typical expression of such aims, see, e.g., "Suicide and Dueling," *Insurance Monitor* (July 1869): 529.

80. Murphy, *Security in an Insecure World*, 180 (quoting *Insurance Monitor*).

81. Ibid., 197 (quoting *Insurance Monitor*).

82. Ibid., 145, 188–197; but see Keller, "The Judicial System," 187–188 (indicating that commercial insurers, particularly the larger ones, did contest suits to a judicial conclusion and that rates were on the rise in the last decades of the nineteenth century, and seeing this as congruent with "their aggressive marketing and investment performance").

83. For statistics on litigation rates, see "The Litigiousness of Life Companies," *Insurance Monitor* 485 (October 1879). While reliable estimates are not easily extracted from surviving sources, insurers regularly aired worries about gaining a reputation for litigiousness in trade journals, weighing the costs and benefits of inserting incontestability clauses in their policies. See, e.g., "The Two Sides of the Indisputability Question," *Insurance Monitor* (August 1879), 396–397.

84. Zelizer, *Morals and Markets*, 109.

85. John M. Wilder, *The Law of Insurance* (Boston: Little Brown and Company, 1891); see also Coe, "The Suicide Clause" (observing that the exclusion clause contains less than two dozen words and the reported cases would "probably not number much more than one hundred in all, yet it would be difficult to find any legal nut that has been cracked in so many different ways").

86. *Borradaile v. Hunter*, 5 Man. & G. 639, 134 Eng. Rep. 715 (1843) (case ultimately compromised); *Clift v. Schwabe*, 3 C.B. 437 (1846); but see *Bayley v. Alexander*, East's Notes, 79; *Morley's India Dig.* 1:362, cited in Coe, "The Suicide Clause," 269 (1818 Bengal case holding that suicide must be understood in the criminal sense and imposing liability on insurer on account of the insanity of the insured at the time of his death).

87. See generally Charles John Bunyon, *A Treatise Upon the Law of Life Assurance* (London: Wildy and Sons, 1854): 69–72.

88. *Borradaile*, 5 Man. & G. at 658–660 (J. Erskine); 664 (J. Coltman); *Clift*, 3 C. B. at 462 (B. Rolfe); 466–467 (J. Patteson).

89. *Borradaile*, 5 Man. & G. at 665–669 (C. J. Tindal, dissenting); *Clift*, 3 C.B. at 457–660 (J. Wightman, dissenting); 472–480 (C. B. Pollock, dissenting).

90. *Clift*, 3 C.B. at 450–451, 454–456.

91. *Clift*, 3 C.B. at 451. Put differently, the counselor maintained that "if the act be intentional, though the result of a perverted will, it is still suicide within the meaning of this policy." *Clift*, 3 C.B. at 452.

92. *Clift*, 3 C.B. at 479–480.

93. *Dean v. American Mutual Live Ins. Co.*, 86 Mass. 96–100 (1862); see also *Gay v. Union Mut. Life Ins. Co.*, 9 Blatchf. 142, 10 F. Cas. 114, 115 (1871); *Nimick v. Mutual Life Ins. Co.*, 3 Brewst. 502, 18 F. Cas. 247, 248 (1871); *Equitable Life Ins. Co. v. Paterson*, 41 Ga. 338, 338 (1870); *Cooper v. Mass. Life Ins. Co.*, 102 Mass. 227, 228 (1869).

94. On this practice, see J. K. Angell, *A Treatise on the Law of Fire and Life Insurance* (Boston: Little & Brown, 1854), 365 (noting that the question of insurable interest can arise where the policy is taken out for the benefit of the father, but that courts do permit a father, wishing to give property to his son,

to make an insurance on his son's life, in his [the son's] name, not for his [the father's] own benefit but for the benefit of his son).

95. *Eastabrook v. Union Mut. Life Ins. Co.*, 54 Me. 224–230 (1866) (J. Kent, dissenting without a written opinion).

96. Ibid., at 227–229; see also *Phadenhauer v. Germania Life Ins. Co.*, 54 Tenn. (7 Heisk) 567 (1872).

97. *St. Louis Mutual Life Insurance Company v. Graves*, 6 Bush 268, 279–281 (1869).

98. *Graves*, 6 Bush 268 at 269–271; 276–277; 288; see also *Phadenhauer*, 54 Tenn. 567 at 570 (court accepting a plea of *moral* insanity).

99. *Smith v. Commonwealth* DUV.224 (1864).

100. *Graves*, 6 Bush 268 at 281–283; 289–290. The formulation here was drawn word for word from *Dean*. Despite their differences, the judges on both sides of the issue found grounds in the record warranting a new trial.

101. *Graves*, 6 Bush 268 at 281–283; 289–290.

102. See, e.g., G. Bliss Jr., *Law of Life Insurance* (New York: Baker, Voorhis & Co., 1874), 372–424.

103. "Current Topics," *Albany Law Journal* 3 (1871): 8, 9.

104. "Proceedings of the American Association of Medical Superintendents," *American Journal of Insanity* (1869): 258–264; "Is Suicide a Sign of Insanity?" *Medical and Surgical Reporter* 26 (June 22, 1872): 568; John Ordronaux, "On Suicide," *American Journal of Insanity* (1864): 371, 373.

105. See, e.g., "The Life Insurance Business: Why the Suicide Clause Is Inserted in Policies—Their Duty to Resist Unjust Claims," *New York Tribune* (September 1, 1875): 2; W. H. Gray, "Life Insurance Companies Accessories to Suicide," *Chicago Daily Tribune* (January 16, 1897): 14.

106. See, e.g., "Suicide and Life Insurance," *Albany Law Journal* (August 19, 1871): 53; "Suicide and Insurance," *New York Tribune* (May 24, 1884): 4.

107. "The Suicide Clause in Life Insurance," *Independent* (February 23, 1871): 8.

108. *Life Insurance Company v. Terry*, 82 U.S. 580 (1872).

109. Ibid., at 580–582; 589; *Terry v. Life Ins. Co.*, 1 Dill. 403, 403, 23 F. Case. 856, 856 (1871). No evidence was offered by either side "touching the conduct of the wife, or the ground or reasonableness of the suspicions of the deceased as to her character." Ibid. The lawyer for the defendant offered background information on this score in a letter to the editor after he lost his case; this letter insinuated that the wife remarried with unseemly haste and further represented that the coroner's jury had adjudged the insured's cause of death to have been "by means of corrosive poison administered *feloniously* by himself." O. H. Palmer, "Suicide and Life Insurance," *New York Times* (May 1, 1873): 5 (letter to the editor).

110. *Life Insurance Company v. Terry*, 82 U.S. 580, 582 (1872).

111. Ibid., at 583 (J. Strong, dissenting without an opinion).

112. See Susanna L. Blumenthal, "The Default Legal Person," *UCLA Law Review* 54 (2007): 1135–1265.

113. *Terry*, 82 U.S. 580, 583.

114. Ibid., at 589.

115. *John Hancock Mutual Life Ins. Co. v. Moore*, 34 Mich. 41, 43 (1876). In surveying the decisional law in the last quarter of the nineteenth century, it would appear that the preponderance of authority across state jurisdictions was in favor of the *Terry* rule, though the application of this rule varied substantially from jurisdiction to jurisdiction. See Frederick H. Bacon, *A Treatise on the Law of Benefit Societies and Life Insurance* (1904): 841–842.

116. *Van Zandt v. Mut. Ben. Co.*, 55 N.Y. 169, 175–177 (1873); *Flanagan v. People*, 52 N.Y. 467, 470 (1873). For other insurance cases explicitly recognizing irresistible impulse as a basis for allowing recovery, see *Newton v. Life Ins. Co.*, 76 N.Y. 426, 426 (1879); *Meacham v. Benevolent Ass'n*, 120 N.Y. 237, 243 (1890).

117. See Stalson, *Marketing Life Insurance*, 401–546.

118. See "Suicide in Life Insurance—Sane or Insane," *Central Law Journal* 4 (1877): 51, 51–53 (puzzling over why American companies trailed thirty years behind the English in inserting such a clause).

119. *Bigelow v. Berkshire Life Ins. Co.*, 93 U.S. 284 (1876). Henry Bigelow took out a policy on his own life on August 22, 1872, in the amount of $10,000. He died on February 8, 1873. The plaintiffs (the insured's wife and (possibly) his son, who were the administratrix and administrator of the dead man's estate) sued for a total amount of $25,000 in damages. The insurer defended by claiming to be liable only for the surrender values on the policies, $457 and $718, respectively.

120. For subsequent affirmations of the point that there is nothing in the provision affecting public policy or morality, see, for example, *Latimer v. Sovereign Camp Woodmen of the World*, 62 S.C. 145 (1901); *Brunner v. Equitable Life Assur. Soc.*, 100 Ill. App. 22 (1902).

121. *Bigelow v. Berkshire Life Ins. Co.*, 93 U.S. 284, 286–288 (1876).

122. Ibid., at 287.

123. *Travelers' Ins. Co. v. Sheppard*, 85 Ga. 751 (1890).

124. *Mut. Benefit Life Ins. Co. v. Daviess' Ex'r*, 9 S.W. 812, 816 (1888).

125. *Bigelow*, 93 U.S. 284, 288.

126. Ibid.

127. *De Gogorza v. Knickerbocker Life Insurance Company*, 65 N.Y. 232, 237 (1875)

128. Ibid., at 236–237, 241–242. For other jurisdictions following this ruling, see *Chapman v. Rockford Ins. Co.*, 89 Wis. 572 (1895); *Billings v. Accident*

Ins. Co., 64 Vt. 78 (1892); *Scherar v. Prudential Ins. Co.*, 63 Neb. 530 (1902); *Scarth v. Security Mut. L. Soc.*, 75 Iowa 346 (1888); *Tritschler v. Keystone Mut. Benefit Ass'n.*, 180 Pa. St. 205 (1897); *Keefer v. Pacific Mutual Life Insurance Company*, 201 Pa. St. 448 (1902); *Seitzinger v. Modern Woodmen of America*, 204 Ill. 58 (1903); *Moore v. Northwestern Mut. L. Ins. Co.*, 192 Mass. 468 (1906); *Haynie v. The Knight Templars and Masons' Indemnity Co.*, 139 Mo. 416 (1897); *Sparks v. Knights Templars & Masons L. Indemnity Co.*, 1 Mo. App. Rep. 334 (1897); *Zimmerman v. Masonic Aid Ass'n of Dakota*, 75 F. 236 (1896); *Union Central Life Insurance Co. v. Hollowell*, 14 Ind. App. 611 (1896); *Bachmeyer v. Mutual Reserve Fund Life Ass'n*, 87 Wis. 328 (1894); *Streeter v. Western Union Mut. Life & Acc. Soc'y*, 65 Mich. 199 (1887); *Kelley v. Mutual Life Ins. Co. of New York*, 75 F. 637 (1896). For a case providing an especially elaborate and influential discussion of the distinction between suicide and accident, see *Penfold v. Universal Life Ins. Co.*, 85 N.Y. 317 (1881).

129. *De Gogorza*, 65 N.Y. 232, 243 (dissent). For other jurisdictions anticipating or following this ruling, see *Pierce v. Traveler's Life Ins. Co.*, 34 Wis. 389 (1874); *Streeter v. Western Union Mut. Life & Acc. Soc.*, 65 Mich. 199 (1887); *Keels v. Mutual Reserve Fund L. Ass'n.*, 29 Fed 198 (1886).

130. "Suicide and Life Insurance," *The Independent* (November 22, 1883): 24. See also Murphy, *Security in an Insecure World*, 191–192.

131. Elliott, "Suicide—Effect Upon a Life Insurance Policy," 378; see also J. W. May, *The Law of Insurance: As Applied to Fire, Accident, Guarantee and Other Non-Maritime Risks*, ed. Frank Parsons (1891), 1:627–628.

132. J. W. May, *The Law of Insurance* (1891 ed.), 627 (editorializing thusly: "The prospect of providing for wife and family may in some states of mind be an irresistible motive, yet it is the very one the company wishes to exclude."). For an alienist agreeing with this assessment, see McFarlane, "The Medical Jurisprudence of Life Insurance," 575–577.

133. Murphy, *Security in an Insecure World*, 191; see also S. V. Clevenger, *The Medical Jurisprudence of Insanity; or, Forensic Psychiatry* (Rochester, N.Y.: The Lawyer's Cooperative Publishing Company, 1898), 212 (observing that "business competition, probably more than anything else, is inducing abandonment of restricting clauses as to suicide on policies").

134. "Editorial Article 6," *Washington Post* (July 13, 1884): 4 ("It is the custom of many insurance companies to treat the claims of suicides the same as other claims, regarding the fact of suicide as *prima facie* evidence of insanity, and make no contest unless the purpose of the suicide was plainly fraudulent. Other companies are far less liberal in the treatment of such cases."); cf. W. H. Lawton, "Suicide and Life Insurance," *North American Review* 179 (1904): 700 (noting that a few companies went so far as to issue policies "incontestable from the date of issue" and estimating that of sixty-nine "old-line" companies

only one refused liability for suicide, all the while agreeing to return the "reserve"; five retained the exception for three years, twenty-nine for two years, twenty-six for one, while another eight gave the insured "full permission to blow out his brains or otherwise make away with himself as soon as he has paid the first premium, secure in the knowledge that his family or estate will receive the full amount of the policy from the company!"); see generally Murphy, *Security in an Insecure World*, 181.

135. Murphy, *Security in an Insecure World*, 145, 193–197.

136. Missouri was the first, doing so in the 1880s; Colorado followed in 1903, North Dakota in 1905, and Texas in 1914. Georgia, by contrast, made suicide a defense by statute if intentionally perpetrated. However, this defense could be waived by contract, unlike the antisuicide legislation pioneered by Missouri. The legality of the Missouri statute was tested and upheld in *Whitfield v. Aetna L. Ins.*, 205 U.S. 489 (1895). See generally "Suicide as a Defense in Life Insurance," *Yale Law Journal* 30 (1921): 401–402.

137. In the application that the insured submitted to the insurer, he warranted that he would not die by his own act, "whether sane or insane," during the first two years the policy was in effect, but this document was adjudged inadmissible at trial because it was not attached to the policy in accordance with applicable state law. *Ritter v. Mutual Life Ins. Co. of New York*, 169 U.S. 139 (1898). Transcript of the Record. File Date: 3/9/1896, p. 21. Term Year: 1897. U.S. Supreme Court Records and Briefs, 1832–1978 (sources accessed via *Making of Modern Law*).

138. Ibid., 53, 118, 121.

139. Ibid., 147; 151–152; 154 (1898). See also *Hopkins v. Northwestern Life Assur. Co.*, 94 Fed. 729, 730–731 (C.C.E.D. Pa. 1899) (extending the logic of *Ritter* to deny recovery to the wife/designated beneficiary of the insured).

140. *Campbell v. Supreme Conclave*, 66 N.J.L. 274, 278–280, 283–284 (1901). However, this was a split decision, generating a quite spirited dissenting opinion joined by five other judges.

141. See also *Lange v. Royal Highlanders*, 75 Neb. 188, 203–204 (1907) (likewise criticizing the reasoning of Ritter and suggesting most state courts allow recovery—at least to third party beneficiaries—in cases of sane suicide where the policy does not exclude coverage on this score); *Patterson v. Natural Premium Life Ins. Co.*, 100 Wis. 118, 121–125 (1898) (refusing to apply *Ritter* where the policy had been assigned with the consent of the company to the children of the insured without deciding whether recovery would be allowed where the policy benefited the estate of the insured); *Parker v. Des Moines Life Association* 108 Ia. 117, 123 (1899) (allowing recovery where the wife was the beneficiary); *Seiler v. Economic Life Ass'n of Clinton*, 105 Ia. 87, 92–95 (1898) (holding that, as against a beneficiary, suicide is not a defense); *Supreme Conclave v. Miles*, 92 Md. 613, 626–628 (1901) (same). But see *Mooney v. Ancient*

Order, 114 Ky. 950, 960 (1903) (following *Ritter*); *Shipman v. Protected Home Circle*, 174 N.Y. 398, 408 (1903) (same, in dicta). The U.S. Supreme Court significantly undercut *Ritter* in a series of cases culminating with Justice Oliver Wendell Holmes's decision in *Northwestern Mut. Life Ins. Co. v. Johnson*, 254 U.S. 96, 101 (1920), effectively declaring the availability of the defense of suicide in insurance cases to be a matter of public policy left for the states to decide and suggesting that the true grounds of the decision in *Ritter* was the fact that the insured purchased insurance with the intent to commit suicide.

142. This commonly used phrase was also the headline under which the *New York Times* regularly reported deaths by suicide in 1880 through 1882, without any editorial judgment as to the moral or legal responsibility of the actor. Another headline from the same paper (published July 21, 1889) illustrates the ambiguity about responsible agency in everyday portrayals of the suicidal actor even more vividly: "Suicide and Its Victims; How the Crime of Self-Murder Is Defended. No Fear of the Hereafter Seems to Disturb the Mind of the Man Bent on Self-Destruction."

143. Lawrence Irwell, "Racial Deterioration: The Increase of Suicide," *Medical News* (October 2, 1897): 421 (also anxiously citing statistics supposed to indicate that self-destruction was "ten times more frequent in the white race than among the colored population"). On the connection drawn between suicide and modern civilization, see Howard I. Kushner, "Suicide, Gender, and the Fear of Modernity in Nineteenth-Century Medical and Social Thought," *Journal of Social History* 26 (1993): 461–490.

144. "Suicide and Life Insurance," *Boston Daily Advertiser* (November 14, 1893); "Suicide and Life Insurance," *The Independent* (April 22, 1894); "Asks His Right to Die," *Chicago Daily* (November 30, 1896); S. Ross Parker, "Suicide and Life Insurance: An Argument," *Green Bag* 22 (1910): 329–332.

145. John J. Reese, M.D., "Original Lectures. Suicide in Its Relation to Insanity," *Medical News* 57 (APS, January 1, 1888); W. H. Gray, "Life Insurance Companies Accessories to Suicide," *Chicago Daily Tribune* (APS, June 1897); G. Boehm, "The Right to Commit Suicide," *Bulletin of the Medico-Legal Congress* (1898); "The Increase of Suicide," *Journal of the American Medical Association* 39 (August 21, 1902): 494–495; "The Increase of Suicide: Life Insurance Said to Be a Great Promoter of This Crime," *Washington Post* (September 2, 1903); "Suicide and Life Insurance," *Boston Daily*; Parker, "Suicide and Life Insurance."

146. Parker, "Suicide and Life Insurance," 331; S. Ross Parker, "Suicide and Insurance," *Harvard Law Review* 49 (1935–1936): 304.

6. BONDED AND INSURED: THE CAUTIOUS IMAGINATION
Ravit Reichman

1. Elizabeth Bishop, *Complete Poems* (London: Chatto and Windus, 1991), 178.

2. E. M. Forster, "Post-Munich" (1939), in *Two Cheers for Democracy* (San Diego, Calif.: Harcourt Brace, 1951), 24.

3. H. Schulman et al., *Cases and Materials on the Law of Torts* (New York: Foundation Press, 2003), 53.

4. "War Damage Insurance," *Yale Law Journal* 51, no. 7 (1942): 1168.

5. François Ewald, "The Return of Descartes's Malicious Demon: An Outline of a Philosophy of Precaution," in *Embracing Risk*, ed. T. Baker and J. Simon (Chicago: University of Chicago Press, 2002), 274.

6. E. M. Forster, "What I Believe" (1939), in *Two Cheers for Democracy* (San Diego, Calif.: Harcourt Brace, 1951), 68.

7. Maurice Blanchot, *The Writing of the Disaster*, trans. Ann Smock (Lincoln: University of Nebraska Press, 1986), 25.

8. Most recently, see Eric Wertheimer, *Underwriting: The Poetics of Insurance in America, 1722–1872* (Stanford, Calif.: Stanford University Press, 2006).

9. Michael Lewis, "In Nature's Casino," *New York Times Magazine* (August 26, 2007): 28.

10. See Lionel Trilling's classic essay on the novel, in which he offered what has become its standard interpretive question: "Who shall inherit England?" Lionel Trilling, *E. M. Forster* (New York: New Directions, 1943), 118.

11. E. M. Forster, *Howards End* (1910; repr., New York: Vintage, 1989), 8–9. Hereafter cited parenthetically in the text.

12. See François Ewald, "Insurance and Risk," in *The Foucault Effect: Studies in Governmentality*, ed. Graham Burchell, Colin Gordon, and Peter Miller (Chicago: University of Chicago Press, 1991), 197–210; and François Ewald, "The Return of Descartes's Malicious Demon: An Outline of a Philosophy of Precaution," in *Embracing Risk*, ed. T. Baker and J. Simon (Chicago: University of Chicago Press, 2002), 273–301.

13. See Ralph Harrington, "The Railway Accident: Trains, Trauma, and Technological Crises in Nineteenth-Century Britain," in *Traumatic Pasts: History, Psychiatry, and Trauma in the Modern Age, 1870–1930*, ed. Mark Micale and Paul Lerner (Cambridge: Cambridge University Press), 34.

14. Prospectus for the Railway Passengers Assurance Company, 1892. National Archives, Kew: Ref. DE/P/E218.

15. I am grateful to Jennifer Schnepf for bringing the significance of these moments to my attention and for her insights on *Howards End* in general.

16. Forster himself likely gained a personal appreciation for insurance's irrational side twelve years later, when he received a letter informing him that a fire had broken out in the warehouse where his travel book *Alexandria: A History and a Guide* was stored. The entire stock of books had been destroyed, his publishers wrote, but since the volumes had been insured, the publishers had enclosed a check for compensation. Several weeks later, the publishers

wrote again to say they had been misinformed and that the books had not been destroyed after all. The discovery of the intact stock of books presented something of a tricky situation, however, since Forster had already been paid the insurance money. In order to address the matter, the letter stated, the insurance agents had themselves set fire to the books after the fact. See P. N. Furbank, *E. M. Forster: A Life* (New York: Harcourt Brace Jovanovich, 1977), 2:113.

17. Quoted in Barry Supple, *The Royal Exchange Assurance: A History of British Insurance, 1720–1970* (Cambridge: Cambridge University Press, 1970), 234–235, n. 4. Originally published in Alan Dent, ed., *Bernard Shaw and Mrs. Patrick Campbell: Their Correspondence* (London: Victor Gollancz, 1952), 132–133. Thank you to Rebecca Summerhays, who was kind enough to share this work with me.

18. Forster, "Post-Munich," 22.

CONTRIBUTORS

SUSANNA L. BLUMENTHAL is associate professor of law and history at the University of Minnesota, where she researches and teaches in the areas of American cultural and intellectual history, Anglo-American legal history, criminal law, and trusts and estates. Her most recent scholarship, which explores the historical interfaces between law and the human sciences, has appeared in the *Harvard Law Review*, *UCLA Law Review*, and *Law and History Review*. Her first book, *Law and the Modern Mind: Consciousness and Responsibility in American Legal Culture*, is a study of insanity trials in the nineteenth-century United States and will be published by Harvard University Press. She is also beginning work on a second book-length project concerning the legal regulation of fraud in Gilded Age America.

LEONARD C. FELDMAN is associate professor of political science at Hunter College, where he teaches political theory. He is the author of *Citizens Without Shelter: Homelessness, Democracy, and Political Exclusion*. His most recent scholarship focuses on political emergency and democratic politics.

CAROL J. GREENHOUSE is professor of anthropology at Princeton University and chair of the department. Her main teaching and research interests involve the ethnography of law, especially in relation to federal power in the United States. She has also taught at Cornell, the University of Indiana at Bloomington, and the École des Hautes Études en Sciences Sociales. Greenhouse is a past president of the Law and Society Association and the Association of Political and Legal Anthropologists. Her main publications include *Praying for Justice: Faith, Order, and Community in an American Town*; *Law and Community in Three American Towns* (with David Engel and Barbara Yngvesson); *A Moment's Notice: Time Politics Across Cultures*; and the edited volumes *Ethnography and Democracy: Constructing Identity in Multicultural Liberal States*, *Ethnography in Unstable Places* (with Elizabeth Mertz and Kay Warren), and *Ethnographies of Neoliberalism*.

S. LOCHLANN JAIN is assistant professor of anthropology at Stanford University. Professor Jain's research is primarily concerned with the ways in which stories get told about injuries, how they are thought to be caused, and how that matters. Figuring out the political and social significance of these stories has led to the study of law; product design; medical error; and histories of engineering, regulation, corporations, and advertising. Her widely reviewed book *Injury* investigates how certain products come to be understood as dangerous while others do not—and what this can illustrate about differences such as race and gender and historically contingent notions such as responsibility and negligence. Jain's current work offers an analysis of the cause and treatment of cancer as a key modality through which American "high-tech" is experienced and explained. Her other research interests include extralegal forms of communication, such as warning signs and medical apologies; queer studies; and art and design. Jain was awarded the Cultural Horizons Prize by the Society for Cultural Anthropology, for best article published in the journal *Cultural Anthropology* in 2004. She was a National Humanities Center Fellow in 2006 and is currently a fellow at the Stanford Humanities Center.

ANDREW PARKER is professor of English at Amherst College. He is co-editor (with Janet Halley) of *After Sex? On Writing Since Queer Theory*, a book-length special issue of the journal *South Atlantic Quarterly* (2007); *Performativity and Performance* (with Eve Kosofsky Sedgwick); and *Nationalisms and Sexualities* (with Mary Russo, Doris Sommer, and Patricia Yaeger). He has also edited *The Philosopher and His Poor*, by Jacques Rancière, and is currently working on a project entitled *The Theorist's Mother: Origination from Marx to Derrida*.

RAVIT REICHMAN is associate professor of English at Brown University. She is the author of *The Affective Life of Law: Legal Modernism and the Literary Imagination*, which examines responses to trauma and war in fictional and legal texts. She is currently working on a book about the modern relation to property in literature and law. Her articles on Holocaust testimony, law and culture, colonial law, and capital punishment, as well as on writers including Albert Camus, Virginia Woolf, and James Joyce, have been published in such journals as *South Atlantic Quarterly*, *Law, Culture, and the Humanities*, *ARIEL*, *American Imago*, *NOVEL*, and *Studies in Law, Politics, and Society*.

AUSTIN SARAT is William Nelson Cromwell Professor of Jurisprudence and Political Science at Amherst College. Professor Sarat is the author or editor of over seventy books. His recent publications include *The Road to Abolition: The Future of Capital Punishment in the United States* and *When*

Law Fails: Making Sense of Miscarriages of Justice, both edited with Charles Ogletree; *Mercy on Trial: What It Means to Stop an Execution*; and *When the State Kills: Capital Punishment and the American Condition*.

MARTHA MERRILL UMPHREY is professor of law, jurisprudence, and social thought at Amherst College. She has co-edited (all with Austin Sarat and Lawrence Douglas) several books, including *Lives in the Law*, *The Place of Law*, *Law's Madness*, *The Limits of Law*, *Law and the Sacred*, and *Law on the Screen*. She is currently working on a project on law and love.

ERIC WERTHEIMER is professor of English and American studies at Arizona State University. He is the author of *Imagined Empires: Incas, Aztecs, and the New World of American Literature, 1771–1876*; and *Underwriting: The Poetics of Insurance in America, 1722–1872*. He has published articles and essays on topics in early American literature and culture in *American Literature*, *Early American Literature*, *Nineteenth-Century Literature*, *Commonplace*, and *Arizona Quarterly*. He is currently director of the Center for Critical Inquiry and Cultural Studies at ASU.